M000223172

IMMACULATE DECEPTION

THE **SHOCKING TRUE STORY** OF
CHRISTINA GALLAGHER AND HER **HOUSE** OF **PRAYER**

IMMACULATE DECEPTION

THE SHOCKING TRUE STORY OF CHRISTINA GALLAGHER AND HER HOUSE OF PRAYER

JIM GALLAGHER

MERLIN
PUBLISHING

First published in 2009 by
Merlin Publishing
Newmarket Hall, Cork Street
Dublin 8, Ireland
Tel: +353 1 4535866
Fax: +353 1 4535930
publishing@merlin.ie
www.merlinwolfhound.com

Text © 2009 Jim Gallagher

Editing, design and layout © 2009 Merlin Publishing
Except
Photographs © of individuals or institutions listed underneath each image
in the plate sections

ISBN 978 1907162 01 5

*All rights reserved. No part of this book may be reproduced or
utilised in any form or by any means electronic or mechanical,
including photocopying, filming, recording, video recording,
photography, or by any information storage and retrieval system, nor
shall by way of trade or otherwise be lent, resold or otherwise
circulated in any form of binding or cover other than that in which it
is published without prior permission in writing from the publisher.*

*The publishers have made every reasonable effort to contact the
copyright holders of photographs reproduced in this book. If any
involuntary infringement of copyright has occurred, sincere apologies
are offered and the owner of such copyright is requested to contact
the publisher.*

A CIP catalogue record for this book is available from the British Library.

10 9 8 7 6 5 4 3 2 1

Typeset by Fairways Design
Cover Design by Graham Thew Design
Back cover image courtesy of the *Sunday World*
Printed and bound by CPI Cox & Wyman, Britain

Acknowledgements

First and foremost, I have to thank my bosses at the *Sunday World* for their support in writing this book and their encouragement for the whole House of Prayer investigation. Newspapers always want investigative journalism in their pages, but often do not give reporters time to do it. This was never the case with my editor Colm MacGinty, managing editor Neil Leslie, news editor John Donlon and MD Gerry Lennon.

Thanks also to my colleagues at the *Sunday World* for their advice, particularly my fellow authors, Eamon Dillon, Niamh O'Connor, Des Ekin, Eddie Rowley, Eugene Masterson, Nicola Tallant, Amanda Brunker, Sean Boyne and the inimitable Paul Williams. Picture editor Dave Dunne was a martyr to the cause. Other colleagues who have to be mentioned in despatches for listening to the moans and groans of a first time author, include Caoimhe Young, whose ears must still be ringing, Esther McCarthy, Daragh Keany and Cathal O'Shea. Photographers Liam O'Connor, Padraig O'Reilly and Val Sheehan stepped up to the plate, as always.

This book would never have been written but for the courage of people like Mike McCrory, Betty and Michael Morrissey and others, who were prepared to admit in public that they had been duped by a charlatan. Admitting you have been made a fool of is never easy – but to do it on such a public platform requires real guts.

Speaking of courage, the House of Prayer investigation would never have got off the ground but for Ireland's number one newspaper and publishing lawyer, Kieran Kelly. In my 30 years experience of dealing with a huge variety of newspaper briefs, I've discovered that they see it as their absolute duty to remove everything of interest from the written material in order to: (a) avoid future lawsuits and (b) enjoy an easier life. This is not the case with Kieran Kelly. A hardened veteran of countless Paul Williams exposés, he never pulled a single story. So thank you *consigliere*.

Thanks also to the team at Merlin, Chenile Keogh, who first approached me about writing the book; Robert Doran for his practical suggestions; and freelance editor Síne Quinn who did wonders with my waffle and got rid of much duplication.

Finally, a big thank you to my friends and family for their unfailing interest and encouragement, including Pat Gallagher, Gerry and Viv Gillen, the extended Harkin family in Donegal, Lynne Kelleher, Stephen Maguire, Dorothy McLaughlin, Ciara and Aisling Riordan, and author Annette Witheridge in New York. Also thank you to Kim, Norah, Betsy, Frank and Mary.

Dedicated to
Mick Gallagher

Contents

Prologue

Christina Gallagher began life in extreme poverty, and has claimed that she could neither read nor write when she left school.

But in the 16 years since she opened her House of Prayer on Achill Island, the life of this 56-year-old separated mother of two has changed beyond all recognition.

To her supporters, she is a holy visionary, who receives regular messages direct from the Virgin Mary and even Christ himself. Tens of thousands of pilgrims have made their way to her prayer centre to be in the presence of a woman who they see as touched by God. Some even claim to have been healed of various illnesses or afflictions, such as cancer, while visiting the House of Prayer. Gallagher claims to have the stigmata, the wounds of Christ. For years she has told her followers of her battles with the Devil to save their souls.

But to her opponents, she is nothing more than a con-woman who, for two decades, has duped the gullible and tricked the elderly into handing over huge amounts of money for 'Our Lady's cause.' Her 'messages' from heaven have got more and more terrifying as the years have gone by, with warnings of mass destruction and death on a global scale, of plagues of locusts feasting on rotting corpses, and of eternity spent in the fires of hell. The only way to be saved, she preaches, is to either visit one of her seven prayer centres (the first in Achill Island, five in the US and one in Mexico) or to give a donation. Those who give generously will get their reward in heaven!

In the meantime, Gallagher has gone from a woman

who owned nothing more than a part share in a modest marital home, to a designer-clad, bejewelled head of an international organisation with a private portfolio of properties bought for herself and her family. She managed all this with no formal income.

For two years she lived secretly in one of the country's most prestigious private developments in a magnificent €4 million mansion in Co. Dublin's plush suburb of Malahide. Her neighbours were millionaire pop stars and wealthy businessmen. None of them were aware of the identity of the mystery woman, who could occasionally be seen driving a BMW with darkened windows.

Gallagher filled another stunning €1 million home outside Newport, in her native Co. Mayo, with every conceivable luxury. She drove only top of the range cars (Audis and BMWs), some costing over €100,000, which she changed regularly. And all the time she would tell her devoted followers that she had no interest in material things and would happily live in a tent.

The astonishing transformation of this so-called visionary, from humble housewife to superstar soothsayer, all took place under the watchful eye of a once-revered priest, Fr Gerard McGinnity. Gallagher's loyal follower and spiritual director, who appears to believe everything she tells him, has alienated himself from his fellow-clerics because of his undying devotion to a woman the Catholic Church does not support. Local archbishop, Michael Neary has stated that the House of Prayer has no backing 'whatever', and has warned foreign pilgrims not to go there.

Now, for the first time, journalist Jim Gallagher, who broke the story about Gallagher's astonishing lifestyle, tells the full story of how this supposedly religious icon became a woman of wealth. By persuading devout Irish and American Catholics to hand over massive donations running into six figures, this self-proclaimed visionary with no job is now a very rich woman.

Speaking to former insiders, once at the top of the House of Prayer's hierarchy, the author reveals how this false prophet fooled and tricked thousands of devout followers. He also interviews victims who handed over huge amounts of money to the charismatic and consummate actress they once admired, before realising it was too late and that they had contributed to a big money-making scam.

He also reveals the less-than-holy lifestyle of this controlling woman, known for her temper tantrums and expletives, who constantly craves to be the centre of attention. The so-called visionary's escapades are revealed in shocking detail.

CHAPTER ONE

In The Beginning...

*'When I saw the poverty in that home, I could not
believe it. I had never seen anything like it.'*

Christina Gallagher, or Christina Ferguson as she was
then, was born into a poor farming family near the
village of Knockmore in Co. Mayo, a few miles west of
Foxford, on 5 June 1953.

She was one of three surviving children to Martha
and Martin Ferguson. With an older sister, Marie,
and a brother Jose, Christina was the youngest in the
family. Times were hard for Christina and her siblings,
particularly as their mother, a devout Catholic, was
sick for most of her life. A small delicate woman,
Martha Ferguson went through the trauma of several
miscarriages. She spent the latter years of her life using
an oxygen machine, as she suffered from a severe form
of asthma. Martha died in 1994, and her husband died
of cancer several years later.

Martha and Martin Ferguson were good honest
people, who were well thought of in the local community.
They did the best they could for their children, although
they did not have much to give other than their love.
Christina was brought up with none of the luxuries she
was to take for granted in her later life, but made do
with the hand-me-downs from her older sister. In fact,
one friend who visited the parents' home after Christina
had already opened the House of Prayer, said she was
horrified by the poverty she saw there.

'Christina's parents were the loveliest couple you could meet. They were old country people, very down to earth, and they were a real sanctuary for the family, very honest people who would not waste anything but did not have anything,' said the friend. 'Martha was sick all her life, and when I went to her house, I was utterly shocked. When I saw the poverty in that home, I could not believe it. I had never seen anything like it. There was no proper floor in the house. It was so basic I wondered how the mother cooked the dinner, because I didn't even see a cooker, just an open fire. I can still see the poverty in my mind.'

The friend recalled that when Martha came to stay with Christina, after she opened the House of Prayer on Achill Island, Martha would always arrive with her cylinder of oxygen. 'She was on it most of the time and would sit in the corner of the kitchen. The little woman was hardly five or six stone in weight; she was so small and frail. She was always sick and was an asthmatic all her life.'

Years later, when a cousin of Christina's from America was having a cup of tea in the House of Prayer, surrounded by expensive furniture and thick carpets, the woman said: 'This is a lot different from the old days when Aunt Martha used to test the tea by pouring it on the floor.' Christina was furious that her cousin had brought up her poor start in life. Rather than accept it as a badge of honour – the visionaries of Fatima and Lourdes were, after all, from humble backgrounds – Christina was embarrassed by her family's poverty. She had done her best to forget those tough early days and did not appreciate people bringing them up in conversation. Once she was living the life of a wealthy woman, she wanted people to think it was a world to which she was accustomed. When Christina was with her closest associates, she liked to see them marvel at her belongings, her jewellery and homes.

But when she started out in life, Christina and her sister, Marie, had nothing. It was their brother, Jose, who was left the small family farm. Gallagher claims in her gushing biography, *Out of the Ecstasy & Onto the Cross*, which was written by her spiritual director Fr Gerard McGinnity, that she spent so much time looking after her sick mother when she was young that she could neither read nor write until later in life (she told Fr McGinnity that she woke up one day and could read and write after praying to Jesus). Her mother was 'so delicate and so frequently ill,' while her father held down a factory job and also worked on the farm at night, that Christina had to take care of the house work and attend to her sick mother, when she came home from school in the evenings, wrote Fr McGinnity.

'At the age of fourteen she began taking on housework and started her first job.' He said she was humiliated when the lady who employed her discovered that Christina could not read or write. Gallagher continued to work as a cleaner and chambermaid in local hotels in her late teens and early twenties. One of the houses she used to work in belonged to the father of the former President of Ireland, Mary Robinson, who was born in Ballina, and whose parents were doctors. As one friend said: 'Christina saw for the first time how the other half lived. She saw a house filled with lovely furniture and must have day-dreamed about living in such a home one day.' But back then, her world was entirely different.

Fr McGinnity wrote: 'As she grew up and eventually got married, she lived a life that was no different to that of any of her neighbours, she was faithful to her religious duties, but had to cope with all the normal efforts, hopes and disappointments.'

This was a rather sanitised version of Christina's life and made no mention of the money she used to make reading palms for people in the area and at local fairs. One local told me: 'She was into reading palms and tea leaves and all that sort of stuff. I used to have visitors come every year, and the first thing they did when they arrived was to rush off and have their fortunes told by Christina.' On trips to Dublin, Christina would head off to Moore Street, in the city centre, to have her own palm read too, even years after opening the House of Prayer.

This hardly fitted in with her pious image as a self-proclaimed visionary devoted to the Virgin Mary. It was also something she probably did not mention to Fr McGinnity – instead exaggerating how religious she was when she was growing up. Through the priest's rose-tinted glasses, Gallagher was the same as other children with the one exception that she 'recognised Jesus as her greatest friend'. According to Fr McGinnity's idealised version of events, when playing with other youngsters, she used to run off during games of hide-and-seek to a quiet spot in one of the fields near her home and spend some time in quiet prayer.

Growing up, Christina began dating a local farmer, Paddy Gallagher, and they fell in love. They got married on 22 July, 1971 in Knockmore Catholic Church. Christina was 18 and Paddy was 25. (Incidentally, for a woman who claimed she couldn't read or write, she seemed to have had no problem signing the marriage register.) Two children were to follow, Mary and Brendan. Paddy and Christina eventually bought a modest bungalow, which they still both jointly own, in the townland of Gortnadreha, near Knockmore. It was a simple three-bedroom bungalow back then, but has since been extended. Christina built a large bedroom at the side and there were other additions to the building, as well as a fountain built in the front garden. For a time, her husband's brother lived in an adjoining extension. Christina's father, Martin, also lived with them for a while after his wife died.

To her supporters, Christina Gallagher was the devoted daughter who lovingly looked after her sickly parents in the last days of their lives. It was a glowing image she promoted in Fr McGinnity's biography. But this is not the complete version of events recognised by those who were close to her. Some of her former followers from the early days of the House of Prayer said that, her husband, Paddy, and her sister-in-law Kathleen, the wife of her brother Jose, did most of the caring.

One former close friend said: 'Jose's wife looked after Christina's mother when she was sick. After the mother died, she then looked after the father. She would drive to Christina's house and pick up the dad, who was nearly blind at that time, and take him to the farm, so that he could potter around there. Then she went back to Christina's house and cleaned up and made dinner. Paddy looked after the dad at night, after he came home from work, and Kathleen minded him during the day.

When Christina bought a new house for herself, outside Newport, Co. Mayo, in 1996 – she had split up with her husband the previous year and had been living in the House of Prayer – she did move her father in, but got some of her staff to come and look after him. One loyal servant, whom we shall call Margaret, said: 'I nursed Christina's father when he was ill in the Newport house. He died there a few years after his wife from cancer. He was a very, very good man, Christina's mum was a martyr all her life.

When the old man died, Gallagher quickly moved his remains back to his own family home for the wake, as she did not want to hold it in her Newport house, where hundreds of local people would have been able to see the opulent style in which she was living. And, of course, they would have wanted to know how she was paying for it, as she did not work.

Gallagher allowed very few people into her Newport home, where she had spent upwards of IR£300,000 adding another floor, extensions, a summer house and even a pond and waterfall. Domestic work was never at the top of Christina Gallagher's priorities, and occasionally she used to get Filipino staff, from the House of Prayer, to come and clean the house for her, some of whom were later sacked. A relative used to look after Christina's grandchildren before they were old enough to go to school. Mary would work at the House of Prayer on Fridays (mainly working on the accounts). At one time, Christina also hired a local girl, a single woman who had had a baby, to come in and do the cleaning. According to one former follower, who had been in the house, she was worked very hard.

In 1985 Christina Gallagher's life was to change forever when she visited Co. Sligo after an apparition there of the Virgin Mary was widely reported. It was a day that was also to have a huge impact on her family and thousands of future followers. 1985 was to become known as the year of the apparitions because there were so many supernatural sightings in Ireland. These apparitions included the famous moving statues of Ballinspittle, Co. Cork, and the appearance of the Virgin Mary in Mount Melleray, Co. Waterford, as well as the Sligo happenings. One evening in September four girls were walking together along a country road, on the way to their homes near Stokane National School in Carns, Culleens, Co. Sligo, when they looked up at the dark sky and saw two brilliant figures in white. They said that one was Our Lady and the other was St Bernadette. All four girls said they saw the apparition and then rushed home, where one of their mothers said they appeared to be glowing. The apparition, which came during a Parish Mission week, attracted huge national interest at the time and a shrine was eventually built on the site that still attracts pilgrims today.

Christina Gallagher wanted to see what all the fuss was about and travelled to the spot where thousands of other visitors had turned up, hoping to catch sight of something themselves. Gallagher later claimed that she too, had a vision at Carns, but not of the Virgin Mary. Her apparition was of the head of Christ in a crown of thorns. He did not speak to her, but she said that she saw it clearly. Fr McGinnity wrote in *Out of the Ecstasy & Onto the Cross* that the apparition was 'real and graphic and incontestable. Christ was in the depths of suffering.' Gallagher was so overcome by the pain of this image that she could 'think of nothing but the horror of sin,' wrote Fr McGinnity, in his inimitable style. Asked to describe what Jesus looked like, she said it was the same face as on the Shroud of Turin, referring to the famous cloth that was said to have adorned the body of Jesus after his crucifixion and onto which his image was transferred. The impact of this vision led Christina to daily Mass, according Fr McGinnity. 'This was clearly a deliberate spiritual preparation by God for what was to come in 1988.'

Sceptics, of course, do not agree. They claimed she saw nothing at Carns – except the enormous potential of such apparitions and their sheer pulling power in drawing people in. As for claims that it led her to daily Mass, this was indeed news to the people who knew her, who to this day claim she does not go to Mass, except when she is trying to impress Fr McGinnity or

other people. One of her former closest friends, who
travelled with her for two weeks in England, several
years later, said they never 'saw inside a chapel' the
whole time they were away.

Now, Gallagher had seen at first hand the power of
what an apparition could do. In a rare interview with
the *Connaught Telegraph* in July 1997, she told reporter
Tom Shiels that Christ had no message for her that day
in 1985. 'I went there looking for peace. I was just like
everybody else up to then, other than that I have been
called by God through our Blessed Mother to give a
message to the world. I am doing the best I can to do
just that.'

Three years after Carns, she claimed her own regular
supernatural experiences began. Gallagher said she
was visiting relatives in Dublin, when she had her first
apparition of the Virgin Mary on 21 January 1988. The
most beautiful woman she had ever seen suddenly
appeared in front of her, surrounded by an enormous
light. The woman was standing off the ground and her
hands were held together in prayer. She then opened
her hands to reveal a clear glass globe, which had
smoke swirling inside it. The woman did not identify
herself, but later gave a message referring to the smoke
of sin issuing from the earth because people were not
responding to her call.

Gallagher started to tell her friends about the vision
when she returned home to Mayo but they were
sceptical. Word began to spread that she claimed to
have seen a vision and she attracted scorn from people
who knew her. She said she had her second vision a
while after the first, when she was visited by both Our
Lady and St Bernadette of Lourdes while she was in
the kitchen of her own home. No words were spoken
on this occasion. A third apparition took place the

following day, 4 February 1988, and this time Our Lady spoke saying: 'Be not afraid. I am the Virgin Mary, Queen of Peace, and I come in peace.' By 28 February the messages were becoming more urgent and more threatening, with the Virgin Mary allegedly warning the world that there was not much time left before 'My Son's Hand will come over the earth in justice.'

People began to hear of the apparitions and would laugh at her. Gallagher's own mother was never convinced that her daughter had developed a direct line to God, but Christina's father Martin was more believing. He was said to worship the ground his daughter walked on and so believed her claims. Gallagher was eventually visited by a Catholic nun, Sister Joseph Mary from Sligo, who had heard about these heavenly visitations and began to help her, taking notes as more visions occurred. Sister Joseph Mary also happened to be a good friend of Fr Gerard McGinnity, a priest who had a keen interest in all things supernatural.

The cleric, who was to become Christina Gallagher's spiritual director, right hand man, and for many people, the real draw at the House of Prayer, was to take a massive interest in this new visionary. Sister Joseph Mary wrote to him about this woman who was claiming to have regular contact with the Virgin Mary, and the nun gave the priest an account of the first messages.

'I read and studied them and I would have spoken to Christina by telephone at that stage,' McGinnity wrote in *Out of the Ecstasy*. 'The content of the messages to date was fine, without any theological or spiritual flaw. It was however, some time before I actually met Christina.' The priest said the visions 'conveyed an urgent but simple message in complete harmony with the Gospels.'

The 'messages' may have been in accord with Christ's teachings, but some were laughable when filtered though Gallagher's personality. One called for 'the healing of disputes through reconciliation with enemies'. This was true brass-neck stuff from a woman who was to become known across the country for threatening legal action against anyone who crossed her or who spoke out against her. Similarly, Gallagher's message from Our Lady for 'refraining from judgement of others' was a beauty, considering she was to expel countless people from the House of Prayer for crossing swords with her.

When Fr McGinnity finally met Christina Gallagher for the first time in her home, the visionary fell to her knees and said, 'Our Blessed Mother is here'. McGinnity was hooked.

In March 1988 the Madonna requested that a special medal be made with the cross and the Virgin Mary praying on one side and the two hearts of Jesus and Mary on the other, weeping tears of blood. When asked by Gallagher what it should be called, the Virgin Mary supposedly said: 'The Matrix.' This was to become a huge seller for the Mayo visionary.

It was around this time, that Gallagher met a woman who was to become a close confidante, and one of her most loyal followers, for the next ten years. The friendship ended only when the devout Catholic woman realised that she had been following a false visionary and that Gallagher was the opposite of the holy image she had so carefully created. The woman gave this author the full story of their relationship, but did not want to be named publicly, because of the harassment she had already received from people in the House of Prayer. We shall call her Esther.

Esther first met Fr McGinnity in the home of a man organising a trip to Medjugorje in the late 1980s, and met Gallagher soon after that at Melleray in

Co. Waterford. 'Christina was supposed to be able to read people's souls but it was just like fortune telling. You hear what you want to hear,' said Esther. 'She took my two hands in hers and then she put her hand in her bag, took out a pen and paper, and put her telephone number on it and told me to keep in touch but not to give it to anyone else.'

Esther was to discover that this was a tactic that Gallagher used again and again to win people over. She would single out a person and then make them feel special. She would tell them that they were the only person she could trust. Or she would come over and whisper conspiratorially in someone's ear, as if sharing a great personal secret.

Esther said that Gallagher and Fr McGinnity were collecting money that day and that she gave the visionary IR£40, which she had saved for a new coat. Christina said to her, 'I could not take that,' but she made no effort to hand it back. 'I had been saving up specially. That was 1989 and it was quite a lot of money then,' said Esther.

The woman, now 72, recalled that Gallagher was wearing a fake sheepskin coat at the time. 'It was definitely imitation. I remember mentioning it to her years later, and she immediately said it was not cheap but real. She didn't like it that she used to be badly dressed. But she used to wear cheap nylon skirts, badly washed jumpers and white high-heels when I first met her. Nobody wore white shoes at the time. She was really poor. She never had anything then but now she wants for nothing. There's a real want in her. She does not buy one thing but two or three at the same time. It was the sorriest day of my life that I met her. It has caused me a lot of heartache and I believe Fr McGinnity has lost his soul completely. He is holding that place together.'

As months went by and the visions supposedly
continued, Christina Gallagher said that the Virgin
Mary had requested 'a little house of prayer', which
'My son Gerard' [McGinnity] would help her to find.
No particular mention was made of Achill Island,
but when Gallagher visited the Convent of Mercy on
Achill Sound, which was up for sale at the time, she
got a feeling of 'great inner peace'. She subsequently
sought the approval of the then Archbishop of Tuam,
Dr Joseph Cassidy, for her plan to open a house of
prayer, which would be a retreat centre for both the
clergy and the laity. She assured him that she wanted
to open this centre 'in complete conformity with, and in
total obedience towards, the Church.' This was rather
ironic in light of the heated battles that were to come
between the two after it opened.

Once the premises were found, a huge fundraising
campaign was launched to buy and renovate the
building. Money poured in from all over the country.
Gallagher and her spiritual director used to visit prayer
groups around Ireland promoting Our Lady's 'little'
house. A woman, called Dymphna, who was a 14-year-
old at the time, recalls attending her local prayer group
in Galway, some 20 years ago with her father.

'There were five or six of us who went, and we
listened to her, and she came across as very quiet and
unassuming. She did not ask for money, but money was
thrown into a pot and it came to IR£80 which was a lot
at the time,' she said. 'The strange thing was that two
weeks later, I got a hand-written letter from her saying
she was looking for money to continue her work, and
that she wanted to open a house of prayer. I thought it
was very strange that she wrote to me, as I was a child. I
showed it to the parish priest in our prayer group, and he
said certainly do not send any money. He also thought it

was strange and he showed it to other adults. I couldn't understand why it had not been written to my dad, but to me. My parents also told me not to send any money. I remember it all vividly because it was so unusual.'

The money continued to roll in, but before the House of Prayer had even officially opened, Gallagher had used some of the cash to buy herself a plush car. A priest had arrived one day in a particularly snazzy model, and as soon as Gallagher saw it, she said, 'I must have a car like that,' according to one of her former followers, who was there that day, Gallagher duly went out and bought one, and actually arrived in it for the opening of the House of Prayer. Fr McGinnity was not overly impressed, but a few weeks later she sent a cheque to Fr McGinnity to buy a car for himself. The priest bought one with a sunroof, because, he said, it was something he always wanted. Former House of Prayer staff said Gallagher also bought cars for her husband, her son and her daughter. Many more would follow over the coming years.

The House of Prayer was officially opened to much fanfare on Friday, 16 July 1993 by the then Archbishop of Tuam, Dr Joseph Cassidy. According to the programme for the opening, 'Mother Teresa of Calcutta has presented a medal to each member of the community of Our Lady's House of Prayer.' But this was an outright invention by Gallagher. Mother Teresa had in fact recently been to Dublin, where Gallagher queued up to meet her along with many other pilgrims. One of her volunteers took a picture of Gallagher and Fr McGinnity with Mother Teresa, and the priest later had it blown up and hung up in the House of Prayer. Gallagher's friend Esther said that when she saw the picture and asked Gallagher if Mother Teresa had been at the House of Prayer, the Mayo woman simply smiled; leaving the impression she had visited. Another former follower said, 'She met Mother Teresa the same as all of us.'

One of Mother Teresa's nuns, Sister Lawrence, was later asked if the Catholic icon had said anything after meeting Christina Gallagher, and she replied that the holy woman from Calcutta had said: 'God help him [McGinnity], the poor priest believes her.'

For the first six months after the House of Prayer opened, Gallagher wore a dreary brown dress, which looked like a nun's or monk's habit, claiming that Our Lady told her to wear it and even how to make it. She can be seen wearing it in photographs from the opening, as she stands proudly between the Archbishop and a beaming Fr McGinnity. But the dress did not survive Gallagher's taste for designer clothes, and soon it was banished to the back of one of her extensive wardrobes. So is Christina Gallagher disobeying one of Our Lady's direct instructions by no longer wearing the brown dress? Or did the Virgin Mary give her permission to add a little Prada to her collection? Many of her former followers would love to know.

Jenny and George (not their real names), a couple from Northern Ireland, did much of the early fundraising work for the House of Prayer. They had been great friends of Fr McGinnity for many years. Jenny was in fact one of just three people listed in the original Land Registry records as being owners of the House of Prayer, along with Christina Gallagher herself and Fr McGinnity. (That was to change in 1998, when another six names were added to the owners' list, including the House of Prayer lawyer and director Donal Corrigan and his wife, Margaret; fellow directors Dick Hogan and Louise Cleary; Gallagher's bodyguard and right hand man Tony Fitzpatrick; and a man called Martin Scally, who has since died. The Land Registry record was changed one last time in January 2003, when the company, Our Lady Queen of Peace House of Prayer (Achill) Ltd, became the official owner.)

As one of just three original owners, it showed the important part that Jenny played in the launch of the House of Prayer. But once the premises had opened, this quietly spoken grandmother did not last long. She became the House of Prayer's first victim – as Christina Gallagher got rid of her after a few months, when she began to question Gallagher's use of the House of Prayer funds. Nevertheless, Jenny remained so convinced that Gallagher was a true visionary that she thought her own expulsion must have meant Our Lady did not want her involved. She was hurt by this but accepted it. Friends said she was such a staunch Catholic that she did not even think of questioning Fr McGinnity.

But to this day, Jenny insists she has never signed any document to stand down as one of the three owners of the House of Prayer or as one of its trustees. If such a document has been signed, she says, her signature must have been forged. The House of Prayer claims she stood down in 2003. She also believes her name was forged on another House of Prayer document. The House's lawyer, Donal Corrigan, sent a letter from the charity's trustees to a firm of solicitors requesting that he represent the House of Prayer in a lawsuit that was ongoing at that time. The letter was dated 19 February 1999 and was sent to a solicitor, regarding an action by a Deirdre O'Toole against Christina Gallagher, the trustees of the House of Prayer and Mid West Radio.

The letter said: 'We the trustees of the House of Prayer authorise Donal Corrigan to take up this file from you' [the other solicitor firm]. It was purported to have been signed by Fr McGinnity, Martin Scally, Louise Cleary, Dick Hogan, Tony Fitzpatrick, Donal

Corrigan, Margaret Corrigan and Jenny. Jenny insists she did not sign that document.

In 2008 Jenny wrote to the Law Society to get the matter resolved. They in turn wrote to Corrigan and asked for a copy of the document in which she supposedly resigned as a trustee of the House of Prayer. According to Jenny, Corrigan did not reply to the Law Society until they had sent two or three reminders. He eventually claimed the document had been lost, but he would forward it if it turned up.

The lawsuit involving Deirdre O'Toole and the House of Prayer, meanwhile, fizzled out. Ms O'Toole was a neighbour of the Achill house, and complained about the constant noise from the roar of coach engines and the loud broadcasting of prayers on loudspeakers. Gallagher attacked her on the local Mid West radio station, and Ms O'Toole subsequently sued. The case never went ahead.

The sad thing for Jenny and George about her departure from the House of Prayer was that when they parted ways with Christina Gallagher, they lost a great friend in Fr McGinnity, for whom they once had huge admiration. They knew the priest long before he had ever met Gallagher, and regarded him as a deeply religious man. Fr McGinnity was a regular visitor to their home and would often bring along one of the visionaries he was interested in at the time. When Gallagher hooked up with him, she too spent much of her time in their home. There were times when the two of them were like permanent guests and the house became the nerve centre for the House of Prayer appeal. Gallagher would regularly get Jenny to drive her to St Patrick's College, Armagh, where Fr McGinnity was teaching at the time, to see the priest. Even when she was away, Gallagher was in continual touch, ringing up to five or six times a day.

While staying there, Esther said Gallagher made herself so at home in Jenny's house with Fr McGinnity, that she would demand, 'we will have a cup of tea now'.

Money and letters of support came flooding into the couple's home and it was Jenny who kept the original books. She would deposit the money in the local AIB Bank, and record it in ledgers. With hindsight, the couple can see now that even in those early days Gallagher was obsessed with money, and was never particularly grateful to people who gave her donations.

'I do not think she answered a single letter, but got Fr McGinnity to write out a standard reply that "Christina Gallagher prays for you,"' said Jenny, who worked endless hours for the cause. She said 'a million medals' went out from her house to different fundraisers around the world. Jenny would give up to one thousand of the specially made Matrix Medals at a time to Fr McGinnity if he was going off to England or somewhere on a pilgrimage or to a fundraiser. The medals were supposed to be 20p each, or five for IR£1, but the priest would just drop them on a table and was happy for people to give what they could. They would be blessed by Fr McGinnity, but in the end Christina told him to stop blessing them. She said they were not getting enough money and wanted to charge extra for blessings. She also introduced a charge of 50p for the medals. 'I thought Fr McGinnity would insist they had to be blessed but he didn't,' said Jenny. 'He gave such a lovely blessing that went on for ten minutes. I was very surprised at him.'

Gallagher was determined to boost profits, so she cracked down on anyone who she thought was not paying enough for her merchandise. She fell out with a religious goods shop, in Dublin, because she felt they were not paying enough for House of Prayer goods.

Jenny said that she used to send boxes of videotapes to a man in Wexford, but Gallagher stopped that too, and said that nothing was to go out unless it had been paid for. Gallagher even claimed that Our Lady had given her a message warning that those people who ripped off the House of Prayer would get rough justice. The visionary claimed that people were 'taking advantage' of the House of Prayer by pirating goods, such as the Matrix Medal and books. So alarmed was Gallagher at this behaviour that she said Our Lady proclaimed a heavenly edict about it, saying, 'those who take from My House, I, as Mother, will lead to the Justice of God.'

One time Gallagher rang to say she had to go to the US and needed new clothes. Fr McGinnity asked Jenny how much he should send her, and wondered whether IR£200 was enough. Jenny suggested that it probably wasn't and that she might need IR£400. But when the priest sent the cheque to Gallagher she was furious at what she saw as a paltry amount, and insisted that she would need double that. According to Jenny, Fr McGinnity was annoyed, but eventually he gave her IR£800. 'That was 1991 or 1992 and it was money meant for the House of Prayer,' said Jenny.

Another way of boosting profits was to have lots of celebration days at the House of Prayer that drew in the crowds to fill the donation boxes. The 16 July anniversary was always a big occasion and could pull in as many as 4,000 people. Then Gallagher introduced another day of celebration, just a few days later on 25 July after 'being told by Our Blessed Mother' to hold a special day of prayer, which was to be called 'Our Lady's Fraternity Day'. On top of that were the regular novenas Gallagher kept announcing on the supposed orders of the Madonna, which meant followers had to turn up for nine consecutive Saturdays. She would then extend the novena again and again.

When there was a big crowd, particularly on the anniversary day, Gallagher would usually have one of her apparitions and would go into a trance for several minutes, which would electrify the crowd. She would throw herself on to her knees, raise her arms to heaven and go into an almost hypnotic state. She would stare above, as if looking at a vision, and her lips would move, as if she was talking to someone but no sound would come out. She would stay in that uncomfortable position, with her arms outstretched and without moving, for maybe five or ten minutes. The crowds would be in awe and Fr McGinnity would immediately lead the worshippers in a hymn to the Virgin Mary. Gradually Gallagher would come around, as if just recovering from fainting, and she would be surrounded by excited pilgrims, who would try to touch her. 'What did Our Lady say? What did Our Lady say?' they would ask her.

Gallagher would eventually smile, as if coming out of a euphoric state and would say that she had to talk to 'Father' first. She would then disappear with Fr McGinnity into the inner sanctum of the House of Prayer for maybe an hour, as the priest wrote down and tried to decipher the Virgin Mary's message. The priest would then come out and read the message to the assembled crowd. Those who were clamouring for it could also get a printed copy.

One of her former followers, Betty Morrissey, saw half a dozen of these trances. 'Her eyes would glaze over and she would be radiant looking. She was the best actress in the world. You would swear she was really seeing a vision,' said Betty. 'She must have had make-up on, because she actually looked like she was glowing.'

After she eventually left the House of Prayer, Betty heard that one of her friends inside, a volunteer, had caught Gallagher practising the position that she held during these trances. But despite going to the House of Prayer for over ten years, Betty Morrissey never saw a sign of the stigmata that Gallagher claimed to have. Practically nobody did. One of the very people to have that experience was Gallagher's friend Esther – and only once.

It was on a Good Friday, and Gallagher told Esther that if she was not down from her room by a certain time, to come up and wake her. When the visionary did not appear, Esther did as she was told, knocking on Gallagher's door. When there was no answer, she walked in calling her name. She walked into the bedroom and saw Gallagher outstretched on the bed 'as straight as a pen' with her arms at her side, as if in a trance. There were drops of blood on both her feet. 'I ran downstairs and got Fr McGinnity and he and Martin Scally and others ran upstairs. They started praying straight away and she came round.'

Back then Esther was very moved, thinking she was in the presence of something supernatural. But today, 11 years after leaving Gallagher, she says it was 'a fix.' She said Gallagher came downstairs half an hour after with plasters on both feet. 'But the next day it was as if nothing had happened. I saw both feet and there was not even a break in the skin. There should have been a scab or something, but there was not a blemish.' She said there was no sign of any other stigmata wounds – on the hands or on the forehead – and she says today that what she thought was blood could have been anything. Another follower, Margaret (not her real name), found an instrument under Gallagher's bed at a later stage, which she thought Gallagher used to make her stigmata wounds. This information was given to Cardinal Seán Brady, Primate of all Ireland, when a group of concerned former supporters of the House of Prayer had a secret meeting with him in May 2008. Esther believes the visionary played her by telling her to come to her room, and when she heard her coming pretended to go into a trance.

Gallagher spoke of her stigmata during an interview on RTÉ's religious programme *Would You Believe* in 1998, claiming that she had received the wounds of Christ several times. The first time she saw it, she said, she looked down and saw a trickle of blood run down one foot and then saw blood start to appear on the other foot. 'I saw a gashed wound appear and open up. The wound got bigger and there was a lot of blood coming, but none came on the carpet and none came on my slippers. Some appeared on my nightdress as little crosses, lots of crosses. There was a towel under my feet and when I took off my slippers there was no blood on the towel either.'

Someone ran for Fr McGinnity, who appeared with a young priest. They all prayed while the novice priest held her hand. One of her biggest devotees at the time, Margaret, took a photograph of the occasion. This photo has since been used countless times in books about the House of Prayer, and in its publicity material.

Would You Believe also carried a clip from a previous Granada TV programme in which Gallagher lifted her fringe to show the camera dark marks on her forehead, like congealed blood. This is the only video 'evidence' of the stigmata ever filmed.

Gallagher told *Would You Believe* that she had not suffered the stigmata recently.

As time went on, Gallagher's fame around Ireland began to grow and many of her visitors came from Northern Ireland, Great Britain and even the US. She became known as the visionary with the stigmata, even though practically nobody ever saw it.

Gallagher was not the only one who was delighted to see people flocking through her doors. There is no doubt that the House of Prayer has been a great boost for Achill Island and its tourism industry over the years. Hotels, B&Bs, pubs and restaurants would regularly fill up at weekends, as coach loads of pilgrims descended on the remote area. Buses of free spending American visitors were particularly welcome to an economy that depended hugely on tourism. Many local business people were happy to take the money, while scoffing at Christina Gallagher's claimed heavenly connection.

CHAPTER TWO

Fr Gerard McGinnity – Devoted or Deluded?

'Fr McGinnity is a priest easy to admire because he was always very pious. But I believe he has been completely taken in by her. He was always naïve and gullible, even though [he is] very smart.'

Following the publication of the Ferns Report in 2005, Father Gerard McGinnity became a martyr figure. The report revealed that Fr McGinnity tried to blow the whistle on a priest who was abusing young seminarians, and it also highlighted the abominable way he was treated by the Church afterwards. This became one of the reasons why many people treated him with reverence. Instead of being lauded for his actions, Fr McGinnity was banished by his Church superiors – who then promoted the offender.

The incident dated back to the early eighties, when Fr McGinnity was a senior dean at St Patrick's College, Maynooth (the most important Irish institution for the training of priests). He was a rising star in the Church, and looked set to be fast-tracked to becoming a bishop.

A group of six students came to him complaining of the activities of one of Fr McGinnity's colleagues at the college, Fr Micheál Ledwith. They said that Ledwith was showing an inappropriate interest in certain junior students. Also a teacher, Ledwith was visiting some students with whom he had no need to have professional contact. Not only did they have concerns about his 'sexual orientation and propensity', but also about his 'extravagant' lifestyle.

In an interview in 2004, Fr McGinnity told the *Sunday Tribune* that the students had already gone to some bishops to express their fears, but they had not been believed. Two of the students had been told, 'Go back and say your prayers'. So the students had come to Fr McGinnity for help, and he conveyed their concerns to a number of the bishops in confidence.

The former Primate of All Ireland, Cardinal Cathal Daly, and the retired Archbishop of Tuam, Dr Joseph Cassidy, were trustees of Maynooth at the time. They have since denied that they received complaints about Ledwith. But former bishop Eamonn Casey does not. He has confirmed Fr McGinnity's story.

After hearing about the complaints Bishop Casey asked to see Fr McGinnity. The priest told the *Tribune*: 'He wanted to know if any of the complaints could be substantiated, and if I could bring in the students who had been improperly approached at that very moment. Once he'd finished talking to me on that occasion, he entered a meeting of the visitors of bishops, and at that meeting it was decided by them to remove me from office.'

Fr McGinnity was ordered to take a sabbatical and went to Rome. When his year was nearly up, a superior travelled to Italy to talk to him. 'He came to see me and he was very agitated and nervous and clearly pained by what he was doing,' said Fr McGinnity. 'The words he said to me, they have always haunted me since. "There are bishops gunning for you," he said. "I can't go back to them without your resignation. Write it down, write it on anything, it doesn't matter."'

Fr McGinnity said he was heartbroken but wrote a letter resigning from his position at Maynooth. Then he packed and returned to Ireland.

Meanwhile, the bishops were busy promoting Fr Micheál Ledwith to the position of president of Maynooth College. They had a different future mapped out for Fr McGinnity. After a spell in a Northern Irish parish, he was sent to a boarding school, St Patrick's in Armagh, to teach religion and to act as dean of the school. To the former senior dean this was a massive come down from working at the country's major seminary.

'For someone who had been in my position, it was outright humiliation, really,' he told the *Tribune*. 'Early mornings, late nights, checking windows, locking doors. I was supervising meals in the refectory, supervising recreational games, making sure that no one was breaking the rules or going into town when they should be in school, making sure that they were in bed at the right time at night, making sure there was toilet paper in the toilets.'

Reporter Sarah McInerney reported: 'His lips curl at this last detail, and the pain of it all shines through.'

Fr McGinnity said that the worst part of it was that people assumed he had done something wrong. There was a lot of innuendo that he wasn't able for the job. 'And nothing was done, not a finger was lifted by anyone in authority to give any other impression except that I was being disciplined or punished.'

The priest said his family was also very conscious of the shame and humiliation of what was happening. They saw how isolated he was and he was concerned not to hurt his mother, not to scandalise her about the Church, so he didn't go into any of the details. 'She knew the basic issues. I hoped she knew.'

Fr McGinnity was left in the school for ten years, bristling with anger, disappointment, humiliation and disillusionment. Meanwhile, he heard that the newly appointed Monsignor Micheál Ledwith was trying to ruin the careers of the students who had complained about him by writing to their bishops and recommending that they not be ordained. His wish was not granted.

In 1994, ten years later, the story was revived when Ledwith was accused of sexually abusing a minor. This time he resigned. Six years later, in 2000, another allegation was made by a former seminarian about incidents in 1994. Ledwith denied both claims. But he received a financial pay-off and pension from the Church, and left Ireland for good to teach in California, where he became a new age spiritualist. The Pope dismissed Ledwith from the priesthood in 2005 at the request of the acting bishop of Ferns, Dr Eamonn Walsh.

Fr McGinnity, meanwhile, was finally moved from the boarding school in Armagh, and sent to a parish in the tiny village of Knockbridge, Co. Louth, where he has remained ever since. He told the *Sunday Tribune*: 'What was done to me would deter any bona fide person from coming forward and warning about a danger to young people. The Church hasn't yet acted positively to try to restore my reputation, my respectability. I am waiting to see them do that, even though I know that they cannot ever restore 20 years of my life, maybe the best years.'

The priest said he did not regret his actions 20 years before, but did regret that that his mother died without ever seeing his name cleared. He still hoped for an apology from the Church, some gesture that would restore his reputation. Did he expect one? 'We'll see. Let's leave it at that, if you don't mind,' he said at the end of the interview.

The apology did, in fact, come the following year in June 2005. But now, four years later, Fr McGinnity's reputation has, in the eyes of many people, been tarnished once again, this time not through the fault of others, but because of his blind devotion to Christina Gallagher.

There are some who claim he has something of a martyr complex and that he has made the most of his past misfortunes. This, they say, allowed Gallagher to manipulate him over the years. Christina inflamed his anger and disappointment at the shocking treatment he received from the Church hierarchy, and she encouraged him to question any critical edicts from the established Church about the House of Prayer.

She also fed his pride by telling him that he was the special one, chosen by the Blessed Mother, regardless of what the Church said. She would tell him that she had received specific messages 'for my son Gerard'. The priest lapped it up.

Former House of Prayer volunteers say that it was at her urging that one hundred demonstrators protested outside the offices of the Archbishop of Armagh, Seán Brady, in November 2005, following the publication of the Ferns Report. They were demanding that reparation be made to Fr McGinnity for the way he had been treated by the Church. They refused to be drawn on what that reparation should be – but Gallagher certainly wanted her spiritual director to be made a bishop. She would have loved nothing more than to have had her own man inside the Church establishment, fighting her cause.

Fr McGinnity was not present at the demonstration, and claimed he had nothing to do with it. But this was not true. Former House of Prayer devotee Mike McCrory, the man who first told this author that Christina Gallagher was not all she seemed, revealed earlier this year that Fr McGinnity had specifically banned him from attending the protest. McCrory was regarded as an official House of Prayer spokesman at the time, and the priest did not want the demonstration to appear organised by them.

'He asked me not to go because, he said, "We want to show them it's a grass roots movement, an up-swelling of feeling. We do not want them to think it's a one-man show." That shows how important I was to them at the time,' said McCrory, on a trip back to Ireland from his home in America, where he now lives.

A statement handed out at the demonstration supporting Fr McGinnity promised that there would be more protests in the future, unless the priest was looked after. It said: 'We demand justice for all good priests, especially for those who stood up for truth and the protection of young people, and who were punished for doing so. We seek justice immediately, especially for Fr McGinnity, who has suffered so much for over 20 years. We have read and heard his story and we will continue to demonstrate until we can see that reparation has been made for the damage that has been done to him. We invite all good priests who have been victimised by their bishops in a similar way to come forward as we seek justice and protection for all good priests.'

Four of the protestors handed the statement into Archbishop Brady's house, although the current head of the Irish Bishops Conference was not in residence at the time. Former followers of Christina Gallagher said they could see her hand all over this protest, which was aimed at boosting the career of her right hand man while at the same time feeding his persecution complex.

Mike McCrory is one of those who refuses to accept the hero status of Fr McGinnity. He said in 2008 that someone should ask the priest why he had stayed silent about what had happened to him in Maynooth for 20 years, until the publication of the Ferns report. 'His was not the reaction of the brave man that he has been painted as.'

McCrory said he had asked the priest that very question two or three years ago, and Fr McGinnity had said, 'Oh, in those days you would never think of questioning the Church. It just wasn't done.' McCrory said he valued the priest so much back then that he failed to ask him what about the days, months and years that followed. If he had really cared he could not have stayed silent. And if he had blown the whistle on the weak Church officials at the time, maybe the whole Ferns episode could have been avoided, said McCrory, 'and Catholics could still love their Church, as I do.'

McCrory said that the priest was 'a wounded man' when Gallagher met him. Other former friends, too, said Christina fed his ego with flattery to keep him onside. Occasionally, describing a vision, she would tell him that she could see 'an angel with a golden arrow pointed' at him, or that Our Lady had passed on yet another message to her 'son Gerard.'

McCrory says Fr McGinnity was so full of pride, it made him feel special. He said he himself had suffered the same weakness when he first went to Achill Island. 'Pride brought me to the House of Prayer. I thought that other people were not good enough Catholics like me to recognise Our Lady. "Our Lady knows she can rely on me," I thought. "I am in the minority but I am special. I have been selected". I think Fr McGinnity is the same. So too is Dick Hogan, one of their biggest supporters.'

McCrory said that when he was still in the House of Prayer he used to ring up every bishop and priest he knew, or whose number he could get hold of, including Cardinal Daly and Archbishop Brady, and he would lambast them for the way they had treated Fr McGinnity. 'I told them they were a disgrace. "It's a sick bird that befouls its own nest," I told all of them. I wanted them to acknowledge what they did and make restitution.'

He said Fr McGinnity was delighted with this when he told him. It was about this time that the whole movement to get the priest promoted was becoming galvanised. 'I did it privately and wasn't asked to do it but I kept him informed.'

McCrory said that the man he regarded as the holiest priest in Ireland, a monk called Fr Athanatius of Mount Melleray, had seen through Christina Gallagher when he first met her, and was not impressed that Fr McGinnity was following her blindly. He said of the priest one day: 'That McGinnity turned out to be a right fruit cake. He is gullible and he is pridefully pious.'

McCrory said a genuinely holy person would not put on airs and graces. 'Someone once said, "The more honest a man is, the less he affects the air of a saint. He knows his own weaknesses." That could explain McGinnity's pride. He got in so deep, I think he was feeding things to Christina for her to say. She could not have come up with some of that stuff herself. But Christina Gallagher used to ring up other visionaries and ask them, "What did Our Lady say to you?" They got the sense that she was looking for stories.'

Fr McGinnity once got very annoyed when he heard another priest was claiming that Fr McGinnity had had a nervous breakdown. He asked McCrory to back him up and refute the claims and speak up for him – but diplomatically. 'You don't want the bishop to think you are my spokesman, which you are.'

Fr McGinnity was also known in many quarters around Ireland for something other than his stance against Fr Micheál Ledwith. He was renowned for his interest in visionaries and the supernatural. It was only a matter of time before he met Christina Gallagher.

The eager priest used to travel up and down the country interviewing numerous self-proclaimed prophets. When he first returned to Ireland from Rome in 1984, he immediately threw himself into this passion. He was first sent to the parish of Stonebridge, between Armagh and

Portadown, in Northern Ireland, where he spent more than a year. His duties were to help the then Primate of All Ireland, Tomás Cardinal O'Fiaich. But McGinnity wasted no time in getting involved with a number of self-proclaimed visionaries, including Beulah Lynch, from Bessbrook, an 18-year-old called Mark Trenor from the same town, and an Australian called Paul of the Cross, who claimed he had a cross which oil came out of. According to former friends of Fr McGinnity, most of these people have since just 'faded away.' They were certainly never authenticated by the Catholic Church.

One former close friend said Fr McGinnity was obsessed with these people, and went so far as to send out Our Lady's supposed messages to Mark Trenor to every parish in Ireland. He got one of his followers to go through the Diocesan Directory of Ireland, which lists every priest in the country, and send every one of them a letter telling them about the wonderful apparitions of 'Our Lady of Bessbrook.' On a trip to Medjugorje he even got up and spoke about Trenor. One priest, a former student of Fr McGinnity's, told me: 'I was in Maynooth in 1984 when a lot of the clergy got these letters from him talking about Our Lady of Bessbrook in Armagh. I can't remember who the visionaries were supposed to be but nothing ever came of it. He has been into this stuff for a number of years.'

Fr McGinnity brought Christina Gallagher to meet some of these visionaries one night. He got so caught up in his trip that he forgot his duty back at the parish (first confessions for first communion). 'He was so wrapped up interviewing Paul of the Cross that he forgot all about the duties he was supposed to be carrying out,' said a former friend who was there at the time. 'Cardinal O'Fiaich called him and told him he was out, that he would be sent to St Patrick's College in Armagh.'

Fr McGinnity was to spend many years at the college, but it did nothing to stifle his interest in the supernatural. Once ensconced in St Patrick's, it was not long before the priest was organising prayer groups in the college, after the school's boarders had gone home for the weekend. Self-proclaimed visionaries from all over the country attended these weekly meetings. Beulah Lynch, Mark Trenor, the Two Patricks from Cookstown, and three female visionaries from Dublin were a few of those who regularly showed up. Some of them would sell their medals and paraphernalia at these events. One regular recalls: 'The Two Patricks used to be one Patrick and a driver. Only one of them was a visionary to start with, but then the other man began having visions and they became the Two Patricks.' They have never been approved by the Church authorities and have been criticised for trying to get money from their followers.

There were some comical moments when some of these supposed mystics were recounting the apparitions they had just had. On one occasion, a man called Martin from Bessbrook, said the Virgin Mary had been in the room and when he began repeating her message to those assembled he turned to one woman and said: 'Our Lady could not remember your name.' Another visionary from Dublin had travelled with Fr McGinnity to Mass and when they got out of the car, she said pointing: 'There's Our Lady now.' 'He would believe anything. The woman was just harmless but he believed her,' said a friend.

Those who knew the priest well said he could spend hours praying in the car. Sometimes he would pray the whole way to Achill or play a tape of prayers on the stereo. 'He was a holy man but even back then he was saying that you must give money to the House of Prayer or you will go to hell,' said one.

Not all these visionaries were happy to see Fr McGinnity devoting so much time and energy to his new star, Christina Gallagher. Mark Trenor, in particular, hated the Mayo woman, and used to say she was a false visionary, said one member of the group. Christina told Fr McGinnity to have nothing more to do with him. Fr McGinnity eventually met up with him and said, 'I will not be dealing with you any more.' He also cut off links with all the other visionaries, claiming Christina was the one true one.

In the past, Fr McGinnity had also been a huge fan of the Swiss mystic Vassula Ryden, who claimed to have visions of the Virgin Mary beginning in 1985. She was later discredited by the Vatican. He also supported an American school headmistress called Teresa Lopez, who claimed she began to have supernatural experiences in Denver, Colorado, in 1990.

Among the visionaries that Fr McGinnity still believed in was the discredited Julie Kim of Korea, whom both he and Gallagher travelled to the Far East to meet. The *Sunday World* published a photograph, on 23 November 2008, of the Mayo housewife smiling next to a beaming Kim. The newspaper revealed that Kim had been excommunicated from the Catholic Church on 21 January of the same year, for preaching what the Church regarded as gross falsehoods. Kim claimed to have a weeping statue of the Virgin Mary and also claimed that the Eucharist turned to visible, bloody flesh in her mouth. Like Gallagher, Kim also claimed to have the stigmata wounds of Christ and to have regular visions from Our Lady. Fr McGinnity was a huge supporter of Kim, even before he met Gallagher. It was this seemingly blind faith in anyone claiming supernatural powers that has made McGinnity a laughing stock to many.

Fr Tomislav Vlasic was another of McGinnity's idols.

Fr Vlasic helped to put the Catholic shrine of Medjugorje on the map, but was defrocked by Pope Benedict XVI in July 2009. The priest had been a hugely controversial figure, particularly after he had a child with a nun in the 1980s and tried to hide it.

In the same way as Fr McGinnity acted as spiritual director for Christina Gallagher, Franciscan priest Fr Vlasic served for several years as the spiritual adviser to the six young Bosnian Croats, who claim to have had more than 40,000 visions of the Virgin Mary in Medjugorje, Bosnia. The Pope had approved Fr Vlasic's laicisation as far back as March 2009, when the priest had requested it.

It was in 1981 that the six children first claimed to have had an apparition of the Virgin Mary on a hillside near Medjugorje. From the beginning, both the Vatican and local Catholic Church leaders were sceptical about the claims. Fr Vlasic wrote to Pope John Paul II in 1984, saying that he was the one who, through divine providence, guided the seers of Medjugorje. But his local bishop, Pavao Zanic, had already expressed his doubts, accusing Fr Vlasic of creating the whole apparitions phenomenon.

Fr Vlasic left Medjugorje in the mid-1980s, after it became public that he had fathered a child with a nun and asked her to keep his own identity a secret. He set up the 'Queen of Peace' community in Parma, which is dedicated to the Medjugorje apparitions.

Fr Vlasic was suspended by the Vatican's Congregation for the Doctrine of the Faith in January 2008. This occurred after he came under investigation for scandalous sexual immorality, and claims that he had exaggerated the visions of the six children. The priest was accused of the 'diffusion of dubious doctrine, the manipulation of consciences, suspect mysticism and disobedience towards legitimately issued orders.'

Fr Vlasic refused to cooperate with the investigation, and was banished to a monastery in L'Aquila, Italy. He was forbidden to communicate with anyone, even lawyers, without his superior's permission.

When he agreed to leave the priesthood, Fr Vlasic was given a set of conditions to observe by the Pope on pain of excommunication, including a ban on giving spiritual direction.

The Vatican has never given the shrine of Medjugorje its formal blessing. Three separate church commissions have failed to find any evidence to support the claims of the Medjugorje visionaries. But thirty million pilgrims from around the world – including tens of thousands from Ireland – have travelled to the small town in the past three decades.

The defrocking of Fr Vlasic came as a blow to Medjugorje followers who had hoped the Vatican would one day legitimise the controversial shrine. It would also be a disappointment to Fr McGinnity, who was one of the first Irish priests to visit the shrine after the initial apparitions. Fr Vlasic was the second spiritual adviser to the visionaries to come under fire.

Perhaps the most enduring legacy of these supposed prophets and their advisers was that Christina Gallagher saw at first hand how it was done and was quick to learn. Fr McGinnity's conversations with some of these alleged prophets with Christina present were filmed back in the 1980s, and the video footage still exists today. I spoke with the man who recorded some of the films, an amateur filmmaker from Northern Ireland, who had not looked at them for 20 years. He was reluctant to show them, because of his loyalty to Fr McGinnity.

Although this man was shocked by what he had read in the newspapers, he still remembered the priest fondly. Though he did say that he had always found Fr

McGinnity to be naïve. He said he was involved with Fr McGinnity, as far back as 1987, and then with Christina Gallagher a year or two later. 'I used to do videos of them, and even went to Medjugorje. I did a lot for him and I liked him a lot. He was a genuine priest, and I felt sorry that a lot of people gave him abuse. But I always found him very, very gullible. He believes everything people tell him.'

He said he had not seen the priest for 12 years, but would love to ask him about the stuff he had read in the newspapers about Gallagher's luxury homes and the massive fundraising appeals.

The man, who did not want to be named, said he videotaped a pilgrimage to Medjugorje with Fr McGinnity, and various interviews around Ireland, including one in Bessbrook, Co. Armagh. He recalled that Gallagher, who was just starting out at the time, sat in when Fr McGinnity interviewed Beulah Lynch, about her apparitions.

'Gerry believed all the visionaries because they were telling him things he wanted to hear. Maybe he was not happy with his own life, and was looking for something else,' said the amateur filmmaker. 'I remember Christina Gallagher said to him once that he was the chosen one, and that Our Lady had asked her to strike up a miraculous medal with two hearts on one side and the Virgin Mary on the other. He got involved in the manufacture of these. I had no time for Christina Gallagher. I did not think she was genuine. From day one I thought she was crazy. I met her in the Lynch house in Armagh and also in Achill.'

The filmmaker remembered one particular visionary who he thought was completely false but whom McGinnity was fascinated by. The visionary was from Australia and was appearing in Bessbrook. He could not remember his name, but it was probably Paul of the Cross. The visionary claimed he had the stigmata on his hands and feet, although the filmmaker never saw them. He was filming a Mass, when this man got up on the altar wearing a robe like a monk's and began talking about his stigmata. 'He was wearing bandages on his hands so I never saw the marks. I was just the cameraman and could hardly ask him to take them off, but I used to joke about him. I didn't trust him. But Gerry McGinnity believed him. He believed everyone. He was gullible. There must have been 12 of these people involved in his life over the last 20 years. They all came to him as their spiritual director. I have not spoken to him about any of this. I always had doubts about different things but I never expressed them to him.'

Another former close friend of Fr McGinnity said the priest was a completely different man back in the eighties. And he said it filled him with despair to see how the priest had changed. 'He was such a good priest years ago. He would be over in the UK doing an all-night vigil and would arrive home exhausted. He really pushed himself and was a very holy man.' He said the priest used to be so busy he didn't have time to worry about normal things like other people, and that even the tax disc on his car was eight months out of date at one time. Fr McGinnity was not interested in anything to do with money but just wanted to get God's message out, he said. 'That's all he cared about. He really was a good priest. His coat at the beginning was all worn and his shoes were worn out. When we pointed this out to him he would say, "I must see to it." But Christina Gallagher completely changed him. She got him a long fashionable coat and pleated trousers. She wanted him well presented. Now, I think he is the biggest villain in Ireland. He is lost.'

A friend of Gallagher's, Esther, said that she was with the visionary one day when she bought the priest two pairs of shoes. Esther thought this was very unusual. She said Gallagher had also persuaded the priest to dye his hair. It was grey when Esther first met him, but was now sandy-coloured.

One man, Neil (not his real name), who has tried to get his obsessed father out of the House of Prayer for years, said he was utterly frustrated that his father could not see through the priest. For all the obsessed followers, McGinnity's connection gave credibility to the House of Prayer. A devout Catholic himself, Neil went on to say that: 'McGinnity supported the discredited visionary Julie Kim from Korea before he met Christina Gallagher. He was acting as Kim's spiritual director. He is like a mad professor and seems to believe in anything that moves. He has supported all types of visionaries. He has been like that for years. He believes in anything, whether moving statues or whatever.'

Neil said that Julie Kim was excommunicated following warning after warning. 'She was into really freaky off-the-wall stuff, yet McGinnity believed in her too. He is the problem at the House of Prayer. Without him Gallagher would not have the following. I know my dad was dubious about some of the stuff she was coming out with, but McGinnity reassured him. There is something strange going on when Cardinal Brady refuses to stop him.'

Whistle-blower Mike McCrory has no doubt that Gallagher has been playing the priest for many years. She has always claimed that the Virgin Mary directed her to him, which appealed to his vanity. For his part, Fr McGinnity says Gallagher proved to him she was a genuine visionary when two members of his family were cured of cancer – because of her intervention.

'Fr McGinnity is a priest easy to admire because he was always very pious. But I believe he has been completely taken in by her. He was always naïve and gullible, even though [he is] very smart,' says McCrory. Nobody was ever drawn to the House of Prayer by Christina's personality or holiness. McGinnity's presence and support is what draws in the crowds. 'She is hidden away, but he is the front man and he does a substantial job selling her. He is brilliant at it. He is the one pulling in people with his personality. Without him she would be nothing. He is the one everyone admires. I've never really seen her do anything, although people still want to be in her presence because of what he says about her. But they seldom see her; she just makes a 10-minute guest appearance at the House of Prayer on some Saturdays.'

Before he met Gallagher, Fr McGinnity used to be invited regularly to talk in the US, because people loved his sermons, said McCrory. When she came along they began inviting her too, but McGinnity just talked about Christina. Even there, she had shown her temper tantrums. One woman who brought Christina to the US complained that she was treated like excess baggage. After the trip, she made a formal complaint to Archbishop Joseph Cassidy about Christina.

Esther has the final word on Fr McGinnity: 'Never once did I hear him checking Christina Gallagher on anything she said or did. She always told him what to do. If she said jump, he would say how high? Whatever hold she has on him, he is putty in her hand. There was one time at the House of Prayer that he begged her to come down and meet the people, because they were waiting for her. He was literally begging her. But she wouldn't go down. I do not remember one person ever standing up to her.'

CHAPTER THREE

The Visionary Entrepreneur

'The cry of double standards must be heard in the deepest recesses of Heaven, and I cannot help feeling that we were all being made fools of by Christina who is showing herself to be a deceiver and a liar.'

Though the House of Prayer continued to grow over the coming years, Christina Gallagher was not without her problems. The most dramatic was the break up of her marriage in 1995. After a row with her husband, Paddy, one night, she stormed out and ended up banging on the door of the House of Prayer. She was let in by one of her devoted followers, a former nun called Sister Treasa.

Gallagher was to live there, upstairs in the living quarters, until she bought the Newport house in 1996. But of course, once she was in residence, the facilities and décor had to be upgraded. When she first opened the House of Prayer in 1993, the upstairs rooms included a number of cubicles. These were planned to be used for visiting priests, who were expected to come on retreat, and as sleeping accommodation for her right-hand man Tony Fitzpatrick. Christina knocked some of these cubicles into a suite for herself, which included a bedroom, her own bathroom and a small sitting room and TV area. She later made more changes, adding a veranda to her living space and putting in her own Jacuzzi and shower steamer in the bathroom. Gallagher was to add two of these steam rooms to her future home in Newport too. She also added a luxurious deep-pile carpet in her bedroom, which one of her followers described as something, 'you and me could never afford.' The carpet was covered in a creamy-white rose design. And of course, there were the obligatory chandeliers.

One guest, who saw the rooms and used the Jacuzzi, said: 'It was plush but gaudy, way over the top. There was a coffee table in the suite and the glass top was held up by angels, which Fr McGinnity bought her. She also had a wine table that had a heart-shaped glass, which Fr McGinnity bought for her too. There was expensive stuff in there but there was no homely feeling. That was back in the 1990s when she lived there, so it could be completely different again by now.'

Another interesting feature in the suite – which the guest did not see, but heard about from a couple who worked as caretakers in the building – was a cloakroom containing a control unit for the TV cameras and audio equipment dotted around the House of Prayer. There, Gallagher could sit and watch what her staff or visitors were up to and pick up their conversations. This was a truly bizarre domestic feature for a woman who claimed to be interested only in the spiritual side of life. It also seemed strange for a woman who boasted that she could see the future that she would need such earthly technology to keep abreast of what was happening under her own nose.

But the House of Prayer was always going to be just a temporary home for this woman who loved the very best of everything, and who had huge amounts of donations pouring through the letter box. A year later she bought the house on a hill outside Newport, on the main road to Castlebar, and threw herself into a massive expansion plan. A friend of Christina's husband, worked on the extension. He added a second floor to the building and various other features, including a summer house at the back, along with a pond and waterfall. A giant wall was built around the property, so that no prying eyes could see inside. An electronic gate and a security camera were also added. Gallagher was splashing out big time, spending over IR£300,000. This was a massive amount of money for a woman who did not have a job and had no visible means of income. And so, of course, she had to keep the project top secret. Only the most unquestioning of supporters, those she knew she could control, were told about it. Her good friend Esther was kept in the dark about the house for two years. She later stayed in the house, and Gallagher took great pleasure showing off the house's many features.

One woman who did see it, however, was an American woman called Marita Wojdak, who ran the House of Prayer's fundraising campaigns in the US. She was shocked at the size and scale of the house and immediately told Gallagher that she would have to get rid of it, because it was bound to cause her major problems in the future. This was not the reaction Gallagher was hoping for, the visionary later confided to Esther. The local media had also got a whiff of this new palace on a hill, and were asking awkward questions about how she could afford it.

In 1998 Gallagher and McGinnity decided to tackle the rumours head on and appeared on *Would You Believe*. In the TV show, she moaned: 'I feel myself held up to ridicule. Why do people in the media have a need to twist the story? Why can't they tell it as it is? There is no sensation.'

Asked if the House of Prayer was wealthy, Gallagher replied: 'No, it is not. It is keeping going. It has a certain amount of money, which we hoped would go to an extension. It is sitting there and it is going to the upkeep of the house at the moment. I never got anyone to give us half a million or a quarter of a million or anything like that. No way!'

Reporter Mick Paelo said there were concerns about the House of Prayer's accountability, because so many people went there. He said that if there were 20,000 visitors a year, and they all gave IR£1, it would add up to a lot of money on top of the trade in the shop.

'Many come and give nothing. Some come who may buy a book or a few medals,' Gallagher replied. Fr McGinnity immediately chipped in that the House of Prayer chapel was the only church he was aware of where there was 'never, ever' a collection plate handed around at Mass, in the five years it had been open. And this was the way Christina wanted it, he said.

The priest failed to mention that day on camera, the personal appeals he had been making for far bigger donations than would ever fit on a collection plate, such as the IR£250,000 needed for an extension to the House of Prayer: an extension for which he had been fundraising for at least three years.

Gallagher told *Would You-Believe* that she could not understand why a big question mark was hanging over her head. She said the House of Prayer had a cheque book and 'every receipt for everything it has got' had to be accounted for to the accountant. Everything was bought through the cheque book to which there were two signatories, herself and the secretary of the House of Prayer.

Fr McGinnity added that the House of Prayer was even more rigorous in its financial dealings than other organisations, because not only were all donations 'recorded and duly audited' by the Revenue Commissioners, but a special book was kept. This 'special book' listed all those who gave donations and was kept in front of the altar (the book has since disappeared).

Reporter Mick Paelo then pointed out that one of the most persistent rumours about Gallagher was that her lifestyle had dramatically changed since she set up the House of Prayer, 'in particular her choice of car.' The camera then panned to a newspaper headline about a new BMW that she had been seen driving, although Paelo did not specifically mention it.

Gallagher replied: 'The car is a Vectra. It belongs to the House of Prayer, not to me. Wealthy? I was never short. My husband was always well able to take care of me and my family before this [the visions] ever happened to me.'

Gallagher did indeed have a company Vectra, which she used to drive to the House of Prayer, but she also had an expensive BMW that she used on personal business and which was kept out of sight at her Newport home. The visionary, suddenly on the defensive, then told the documentary team that her apparent wealth was all down to a book she had written, which certainly never set the bestsellers list alight.

She said: 'Regarding a wage, I had no wage from this, good, bad or indifferent, and maybe this is a good programme to get the story cleared once and for all, publicly. I went to my accountant and I said this is unfair, I have been doing this so many years on the road and I am drawing from my husband, and I do not think God or man would expect me to continue. I have been six or seven years or maybe more and I was getting nothing, apart from what my husband gave me to keep me continually giving, giving this message. Finally, [the accountant] said there was one way: you can draw from your book. You can draw royalties from your book, so I got a substantial amount of money from royalties for my book.'

Gallagher then told the TV programme that the

wall around her Newport home was to stop people snooping. 'The big wall is a prison to keep people from writing what is in your personal private rooms.' She said this was something she had to endure.

But Gallagher now intended to get rid of the house, after the telling off she got from Marita Wojdak. An English lawyer based in Derby, John Beighton, who had been a big supporter of the House of Prayer for the previous two years, and who travelled over to Achill regularly, was asked if he could help to find a buyer for the house in England around 1998. The house was videotaped and Beighton, a convert to Catholicism, was told to approach the rock star brothers, Noel and Liam Gallagher of Oasis, to see if they would be interested in buying it. The brothers often holidayed in nearby Charlestown, where their mother came from. This gives a clue as to the comfort of this mansion, when it was thought that millionaire rock stars might be the only ones who could afford to buy it. Whether or not Beighton got in touch with the brothers is unclear, because the house still belongs to Gallagher. Beighton quit the House of Prayer shortly afterwards – following a confrontation over Gallagher's wealthy lifestyle. Beighton has refused to discuss the House of Prayer for the last ten years. But at the time he told fellow devotees that if he managed to sell the Newport house, Gallagher had demanded that IR£100,000 of the money be in cash.

The row, which saw Beighton walk away for good, involved him and seven other supporters. It happened after an American called Chuck McNerney was made manager of the House of Prayer in 1998. Chuck resigned after just five weeks. He claimed that he was not allowed to do his job properly and was shocked when Christina Gallagher would not even permit him to open the post. She insisted that opening the mail –

much of it filled with cash donations – was her 'only joy.' McNerney thought this was ludicrous. He also wanted to introduce a proper financial management system and a proper computer system, which would have prevented the possibility of fraud. Gallagher strongly opposed his proposed improvements. He quit, claiming he could not work with the visionary, and objected to her dictatorial style. He said she was also far too controlling and had introduced a whole wave of petty restrictions, including banning him from going to the pub for a drink.

McNerney had planned to sell a property he owned in Denver, Colorado, and to move full time to Achill to live in the House of Prayer. Instead, he moved back to the US.

Other followers were not impressed by the way McNerney was treated. Things came to a head on 18 September 1998, when a group of eight supporters, including McNerney, who was still in Achill, gathered in the House of Prayer to confront Gallagher and Fr McGinnity about concerns they had over her lifestyle, her finances and her conduct. Among the group were Beighton, Leon Dawson, Wilf and Sandra Dawson and Carmel Sisson. But the group received no satisfactory answers to their questions. Instead Christina Gallagher threw a tantrum at being quizzed. She called them traitors and said there was nobody she could trust.

They had asked her about a relationship she was having with an Englishman called Lawrence 'Chalky' White. She had met Chalky while on holiday in Devon, and had brought him over to Ireland to stay with her in Newport. Her supporters were uncomfortable with this new relationship, as Gallagher was married, although she had been separated from her husband Paddy for some time. But Gallagher continued to deny any such separation while appearing at the House of Prayer. In fact, she had blatantly lied by claiming in public that she and Paddy were still very happy together. This was an image she was desperate to keep up because of her role as a Catholic visionary. But some of her staff and supporters concluded that her over-familiarity with Chalky, and his attitude to her, suggested they were more than just good friends. This was confirmed to me by Gallagher's one-time close friend, Esther, who was with the visionary when she met Chalky in England the previous month.

During the confrontation, a furious Gallagher insisted that her relationship with Chalky was an innocent one and she lashed those present for not trusting her. The group of eight left the meeting frustrated that they had received no real answers to any of the issues they had raised.

John Beighton was so disgusted at the way they were dismissed by the visionary that he wrote a scathing eight-page letter to Gallagher and Fr McGinnity, expressing the concerns and fears of the group.

He said in the letter, dated 1 October 1998, that he was acting in his capacity as a supporter and volunteer at the House of Prayer, and as a trustee of a charity that had given financial support to the Achill House. He said he had also received representations from various other people who had given money to the charity. He said serious questions had been raised about the financial running of the House of Prayer and of Gallagher's lifestyle. He also said he would much rather have had a proper face-to-face discussion with the visionary and with Fr McGinnity. This had proved impossible at the 18 September meeting, because Gallagher would not address any of the issues raised. He said she had just dismissed these real concerns with 'petulant' statements about being 'betrayed.' This was a reaction which was unacceptable.

Supporters who had given their lives to the House of Prayer should be allowed to raise legitimate concerns and get proper answers without being called a Judas, he said. He demanded answers to various matters, such as the financial management of the House of Prayer. He said he was shocked by the lack of control over the finances. He stated that Gallagher had recently admitted to him that she was unsure of the trustworthiness of some of the staff.

John Beighton wrote: 'This causes me grave concern.' He demanded to know what system was in place to prevent such irregularities happening and asked how abuse was prevented. As far as he was aware, there were no proper accounts kept at the House of Prayer for donations in cash or by cheque that arrived by post or by hand. He asked if records existed for cash raised in the donation boxes and which bank account this money went into? Who handled these donations and what system was in place to prevent fraud or abuse? He asked why Gallagher had not implemented the recommendations made by Chuck McNerney in his short spell as manager.

The lawyer said he and the people he represented were worried about the fact that some workers were being paid in cash every week, and they were concerned that they were all properly being accounted for through the PAYE system.

Beighton said he understood that Gallagher's daughter, Mary Gorman, had been receiving cash from the charity, and also had a brand new Opel estate car. He believed she was also in receipt of state benefit and asked if she had declared the cash payments to the benefits office or were this payments being treated as gifts. He said he understood Gorman had only recently been put on the PAYE system in some years after the House of

Prayer opened. So were other employees being paid in cash? The lawyer asked where the cash came from to pay these employees.

Beighton demanded to know how many cars the House of Prayer owned and who used them. 'Why does Mary Gorman have a brand new car when she visits the house only once a week from Ballina?'

He said he believed there were six cars. He asked if Christina Gallagher's BMW was a charity asset. He wanted to know whose name it was registered under, how much it cost and when it was bought. 'I understand that it is a top of the range BMW 7 series. If it was owned by the charity or purchased with money from the charity, how can this possibly be justified?' he asked, particularly as the charity had just bought her a brand new 1998 Opel Vectra. He asked if the BMW was a charity asset, why was it 'hidden' and why was it never used to drive to the House of Prayer. He also asked why Gallagher, in a recent radio interview, had refused to admit its existence.

'If she has nothing to hide, why does she not show clearly where the money came from for the car in the first place?' He said this would end the spread of any rumours. But if the charity did not buy the BMW, where did Gallagher get the money to buy it 'as she does not work and it cost around IR£40,000?'

Beighton then asked about one of the charity's cars given to an employee, who used to run the House of Prayer shop but had left in July. Where was it now, he wanted to know? If he had been allowed to buy the red VW Polo, where was the money?

He also asked about gifts made directly to Christina Gallagher over the past ten years. He said that with so much criticism and innuendo in the media about Gallagher becoming 'a rich woman', he was sure she would welcome the opportunity to make 'a full and frank disclosure' of any gifts she had received and also of her personal assets. This would end public speculation once and for all.

Beighton said that he had discovered from Chuck McNerney that the House of Prayer had IR£500,000 worth of goods in its stock room. He wondered how it could possibly be justified that so much money was tied up in these goods. He also asked why so many copies of Gallagher's biography, *Out of the Ecstasy & Onto the Cross*, had been paid for and stockpiled.

With regard to the management structure of the House of Prayer, he could see that Christina Gallagher was clearly at the top of the tree. He wanted to know how the charity was managed; when did the trustees meet and why did Gallagher appoint staff without consulting the trustees? 'Is she not accountable to the rest of the trustees?' He said it was up to all trustees to ensure the proper management of the charity. He asked if they were up to the job or just Christina's 'puppets'. 'If so, clearly the system is open to dictatorial abuse by Christina.'

Beighton said that Gallagher's refusal to allow McNerney to open the mail in his brief spell as manager opened a huge can of worms. He said it was beyond all justification for a manager of any business or charity to be banned from opening letters. All it did was create suspicion in people's minds as to why Gallagher, or her daughter Mary, or Tony Fitzpatrick, were the only ones allowed to open mail. This was even more alarming because of the large amounts of cash and cheques that arrived in the post. 'My understanding is that many of the cheques are payable to Christina personally.' Beighton said the trustees had clearly failed to put in place proper procedures to prevent fraud or the possibility of fraud, which was a cause of great concern to supporters of the House of Prayer.

The solicitor then turned his attention to the 'high powered microphones and cameras placed in every room' at the House of Prayer, which were an 'intolerable intrusion' for employees and volunteers. He reminded Gallagher and Fr McGinnity that he had told them at the 18 September meeting that this high-tech equipment was not conducive to creating a sense of trust in the House. Gallagher had sworn that the cameras, in her own words, 'were not working and had not been working for at least a year.' But he had since discovered 'beyond doubt' that the system was up and running, and was being used by Gallagher, her daughter and Tony Fitzpatrick to spy on staff and volunteers. 'Not only did that come as a great surprise and shock to us that Christina had lied to us, but we were dumbfounded as to why she saw the need to do this to us.'

Beighton again raised the question of Gallagher's relationship with Chalky White in the letter, claiming it was pure hypocrisy for her to criticise her supporters for not trusting her, while lying to them about the cameras and audio equipment in the House of Prayer. 'The cry of double standards must be heard in the deepest recesses of Heaven and I cannot help feeling that we were all being made fools of by Christina, who is showing herself to be a deceiver and a liar,' wrote Beighton.

Gallagher had claimed that the reason for installing the cameras in the first place was to prevent theft, though there was no evidence of any thievery at that time. Beighton pointed out that the camera equipment was of the highest quality. Some of it was disguised as infra-red sensors to give the impression it was part of a burglar alarm system. 'The aim was in fact to eavesdrop on every conversation in the sensitive areas of the House, such as the dining room and the kitchen.'

The solicitor said he had personally examined one of these so-called sensors to uncover the deception going on. He said no such complex system would be justified in preventing theft – cameras alone would have been sufficient. So it was clearly meant to listen in on 'every possible conversation' between volunteers and staff in the House of Prayer. Why was Gallagher so interested in what people were saying? Did she have something to hide? he wanted to know. Why did Christina lie about the cameras? Beighton said that surely this was not the atmosphere that Our Lady wanted to create in her House of Prayer.

Finally, Beighton asked about the plush Newport house that Gallagher bought in her own name and that of her daughter Mary in 1996. He wanted to know why the visionary had claimed in public, several months previously, that the house was for herself and her husband Paddy to live in. She also said her son Brendan was going to move into the old marital home near Knockmore, Foxford. 'The facts do not support this statement made by her.'

He said Paddy was still living in the old house. Their son Brendan had moved into a new house that he had bought himself with, Beighton had heard, help from Christina. 'Please provide details,' said the solicitor. He then asked where Gallagher got the money to buy the Newport house, and where did she get the IR£300,000 to IR£350,000 that she had since spent on the property. He said these were private matters, but they had caused 'the people of Ireland much disquiet when they see a house worth IR£350,000 to IR£400,000 in her sole possession and they know she is not working.'

The lawyer then asked if Gallagher had bought or

contributed to her daughter's house in Ballina. 'If so, where did the money come from?'

He ended the hard-hitting letter by insisting that Gallagher answer every single point he had raised or he would have no hesitation in going to a higher authority. 'She ignores them at her peril. It is not me to whom she will answer to finally.'

What was Gallagher's response? Did she give a full and frank explanation to the many questions Beighton had raised? Hardly. The solicitor got a legal letter from the House of Prayer lawyer Donal Corrigan threatening him with a libel lawsuit. Corrigan said all the accusations were 'false, without foundation and grossly defamatory.' It was business as usual at the House of Prayer.

Years later, Fr McGinnity was to claim that John Beighton had withdrawn the letter. Whether he did or not we do not know, because the solicitor now refuses to talk about the House of Prayer. If he did withdraw it, perhaps it was because of the threatened legal action against him.

But who was this Chalky White character who had suddenly appeared on the scene? The one person who knew all about him was Gallagher's friend Esther. She had been forced to spend a couple of weeks with the couple on a trip to Devon, several weeks previously. Gallagher had suddenly announced that she had to get out of Ireland, because an American businessman called Phillip Kronzer was coming to 'destroy' her. He had set up an organisation called the Kronzer Foundation to investigate false religious movements and cults. Kronzer had lost his wife to a cult. Christina heard that he was now coming to confront her. Gallagher begged Esther to go with her to avoid Kronzer, and Esther agreed. The two women had only just returned from a weekend in Dublin, when they got the call about Kronzer. Gallagher had hooked up with her sister, Marie, while in the capital, and they had gone to have their fortunes told, leaving Esther behind.

Esther had been a friend of Gallagher's since 1989, almost a decade. She had been a regular visitor to the House of Prayer from her home in Northern Ireland. Once Gallagher had persuaded Esther to go to England, Gallagher rang Fr McGinnity and told him to get as much money as he could lay his hands on. Esther remembers going to the bank twice in England and changing IR£2,000 each time into sterling for Christina. 'But she had more than that because she changed some on the boat,' Esther recalled. 'She bought drink to bring to Chalky, all sorts of clothes, aftershave and a watch. She could have had IR£6,000.'

Esther said that Gallagher paid for everything in cash. She never used credit cards. 'I paid a hotel bill with my Switch card but she paid me back in cash. When she went to pay for something she would always turn her back to you when she opened her bag. It was always cash, cash, cash.'

The two women travelled to Rosslare on 9 August 1998 and boarded the ferry. They stayed in the UK for two weeks. Gallagher tried to cover her tracks by booking her ticket in Esther's surname. She also used the first name Bridget, and gave her address as Shamrock Park, Sligo.

They landed in Pembroke, where to Esther's surprise, a man was standing waiting for them. She was less than impressed. Chalky White had what Esther described as long dirty-grey hair. He was unkempt looking. She thought he looked like a drunk. Despite his appearance, Gallagher seemed fascinated by him. They went to a pub, which Esther described as very rough, 'like a long-distance lorry drivers' place,' where they had accommodation booked for the night. 'Her room was not near mine,' said Esther.

They spent only one night there. The next day all three of them got a taxi to the railway station to get a train to Paignton, in Devon. Christina suddenly decided she couldn't be bothered with the train, and said they would take the taxi all the way from Pembroke to Paignton. The fare cost £240! Esther asked why they were going to Paignton and Gallagher replied: 'It is the most Protestant part of England, and nobody will recognise me there.'

Esther said: 'She did not say why she didn't want to be recognised. But strangely enough she was recognised at one point by an Irishman, who said, "I know you. You are Christina Gallagher." She denied it but the man said, "Christina, I know all about you. I have your book."'

Esther discovered that Gallagher had been in Paignton several weeks before, and that was when she first met Chalky. On the first trip she was staying with her sister and two nieces. Her sister owns holiday apartments in the town. Esther said: 'Christina must have had a row with her sister, because she stormed off and was sitting down crying, when this Chalky came along and comforted her, and asked her to go for a coffee or a drink. That is how they first hooked up.'

When they arrived in the seaside town, they booked into the Inn on the Green for three nights. 'We were in rooms 79 and 80, and I still have the receipts,' said Esther. After going to bed that night Esther could still hear voices and noises from Gallagher's room. At 2.30am she eventually got up and went in. She saw the visionary and Chalky lying on the bed in their clothes. Esther said to Chalky: 'Don't you think it's time you went home?' But Gallagher exploded with anger saying: 'Get out the f**king door and mind your own f**king business!'

The next day Esther found that Gallagher had changed rooms to another floor, well away from hers, claiming the first one was not big enough. When they checked out, Chalky came out and said one of the staff had complained that they had booked rooms for only two people but three had stayed. The group then moved into another hotel, the Palace, and again Gallagher made sure she was on a different floor from her friend. Even though they were in a holiday town, Esther said she did not enjoy her stay in Paignton. 'I was 63 and I had to sit in a bar every night with her, and it was not very nice. I do not drink, but she was knocking back the double Bailey's and ice.'

During the day Gallagher went on a shopping spree. Esther still has the receipts which confirm that on 11 August the visionary bought a pair of trousers for £78 and two suits for £317. The following day, she bought three pairs of shoes and another suit for £319. 'I nearly died when I saw them, as you would only wear them at a country and western club. One suit had the back cut out like she was an actress or a model, and it was not something you would expect a visionary to wear.'

But if she was shocked by that outfit, it was nothing compared to what she saw Gallagher wearing next. 'She also bought a leopard-skin catsuit. I was not with her when she bought that. She danced and shimmied away in it. I had to go with her every time she went to the loo to unzip her. I took a giggling fit at one point, saying if we left the cubicle together people might say: "there's two lesbians." Christina was a size 14 but she bought a size 10, so you can imagine how tight it was. I went back with her to the same shop because she wanted to buy another one, but they only had one left, a 14.'

Esther said Gallagher wore the leopard-skin catsuit in the bar at the Inn on the Green, where she got a date with a computer teacher from the local college. By Esther's account, he was an attractive man. The next day when Gallagher came down ready to meet him, she was wearing 'rings galore and was covered in make-up.' Even Chalky used to joke at her for wearing too much make-up. 'Anyway, she came down and said, "see you later." When she came back, a couple of hours later, she was fuming. She complained about his "bloody wreck of a car", which was covered in dog hair, and the fact he brought her for a hamburger.' Gallagher later told Esther that she had passed herself off as a writer and property developer. This claim was not entirely untrue, as she did co-author a book with Fr McGinnity. She also knew about property development, as she had recently carried out lavish extensions to her home in Newport.

Esther was surprised that even though Gallagher claimed to be besotted with Chalky, she still wanted to meet other men during this holiday. Gallagher spent one night dancing in the Palace Hotel with a man called Kevin, as Chalky looked on with a hangdog expression. She told Esther, 'I have to have him,' even though she spent much of the time eyeing up a different man at the bar. When Kevin was finally leaving he came up to Esther and said: 'I told your friend I was not interested. I have been living with my partner for years.'

While they were still in Paignton, she had taken Chalky off shopping and bought him every colour of shirt that the shop had. They were very expensive. She also bought him a pair of trousers.'

Esther said that Gallagher also picked up lots of property brochures. Gallagher stunned her friend by claiming that she wanted to open a nightclub like the Inn on the Green and put Chalky in charge. 'She wanted to live in Paignton. I never saw anyone so fascinated as she was by Chalky. She said she would give the House of Prayer to some religious order and they would give her money and she would come over once a month. She was full of hot air!'

Esther said Gallagher was impressed by the Inn on the Green as it was a thriving business with bars, a restaurant, a nightclub, apartments and bedrooms. 'It was a money-making place and it was not run by English people. I think they were Turkish.'

Gallagher also confided in Esther that she had given her sister £10,000 in 1998 towards holiday apartments in the English seaside town. 'But I suspect it was a lot more than that,' said Esther.

When Gallagher and Esther returned to Ireland on 25 August 1998 they stayed for a night in the Glenview, Co. Wicklow. 'It was very plush and as soon as Christina saw it she said, "I am not f**king paying for this!"' She had no problem staying in the lap of luxury herself, but she did not want to pay out for her minions. In the end it was Fr McGinnity, who arrived to meet them, who paid for the rooms.

Gallagher had given Esther strict instructions not to talk about anything that had happened in England to anyone. But Esther, a deeply religious woman, had been mortified by what she had seen in the previous two weeks. It had spelled out to her in the clearest possible terms that Gallagher was not the holy spiritual woman she pretended to be. She realised that she had been following a false visionary for the past decade. 'We were away from the 9th to the 25th and I never saw the inside of a chapel until I came back home again,' said Esther. 'Christina never said one prayer in that time. When I mentioned to her that we had to find a church she just looked at me and said, "They turned their back on me, I am turning my back on them." I have never once seen her praying, unless she was trying to impress somebody. Christina does not go to Mass at all.'

Following their return to Ireland, Fr McGinnity wanted to say Mass for them in his hotel room. But Esther was not happy unless she first went to confession. Gallagher told her to wait until afterwards, but Fr McGinnity brought her out into the hall to speak with her privately. Then Esther told him everything that had happened in England. Esther was expecting the priest to be shocked by what he heard, but she said he did not express a single emotion. Later, when they were back in the House of Prayer, the priest asked to speak to Esther and took her to the dining room. There he asked her to repeat everything about what had happened in Paignton. Again he showed no emotion. A year later, long after she had quit the House of Prayer, it suddenly hit Esther that the priest, in her view, had deliberately brought her to the dining room, so that Gallagher could listen in to everything that was said on the audio equipment.

While they were in England, Gallagher had been in constant touch with Fr McGinnity. At one point Gallagher told him that a wealthy elderly woman in Galway was promising to leave the House of Prayer IR£2 million in her will. She was in hospital at the time. Esther later heard that the woman may have left Gallagher even more money, although this was never verified. But Gallagher did tell Esther that the woman's parish priest warned her not to do it.

A week after they arrived home, Esther got a call from Gallagher telling her that she had to come down to Mayo. Esther said she couldn't, but the visionary insisted and asked her, 'Do you know who is here? Chalky!' She said Esther was the only one she could trust, and that (when she came down) she had to call him Lawrence.

Gallagher then delivered this bombshell: 'He is going to be taking charge of the House of Prayer.'

Esther said: 'I couldn't believe it. He was twice divorced, and looked very rough when I first saw him and he didn't work. But she was getting him ready to come and live in Ireland. She was crazy about him but she had still wanted to dance with all the other men she met in England. I actually felt sorry for him, watching him behind a pillar mouthing the words, "I love you" to Christina as she danced with someone else.'

Once she had decided that Chalky was going to move to Ireland, Gallagher started looking in estate agents windows at large properties. Esther asked her what she would do with such a place and the visionary said she would put Chalky in it. 'She was looking for a big place that might get a grant to do up. She was very switched on,' says Esther.

Esther said that Gallagher tried to clean Chalky up by dying his hair. But she could not do much about his badly stained teeth, which had been discoloured from heavy smoking. Chalky went with Gallagher to the House of Prayer and to her home. He was also her guest at the wedding of her son Brendan in September 1998. It must have been an interesting afternoon as her husband Paddy was obviously there too.

Esther recalls that during the reception, the elderly House of Prayer director Dick Hogan came to her table and asked who this Lawrence man was. The devoted supporter of Christina Gallagher would have had a coronary if he discovered the married holy visionary he worshipped had a twice-divorced English boyfriend who she wanted to run the Achill prayer centre. One of the wedding guests actually photographed Gallagher kissing Chalky outside the chapel.

Esther left the House of Prayer for good after

attending the wedding. She told Christina Gallagher
that she would never be back. Esther was so upset by
everything she had seen in England that she actually
lost her faith for a time, although she has since gone
back to the Church. But she says if Gallagher arrived
at her house now she would not let her past the door.
Looking back, she says she finds it hard to believe she
fell for it all.

Esther said she should have seen through Gallagher's
self-obsession much earlier. Even when the House of
Prayer closed down temporarily in 1998, Esther said
that Gallagher was moaning: 'Nobody has asked if
I'm okay or if I have a pair of shoes to stand in.' At
one point she complained that Our Lady and Jesus
had turned their backs on her. 'There is nobody more
important than her.' It was also incredible the number
of times 'Our Lady' suddenly appeared with a message
when Christina needed her. 'When you think back on it
now, you wonder how you were so gullible. How did
we fall for this stuff? But we thought we were doing
Our Lady's work.'

It also helped that Gallagher had Fr McGinnity
standing behind her every inch of the way, keeping
alive her image as a devout holy woman. Esther recalls
that there was a celebration in the House of Prayer on
Gallagher's 25th wedding anniversary in July 1996. Fr
McGinnity even gave her a papal blessing! And yet
Gallagher and her husband had separated the previous
year, which the priest must have known. When she
bought the house in Newport that year, there was
always a room ready for 'Father'. Even a blind man
would have noticed that the husband didn't live there,
but the priest helped Gallagher to keep up the façade.

The last contact Esther ever had with Fr McGinnity
was in October 1998, after he had received the hard-

hitting letter from solicitor John Beighton. The priest rang to say they were shocked by what they had read and that it was libellous. But a feisty Esther told him: 'You won't get a penny off me. Someone needs to go to confession – and it's not me.' McGinnity never rang again.

CHAPTER FOUR

A Devoted Couple

'We were going to suffer if we had money; if we had property to sell, we were going to suffer very much in this life and we were facing eternal damnation in the next if we did not contribute to this worthy project.'

Betty and Michael Morrissey live in a comfortable bungalow in the tiny village of Knockanore near the Co. Waterford-Co. Cork border. It's a remote but picturesque area of green fields and gentle hills where not a lot happens. Signs everywhere point to an alternative 'scenic route' on the local road system, but the main network itself is nothing more than a maze of country lanes. In the village there are no shops, just a church, a school and a pub. The nearest place to buy milk is 16km away, so the couple do most of their shopping in Youghal.

The Morrisseys live alone with their three Alsatian dogs. They say they would sell up and move somewhere smaller but for the dogs. They have no children and they were both only children themselves, so there are no big families in the background. They are the type of people who would be considered to be the backbone of small rural communities: honest, generous, loyal and hardworking. If anything sets them apart it is that, as devout Catholics, they take their faith a little more seriously than most. They would scoff at the notion that they are 'holy Joes' but the couple have for years attended regular prayer meetings in people's homes. Their faith is so important to them that they eventually built a prayer room in their own house.

Betty, who is 69, and Michael, who is ten years older at 79, would probably have lived out their days quietly and unknown to the rest of the country but for one thing – their link to the House of Prayer.

Former devoted followers of Christina Gallagher and Fr Gerard McGinnity, the couple handed over nearly €150,000, practically their whole life savings, to the two religious figureheads over a ten-year period. This was an astonishing amount of money for anyone to give, let alone an ordinary couple with no massive reserves. But the big-hearted couple were determined to do some good in the world while they were still alive. Their story is perhaps typical of the way good, devout, generous people across Ireland got sucked into the House of Prayer scam.

Betty Morrissey has a lively personality with a good sense of humour. She occasionally bursts into laughter while telling their story, often at the expense of themselves, for being so foolish. Even today she is incredulous that she fell for all the lies. Dressed in jeans, she looks much younger than her years. While she talks, Michael, a retired builder, paces up and down the room, intent that the whole story should finally come out and that nothing be omitted. It is obvious that Betty and Michael are completely devoted to each other and one would be lost without the other.

Betty reveals that they first heard about the House of Prayer while attending a prayer meeting in Cork City. This was a gathering they would join occasionally, if Michael happened to have business in the city. 'We would just drop in when we felt like it,' says Betty. 'At the entrance to the room where the prayer meeting was held was this donation box for contributions for Our Lady Queen of Peace House of Prayer in Achill Island. That was the first we heard of it. It was 1995 or maybe

1996. I know the House of Prayer opened in 1993, but we had heard nothing about it until then.'

Betty said that at the end of every prayer meeting there would be a 'big promotion of Christina' and that the people there would be told what a wonderful person Christina Gallagher was, how privileged they were to have this visionary in their country, and that if anyone was in a position to make any donation for the upkeep of the House of Prayer it would be very much appreciated. Betty said the couple who ran the meeting were huge followers of the House of Prayer, although the man has since died and the woman is no longer a believer. But at the time they had a big collection of books, videos, cassettes and other goods for sale. Betty said she decided to buy one of Gallagher's books entitled, *Please Come Back to Me and My Son*. Betty said she was very impressed by it, and became very curious about the House of Prayer.

The Cork couple leading the prayer group ran regular buses to Achill and Betty decided to go. Michael, on the other hand, had no interest in travelling all the way to the West of Ireland, especially by bus. Betty said she went a few times on the coach, but there was no budging Michael. He was not interested. Ironically, the very first time she travelled to Achill, the bus passed a stunning house behind high walls outside Newport in Co. Mayo.

'I saw this huge mansion with cut stone, a very elaborate house with great security around it and CCTV... and I said to the person beside me on the bus, "This has to be a drug baron's house", because at that time there were very few big houses around that part of Mayo so it really stood out.' It was two years later that Betty, to her horror, discovered that the 'drug baron's house' belonged to none other than Christina Gallagher.

Betty remembers that first occasion well, because at the time she and Michael were trying to get planning permission to build a higher wall around their own garden to keep their dogs in. She recalls being shocked at how this house got planning permission for such a high wall.

Betty recalled that her first visits to the House of Prayer were less than memorable. Their bus would arrive at around 11.00am and they would then attend a Mass said by Fr McGinnity. From 1998 the Church banned the saying of Mass, Confessions and all other sacraments at the House of Prayer. But back in 1996 Masses were still being said. They were long-drawn out affairs, and would take twice as long as a normal service, says Betty, who confessed that she was often extremely tired from her early start and the long journey. But she said she would see everyone praying fervently and the whole place gave off a reverent atmosphere.

'At that time Christina wasn't coming there much at all, and I didn't meet her for ages. There was just a small shop and everyone used to go towards this shop buying souvenirs, and of course this eejit would be buying souvenirs for everyone she knew nearly. Oh when I think of the money I spent in that shop!'

Betty said she used to travel to Achill every month or six weeks. She kept pressing Michael to go, but he refused to travel by bus. Eventually he agreed to go by car, and they began driving up themselves. This gave them much more independence. Betty said Christina Gallagher made a big impression on her when she finally did see her. 'She seemed to have an aura of holiness around her face, and then the first time I saw her going into this kind of ecstasy, you would really believe she was seeing something from heaven. And of course the crowd would all be singing hymns to Our

Lady and it would all be very emotional. You just got carried away by the whole thing, at least I did. I really believed. I was very impressed, very impressed.'

Betty remembered that the first mention of donations came when they attended a prayer meeting organised in Whitechurch, Co. Waterford. This meeting was actually filmed and the video later went on sale in the House of Prayer shop. Fr McGinnity was appealing for IR£250,000 to build an extension to the House of Prayer, because Our Lady 'wanted' it to be a retreat house for priests and it was too small, he claimed. Betty and Michael gave a total of IR£21,100 to that project, handing over two donations of IR£10,000 and then a IR£500 and a IR£600. The cheques were given over a two-month period.

'It was a lot of money, but at that time we had sold the house that Mike had originally lived in,' says Betty. 'We had actually gone to Christina and Fr McGinnity and said we would like to help, but we wanted to give some money to the Third World. It was 1996 and we wanted to do some good while we could. Christina said straight away: 'There are plenty of people to contribute to the Third World but very few to contribute to the House of Prayer.' And Fr McGinnity nodded. I believed her because I thought the House of Prayer was not well known and there was such publicity for the Third World and all the famines that were happening.'

The couple said they began to get a little worried when two years went by with no sign of the extension going up. In 1998 the House of Prayer closed temporarily, after a standoff with the Archbishop of Tuam, Dr Michael Neary.

'Nothing was happening with the building. We were anxious about the money,' says Michael, who as a former builder, would have taken particular interest

in any extension. The couple felt that maybe someone
had run off with the cash, a belief that Gallagher did
not dispel when they kept questioning her about the
extension. Gallagher also claimed that there were
problems with the planning permission. But much
later the extension did go up, after the House of Prayer
reopened. People began to gradually drift back. But
now there were no Masses or confessions, because
the Church had changed its stance on the centre and
had withdrawn its initial support. The hierarchy had
backed it when it thought the House was going to be a
retreat centre for priests and a place of quiet meditation
and prayer. But the archdiocese now realised it had
become something completely different: a place of
pilgrimage with Christina Gallagher at the centre. This
was something the local Church authorities were not
comfortable with.

The Archbishop of Tuam wanted to incorporate the
House of Prayer into the diocese, over which he had
control, but Christina Gallagher would not play ball.
She had no plans to hand over her baby to a third
party.

While this battle was going on, Betty Morrissey learnt
something that shocked her to the core. She was told
by friends that the huge Newport house belonged to
Christina Gallagher. 'We just could not believe it,' recalls
Betty. 'I felt absolute shock and disbelief. I said how could
a visionary want to live in such a palatial residence?'

Betty's amazement was heightened by the fact that
she had read in Christina Gallagher's book that the
visionary had no interest in material things. Although
Gallagher claimed she once dreamt of having the best of
everything, she said she had put those shallow notions
aside, and now wouldn't have a problem if she had to
live in a tent. 'And it was this book which had really

influenced me to go to the House of Prayer,' said Betty incredulously.

Betty heard that the Newport house was so luxurious that the press were trying to get inside to photograph it, and that it was generating a lot of local publicity. 'Michael knew from the outside, being in the building trade, that it was a very expensive house, very plush,' says Betty. She was so horrified by the discovery that she decided to distance herself from the House of Prayer. Even on the usual 16 July anniversary, when there is always a big celebration, Betty refused to go inside.

'Michael went up but I wouldn't go beyond the local church. I stayed in church trying to say a few prayers, and I thought it was all wrong to go up to the House of Prayer. I can't tell you the effect it had on me that she would want to live in a place like that.'

After a long day, Betty went to find her husband. She was walking aimlessly around the car park when she suddenly realised something was happening right next to her. 'Christina appeared almost beside me and she went into what I call a trance, but which she terms ecstasy. She fell to her knees, and her eyes raised up to heaven, and you felt she was really seeing something,' said Betty. The stunned pensioner said that all her doubts suddenly evaporated, and that she felt privileged to be there, watching all this happening just feet away. Gallagher had been circulating amongst the pilgrims when it happened, and now people were rubbing her arms and bursting into hymns to Our Lady. Betty felt a complete hypocrite for ever doubting the visionary. Later, Betty said to her husband that there must be some kind of explanation as to why this holy woman was living in such a palatial home, and that maybe it was down to the husband Paddy. Perhaps it was him that wanted to live in a big house, she argued.

Betty was 'sort of dragged back in' to the Gallagher fold, and the couple continued to attend the House over the next few years without incident. Then one day in 2004 Fr McGinnity rang Michael at their home. It was a fateful phone call that would eventually smash all links between the Morrisseys and the house.

'Our number is not listed, and there's no way he could have got hold of it only from Christina,' said Betty. The priest asked Michael if he would be prepared to meet him and said that he would come down half way to Co. Waterford. One of the Morrisseys' friends on Achill was ill at the time and they wanted to visit her, so they said it would suit them better to meet on the island, and that they would go to the House of Prayer that weekend. The couple thought that the meeting would be about setting up a House of Prayer in the Munster region, as one of Our Lady's requests to Gallagher was supposedly to set up a chain of houses around Ireland.

'When Michael met Fr McGinnity he arrived out with a sheaf of those messages [apocalyptic messages supposedly given to Christina Gallagher from Our Lady] and he started reading them out to Michael. Michael got so fed up he said, 'Father, sure I know those messages off by heart. What is the point of all this? Is it money you want?' And Fr McGinnity said, "It is."'

Betty says she and Michael are now convinced the terrifying messages were just to psyche Michael up to give money. Both of them had heard them many times before. The messages predicted death and destruction on a massive worldwide scale, and warned that anyone who had the means to help the House of Prayer, but refused, would suffer eternal damnation.

Michael said he was dumbfounded to hear the House was in financial trouble and that he was being asked to help again. He asked for time to think. Michael recalls that he then asked how Christina was, as he had heard that she was not well. Fr McGinnity replied that she was very poorly. 'And worse than that,' he said, 'she has to sell her house.'

Michael was shocked by this revelation. But he suggested that the sale of her house would surely ease any money problems she had. But Fr McGinnity told him that any cash from the sale of the house would go straight to the bank. Michael was told that the money the priest wanted was to help buy a new home for Gallagher. To Michael and Betty this piece of news explained away many things. They came to the conclusion that the visionary lived in such a plush home because she had an extravagant husband and that he must have pushed her into this situation of debt.

'I decided that it was he who was to blame for the elaborate house she was living in,' says Betty. 'That was the only reason I agreed with Michael that we should help. That was when Michael gave €40,000. We blamed the husband.'

Michael had also heard rumours that Gallagher's marriage was breaking up and that if this were true, it would be reasonable to be selling the house. Unknown to the couple, Christina and Paddy had separated in 1995. Her estranged husband lived in their old house and she lived in Newport. Gallagher had also been claiming to anyone who would listen that she had been getting terrible hassle from her neighbours, and had to sell up. And yet when Mike McCrory later went to visit the neighbours he would discover that they had never even met Gallagher. She would drive straight through her electronic gates without stopping.

Michael and Betty Morrissey made their €40,000 donation two weeks after being approached. They said they didn't think anything of it when Fr McGinnity asked for the cheque to be made out to him. The priest would reveal at a later meeting that the House of Prayer was 'having a bit of trouble with the Revenue Commissioners', which would be sorted out soon. Michael said: 'I didn't ask any questions because I trusted the man 100 per cent. I was going to make the cheque out to the House of Prayer, but I trusted him or I wouldn't have given it to him otherwise.'

Months later, the couple were at the House of Prayer one Saturday afternoon when the manager, Noel Guinan, asked if they would be prepared to go to a special meeting in Mullingar, Co. Westmeath. The couple were shocked as it would involve another long drive from their home in the middle of the week. They were reluctant to agree, but Guinan said that all the biggest supporters of the House of Prayer would be at that meeting. When the Morrisseys pointed out that it would be very expensive and that they would have to pay for a B&B, Guinan revealed that the accommodation was being provided for free.

They eventually agreed and drove up to the meeting, which was in a nursing home in Multyfarnham, just over three kilometres outside Mullingar, in May 2005. The Morrissey's didn't know any of the other people there, and they felt the others did not seem to know each other either. 'We were waiting for ages for Fr McGinnity to turn up but he finally arrived with this Noel Guinan and a woman called Majella Meade from the House of Prayer,' recalls Betty. 'First this picture was placed on the table of Our Lady crying tears of blood. Fr McGinnity produced the rosary beads, and we were tired and fed up after the long drive, and we were hoping he would only say one decade but he proceeded to say this whole long rosary. His rosary takes almost an hour. By the time this was over, this Majella Meade came forward and started reading very threatening messages out of a book, a compilation of Our Lady's messages [to Christina Gallagher]. To say the messages were threatening was an understatement. We were going to suffer if we had money; if we had property to sell, we were going to suffer very much in this life and we were facing eternal damnation in the next if we did not contribute to this worthy project that Our Lady wanted, a project that was going to save millions of souls.'

When the couple heard that the project was to save souls, the only way they could rationalise it was to think it was in connection with the establishment of the chain of houses in America. Someone then asked if it was in connection with the American Houses of Prayer and Fr McGinnity hesitated and said, "Partly". Papers were then circulated around the room and people were asked to write down the amount of money they were prepared to give.

'We pledged €100,000,' said Betty. 'We didn't have it to give; no way did we have it to give. But it was like mass hypnosis. I can't explain it any other way. We were in this mind-frame of foreboding for the future, and feeling very insecure, feeling that we really had to give the money. Wherever we got it from, we had to give it. People were openly discussing their financial situation. People were talking about money they had put aside for their children's education and that they would find it very hard to take money out of that.'

One particular man said he had sites to sell and that he could not do that overnight, that there would be a legal process to go through. But Fr McGinnity asked him if he would go to his bank manager and get an advance against the sale of those sites and the man said he would. 'They were all struggling to find ways to give the money. They were all falling over backwards to find ways of doing it.'

Michael said: 'It shows how brainwashed we were. One poor man working for a wage was giving money every week from his pay packet – a big part of his money.'

The couple said there were 25 to 30 people at the meeting and there was a roll call at the beginning. 'Everyone was hand-picked,' Betty said. After the money was pledged, Noel Guinan collected the papers and totted up the total, which amounted to roughly €1.5 million. 'And no way was Fr McGinnity pleased with that, out of just 25 people,' said Betty incredulously. 'This is crazy stuff when you think back on it!'

The priest told his captive audience that he hoped to reach a target of €2 million, and appealed to them, 'if there was any way' they could manage to give a little more. The papers were passed around again. The Morrisseys kept their pledge at €100,000, but other people upped theirs because, although the total did not hit €2 million, it did get to €1.8 million. That was the final figure. It was then that Fr McGinnity mentioned that the cheques should be made payable to a John Rooney.

'And this is the most amazing thing,' says Betty. 'We were so brainwashed, we were so hypnotised, or whatever was wrong with us, that nobody asked who this man John Rooney was.' The couple assumed that he must be the man coordinating the American houses, although they did not know for sure as nobody told them.

'We were so terrified coming out of that meeting,' says Betty. 'We were so drained. We did not know where we were going to stay for the night. We were brought to a location very, very near. I thought it was in the grounds of the nursing home but it wasn't. It was late at night and there is a series of holiday cottages there and we were accommodated in one of those.

We were really drained out, asking ourselves why: were we put under such intense pressure? It was the way the whole thing was orchestrated. It was the psychology used. I can't convey to you the atmosphere that was in that place that night.

'We were most unhappy. How could we have pledged €100,000? How could we be so stupid? What kind of psychology had they used on us, that we were prepared to give money we had no hope of raising?'

Betty said part of their naivety was down to the fact that the project was to 'save millions of souls.' She explained that being of a religious nature, this was the best way to appeal to them. She felt everyone there was chosen specially, because they were religious people and would want to help. 'People asked why the project was so secret? Why couldn't Fr McGinnity disclose what it was about? He said it was just so secret that if it was disclosed it would be blocked,' said Betty.

As soon as they got out of the meeting they began to discuss ways of raising the enormous amount of cash they had pledged, including selling their car. Michael had an old work van that would have to do them from now on, she said. But they both agreed that there was no way they could possibly raise the €100,000 they had promised. Still reeling from the shock of it all, the couple agreed between themselves that they would try to give €50,000.

Michael recalls that he had already decided in advance that if the meeting turned out to be about money, then he was going to get up and walk out. 'At that stage I was getting fed up with it. But I didn't walk out. I was glued,' he said. He is convinced today that others at the meeting could not have come up with all the money they promised either, as €1.8 million would be too much for such a small group to give. No money changed hands that night, so nobody knows for sure how much was eventually donated, except the House of Prayer leaders themselves.

Betty recalled that after the meeting was adjourned people stopped for a cup of tea, but the atmosphere was one of stress. Nobody relaxed or chatted. 'Everybody was uptight about the situation except Fr McGinnity. He was beaming all over and shaking hands with everybody and thanking them for coming.'

The worried couple eventually retired to their bed for a sleepless night. Two weeks later they were on their way back to the House of Prayer, and they knew that they were going to come under fierce pressure to deliver the cash. When they arrived in Achill they were met by the manger Noel Guinan, who asked them if they had the money with them.

Betty told him: 'Noel, it would be very hard for us to give it. I'm sorry; we have committed ourselves to something that was just out of our reach completely. We pledged €100,000 and now to give even €50,000 would be a very, very great effort.'

She said Guinan was not happy with their reply but had to accept it. As Betty chatted to Guinan, Majella Meade suddenly appeared on the scene. The Morrisseys were usually wary of her, as she was the one who often read out the apocalyptic messages. While Betty talked to Noel Guinan, Meade zoomed in on Michael. Even today he can't recall exactly what she said to him, but the result was that minutes later he was getting out his cheque book.

'At this stage I was just fed up,' he recalls. 'Betty was all against paying any money that day. She decided to leave her cheque book at home, just in case, but I had my own cheque book in the car.' After being pressed by Meade, he found himself revealing this fact to the Gallagher devotee.

'Of course this Majella then couldn't get down to the car fast enough,' says Betty. 'She actually took the cheque book out of Michael's hand. She wrote 'John Rooney €50,000.' That is her writing on the cheque – and Michael signed it. She practically forced him. I was very unhappy and we had a major fight on the way home.'

Even today Michael is mystified as to why he did it. But he says he was so stressed out by the relentless pressure over such a long period of time that he just wanted to get away from Achill and go home. 'Before that, for months and months – maybe 12 months – I was criticising the House of Prayer to Betty, but she wouldn't listen to me,' says Michael. 'I was saying, look, I have done more for the House of Prayer than the House of Prayer is ever going to do for me, which turned out to be true.'

Amazingly, the €50,000 was not the last donation the couple were to give the House of Prayer. Months later, Michael was to hand over a further €8,000 to Fr McGinnity for the very same cause, the secret mission to save 'millions of souls.' What possessed him to do such a thing when he was so unhappy about handing over €50,000? 'The way our solicitor summed it up was that we were under a spell,' says Betty. 'What on earth was wrong with us? We said the only conclusion was that we were under a spell. But Fr McGinnity was so plausible. It was an on-going thing every time you went up there. "Would there be any way you could help us?" he would say. "If someone could help with the project… If there was any way anybody could help…"'

Betty and Michael were finally to bail out of the House of Prayer completely the following year, 2006, when once again they were being pressured for more money. This time it was for something called the Blue

Ivory Trust, which at that point they had never heard of. The couple said that an announcement was made one Saturday afternoon that there would be a meeting after the usual afternoon prayer session and that if anyone wanted to find out what the Blue Ivory Trust was about they could attend.

Michael immediately told his wife that there was no way he was going, and he went off for a pint in a local pub. But Betty said her curiosity had been piqued, so she went along. The meeting began when Majella Meade stood up and started reading threatening messages from the same book she had used in Multyfarnham. Meade then told the crowd that Christina was finding it very hard to maintain her house in Newport, and that she was having great problems with her neighbours. She said that a few of Christina's supporters had got together to form a legal trust called the Blue Ivory Trust, which would buy Christina's house from her to get her out of her financial difficulties. The house would be held as a shrine to Christina, and if the required sum of money wasn't realised, people would be refunded their money.

Betty recalls that Fr McGinnity was standing by saying nothing and that somebody asked him, 'Father, is this message from heaven?' And he nodded his head and said, 'It is.'

His answer was like a punch in the stomach to Betty. She said she felt physically sick, because she had discovered that Gallagher had been trying to sell the house privately some years before in upmarket property magazines, in England. The house was so elaborate that she could not put it up for public auction or people in Ireland would see the style in which she lived. A priest saw the adverts in a property magazine in England and told friends of the Morrisseys. Betty's shock was, of course, made all the worse by the fact that she and her husband had been persuaded to hand over €40,000 to help buy a new home for Gallagher two years earlier. Now, here were her supporters again trying to raise yet more money for the same purpose.

As the shock sank in, Betty was aware that other people were only too keen to pay up. Some were in a hurry to get back to their buses and were trying to write cheques up against walls with their biros. 'They were just falling over backwards to contribute and I felt so sickened by the whole thing. I went to find Michael who had gone to the pub, and I had a stiff whisky, I can tell you. And I said to him, 'This is such a racket.' I said, 'We have to pull away from this. It is a complete racket.' He said, 'Didn't I tell you that all along.' There was deception all the way through. They have betrayed people's trust.'

The couple attended the House of Prayer only one more time, in July 2007, when they travelled to Achill to meet friends who lived on the island. Betty said she decided to go into the House of Prayer more as a spy than a pilgrim to check out what they were up to. What she saw once again shocked her. 'I was so horrified because there were dustbins – actual dustbins – in strategic areas around the place, at the entrance and several places around the car park marked "donations". I couldn't believe my eyes. It was the first time I had seen that.'

She also found a row of portacabins erected by the side of the car park, another first for her. She went into each one to see what was going on and found that they were all collecting money for different things. The first one had a follower of Christina Gallagher's collecting money for the Blue Ivory Trust, surrounded by photos of the Houses of Prayer across America. In the second, four or five women were taking down the names of people in a long queue who wanted to order the House of Prayer's *News Review*, a new monthly magazine with an annual subscription of €30 a year. 'There were crowds going in, it was unbelievable.'

The next cabin was dedicated to a new project, An Endless Rosary, which was to be launched in the House of Prayer for people's intentions for the living and the dead. If you paid €50 for a bead your intentions would be remembered for ever more in this endless rosary that would be held in the House of Prayer. 'Even though I was shocked I still bought a bead.

'I think I did it as a cover for the fact I was spying,' says Betty. 'I said, "I need a receipt for this." The woman said I would be forwarded a receipt, but the receipt never came. There was no receipt book at all, and lots of people were paying €50.'

It was the last time Betty ever set foot in the place. Six months later, from January 2008, the *Sunday World* articles began appearing, confirming the couple's worst fears. The newspaper's first article, about the new €1 million house Gallagher had bought outside Ballina for her daughter, was a huge surprise. But that surprise was nothing compared to what she felt two weeks later when the *Sunday World* uncovered the Malahide mansion. Like thousands of other people around the country, Betty was stunned. But unlike them, she knew that she had been swelling Gallagher's coffers for a decade, and she was now left with the awful suspicion that she had been doing nothing more than funding the supposed visionary's millionaire lifestyle.

Betty had been sickened enough to find out that Gallagher had been living in the luxury house outside Newport, but the magnificent house on a private estate in Malahide was in a different league altogether. Betty said the story was a complete bombshell.

Christina Gallagher with a pet bird on her shoulder at the House of Prayer.

Gallagher and her estranged husband, Paddy, put on a charade for the House of Prayer followers, by celebrating their 25th wedding anniversary at the Achill centre.

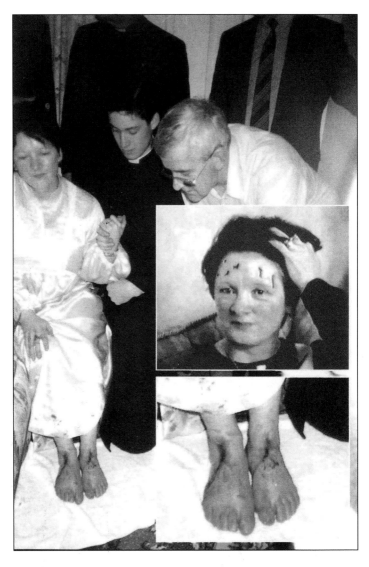

Gallagher shows off her 'stigmata' wounds of Christ in 1995. Critics claim the wounds were self-inflicted. Very few followers have seen any evidence of her supposed stigmata.

Christina Gallagher on holiday in Devon, in August 1998, where she met up with her companion Chalky White.

Christina Gallagher photographed with the discredited visionary Julie Kim, from South Korea. Kim was excommunicated from the Catholic Church, in January 2009, for preaching falsehoods.

The House of Prayer in its heyday, when thousands of people used to visit on the anniversary days. This photo was taken before the exposés began in 2008.

© *Sunday World*

Some of the paraphernalia on sale at the House of Prayer, from pens and videos to statues and pictures.

Christina and her estranged husband, Paddy, in happier times with their granddaughter.

The House of Prayer manager, Noel Guinan, with Christina Gallagher at a Christmas party.

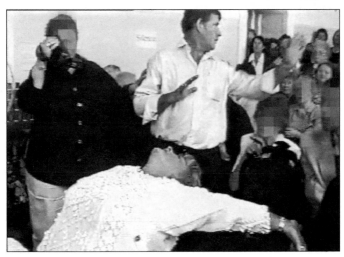

Christina Gallagher goes into 'ecstasy' at the House of Prayer. These are the moments in which the self-proclaimed visionary allegedly gets her apocalyptic messages direct from heaven.

Fr Gerard McGinnity
leaves his parish church in
Knockbridge, Co. Louth.
Gallagher's spiritual director
refused to say a single
word to help clear up the
unexplained controversy
over Christina's huge wealth.
© *Sunday World*

Fr Gerard McGinnity with the woman he idolises.

Fr McGinnity with American money man John Rooney, the official owner of Gallagher's fabulous Malahide mansion.

Whistle-blower Mike McCrory, the man who started the investigations into the House of Prayer.

© Sunday World

Betty's disgust turned to fury the following week when the *Sunday World* revealed that the fabulous mansion was actually registered to the name of Gallagher's chief American fundraiser, John Rooney, the man to whom her husband had been asked to make out a cheque for €50,000 in June 2005. This was just a few months before the mansion was snapped up in the name of Rooney.

'When I heard the owner was John Rooney, something snapped inside my head,' recalls Betty. 'I felt sick. I will never forget the shock. Did our money go straight into buying that house for Christina? I presume it did. How many collections were held around the country for that man?'

When the Morrisseys first agreed to talk to me in January 2008 it was on an off-the-record basis. They did not want to be named. Michael had a heart condition, and Betty did not want to put him under any more stress than he was already suffering. Also Michael was very reluctant to go public, being content to put their money losses down to a bad experience. He was keen to put the whole thing behind him and move on with his life.

In their first interview, published in an article on 27 January 2008, Betty revealed how they had planned to give thousands of pounds to the Third World, but instead got duped into giving it to the House of Prayer. This was something she was very angry about. 'I really hold that against Christina because we wanted to do some good with the money. It is so sad,' said Betty at the time.

'We could not see any sense in this Blue Ivory Trust and we also felt that what Fr McGinnity was saying was just not true. There was no dwelling on the spiritual at all. He just talked about Christina and how much she was suffering. It was completely overdone. He is like a man hypnotised,' she told the newspaper. 'But whatever Fr

McGinnity says, people will believe. People who go there are brainwashed and I can see that now, standing back. They are not open to argument. It is the saddest thing. They are a cult and we were complete idiots. We know we have been made fools of.'

Many others had been hoodwinked too, said Betty, who accused Christina Gallagher of deliberately preying on people's religious beliefs, and of targeting individuals who she thought had money. The Morrisseys believe hundreds of people all over Ireland must have signed cheques to John Rooney, and that the money went straight into buying the Malahide mansion. Even if it didn't, they argue, what was the House of Prayer doing collecting money from pensioners like themselves when they owned a €4 million mansion, which they could sell to raise funds?

'Why don't they sell that? Or Gallagher's daughter's €1 million house?' Betty asked. Weeks later, in March 2008, the couple again spoke out after getting copies from their bank of two cheques they had written to McGinnity and Rooney for €40,000 and €50,000 respectively. Once again they agreed to talk on condition of anonymity. The *Sunday World* published the cheques, with the Morrisseys' name blanked out, on March 30 in an article called 'Holy Cash Cow.' A sub-heading read: 'We uncover dodgy links between cheques and Gallagher's house. The story said the cheques added up to a scandal for 'holy' woman Christina Gallagher and were proof that the finances of the self-proclaimed visionary and of her Achill Island centre should be investigated.

The story caused a sensation. Other national newspapers, including the *Sunday Tribune*, the *Sunday Times*, the *Sunday Independent*, the *Irish Independent* and the *Irish Mail on Sunday* were all now vigorously following up the House of Prayer story. RTÉ's prestigious *Prime Time* programme decided to devote half of one of their shows to the House of Prayer. A TV crew travelled to Co. Waterford to interview Betty Morrissey with her face blacked out. One of the crew was so moved by Betty's story that he began to cry during the visit, Betty revealed. The next day the same crew interviewed this reporter in the offices of the *Sunday World*.

The segment went out on air the following night, Thursday 3 April 2008. A *Prime Time* reporter was seen knocking on Fr McGinnity's door in his parish. The priest answered the door saying he was on the phone and would come out shortly to talk. He never did – and refused to answer the door again. Hundreds of thousands of TV viewers had seen him lying on camera.

Michael Morrissey said after watching the show: 'If McGinnity had any standing at all he would have appeared on the programme. If you believe in something you should be able to defend it. But then he would be defending the indefensible, so how could he?'

For the Morrisseys, this would probably have been the end of their part in the House of Prayer saga. They felt that they had done as much as they could to expose Christina Gallagher and to stop her ripping off other people around Ireland. It was now up to others to pick up the baton. They were still adamant that they did not want to be named. But that was to change because of a blunder by Fr McGinnity. The Morrisseys still had friends in the House of Prayer and when they heard that the priest was telling his usual Saturday afternoon congregation that the cheques in the newspapers were a forgery, and that everything in the press was a lie, they saw red.

They found it almost impossible to believe that a priest they once trusted completely and to whom they

had handed over their life savings was now claiming
he had never received any money from them, and that
the cheques they in fact signed were forgeries. The
couple were completely outraged and Betty Morrissey
finally decided to go public. Her husband Michael
was now totally up for it too, so incensed was he that
Fr McGinnity was basically calling them liars after
everything they had done for the House of Prayer. They
felt utterly betrayed.

The *Sunday World* printed their story with
photographs on 4 May 2008 under the heading: 'We
were threatened with eternal damnation if we didn't
give €150,000 to the House of Prayer.' The Morrisseys
explained how they were seduced and cajoled into
handing over €150,000 during a 10-year period. They
told how they were put under massive psychological
pressure to find the cash, even though they could not
afford it. They revealed how McGinnity relentlessly
targeted them and many other elderly people and was
now 'blatantly lying' about not receiving money. Two
of their cheques had been made out to him at his own
request, they said.

In the same article, the couple said how shocked
they were to learn that the priest had even lied to
his own superior, Cardinal Seán Brady, head of the
Armagh Diocese, about his involvement with Christina
Gallagher. They had learnt that Fr McGinnity had
recently been called in by the cardinal and quizzed about
his role in the House of Prayer, following a number of
complaints from Catholics around the country about his
involvement. People wanted to know why a parish priest
in Knockbridge, Co. Louth was being allowed to leave his
own parish every weekend to preach in a controversial
prayer centre that had no Church backing and which was
in a different diocese on the other side of the country.

But Fr McGinnity evidently lied to the cardinal by claiming he played no part in fundraising at the House of Prayer. We know this because of a letter Cardinal Brady subsequently wrote to at least one of the people who had complained about Fr McGinnity's presence in the House of Prayer. In his reply, Cardinal Brady said he had discussed matters with Fr McGinnity 'who has sought to assure me that everything is in order and that he is not directly involved in the raising and administration of funds.' The Cardinal continued: 'I was told that where family members object to a relative donating, the money would be returned.' Cardinal Brady ended by saying: 'I wish to underline that Fr McGinnity has neither sought nor obtained my approval for his involvement with the House of Prayer.'

To the Morrisseys, and to many other opponents of Christina Gallagher, this was a cop-out and was a hugely disappointing response from the head of Ireland's Catholics. The Church, which had been strongly criticised by many people for not doing more to stop Christina Gallagher in her tracks, appeared to be sitting on the fence yet again. Betty Morrissey said as much in the 4 May article: 'If the Church had acted sooner, we and many others would still have our money in our pockets.' They also found it risible that the House of Prayer was claiming it would return donations at the request of any family members.

Dejected that no official Church action was being taken against Christina Gallagher and the House of Prayer, the Morrisseys decided to take matters one step further themselves. So they made an official complaint to the gardaí in Co. Mayo about the organisation. They made an appointment with gardaí in Westport, and subsequently travelled to the West to make a full statement claiming Gallagher and Fr McGinnity had taken money from them on false pretences. But the battling couple were not content with that. Now fired up by all the lies that they had discovered Fr McGinnity was telling, they also decided to take a civil action to get their money back. They consulted a lawyer in Waterford, who agreed to take their case. The solicitor asked this reporter for copies of the extensive records I had collected over recent months, including the land records for Gallagher's portfolio of properties.

The day the writs were served was one of the most dramatic days in the history of the House of Prayer, and was captured live on a secret camera. The *Sunday World* had already decided to send an undercover reporter and photographer into the House of Prayer, on Wednesday 16 July 2008, because it was the 15th anniversary of the opening of the house and Christina Gallagher usually claimed to receive a message from Our Lady on that day of celebration. I had also discovered that the Morrisseys' lawyer was going to travel to Achill that same day and serve the writs on Gallagher and Fr McGinnity inside the House of Prayer. This was obviously something not to be missed.

Despite her claims that she has foreseen virtually every global calamity of recent times and that she is guided by Our Lady, Christina Gallagher did not see the writs coming. She was taken totally by surprise when the solicitor put his hand on her shoulder and handed her the High Court summons accusing her of wrongfully taking a six-figure sum from the Morrisseys. Veteran *Sunday World* photographers Padraig O'Reilly and Liam O'Connor, along with reporter Cathal O'Shea, were present to capture the look of bewilderment on Gallagher's face. A few seconds later the lawyer served a second writ on Fr McGinnity, who was so enraged he refused to accept it, flicking it up into the air in anger. As the summons fell to the ground the solicitor was quickly approached by Gallagher's security staff and asked to leave the building. The whole astonishing scene was captured on camera, and the dramatic footage was later posted on the *Sunday World* website.

The afternoon's events must have left the House of Prayer hierarchy in shock. In the 15 years they had been open for business, this was only the second legal action taken against them.

The Morrisseys knew that their lawsuit was very unlikely to end up in court. Everyone guessed that Gallagher would do anything to stay out of the witness box, where she could be grilled about her wealthy lifestyle and her collection of houses. But few people could have guessed how quickly the matter would be resolved. Just one month after the legal papers were served on Gallagher and Fr McGinnity, the Morrisseys were given their money back in an out-of-court settlement. So too, was another victim, Paddy Woods, who hired the same lawyer to retrieve his €100,000.

It was an incredibly speedy resolution and showed how desperate the House of Prayer bosses were to bring the matter to a close. All parties, as is legal custom, had to sign confidentiality clauses in the agreement, which effectively banned all sides from discussing the settlement. But I discovered that Gallagher and her organisation had paid out a massive €250,000 to the two parties as a settlement and in legal fees.

Meanwhile, Fr McGinnity had begun telling the gullible faithful in Achill that there had never been any writs against the House of Prayer and that it was all a media hoax. On 24 August 2008, the *Sunday World* carried the story about the €250,000 settlement – and for good measure published the High Court documents that showed that Gallagher, McGinnity, John Rooney

and the House of Prayer had all been named in the
action taken by the Morrisseys. Again, the once
respected priest, Fr Gerard McGinnity, had been caught
lying through his teeth. He was not the only one.
Gallagher herself and other followers were often telling
the Saturday afternoon faithful that a huge lawsuit
had been filed against the *Sunday World* and that the
House of Prayer was going to get a massive windfall
in damages. In reality no lawsuit was ever filed. But
sadly, many of the elderly House of Prayer followers
swallowed everything they were told.

CHAPTER FIVE

Dissenting Disciples

'Your stories were a bombshell to so many people. But Christina Gallagher did not put a gun to people's heads. They gave money willingly.'

After they first went public, Betty and Michael Morrissey were besieged with telephone calls, many from House of Prayer officials calling them traitors. It got so bad that they stopped answering the phone, if the caller's number did not show up on their caller ID phone system.

The elderly couple were put under enormous pressure, but did not regret coming forward to talk about their experience. As they saw it, they had right on their side, and an alarming story to share. They also hoped that by telling their story they might prevent other people from being drawn in or cheated by the House of Prayer.

What they certainly did not expect was for two of Christina Gallagher's cronies to turn up on their door one morning – several hours drive away from Achill Island – in a desperate bid to woo them back into the fraternity. Arriving unannounced, a man, unknown to the Morrisseys and a woman they vaguely knew, said they wanted to arrange a meeting between the Morrisseys and Gallagher, Fr McGinnity and Majella Meade. Understandably, the Morrisseys were annoyed and quite taken aback. The couple did not let them through the door.

'I got a call early one morning from a man called Barry, who said he was outside our house. I looked and I saw the car,' said Betty. 'He was with a woman called

Josie Butler, from Tipperary, who I knew. In my statement to the gardaí, I had given her name, as one of those organising the John Rooney fundraising meetings.'

Betty said she felt intimidated by the unexpected call, and told the visitors that there was no point in having a meeting. The only meeting that they would have would be in front of their solicitor. The man called Barry rang again the next day and the day after that. On his last call he said, 'We will give you a few days to think about it.' But Betty told him that they did not want to go back to the House of Prayer and, in fact, never wanted to go to Achill again. She felt the unexpected visit was just a desperate ploy to silence them. 'I couldn't believe it when they just showed up. It just shows their cult-like mentality again, they put you under such pressure and try to control you,' she said.

By this stage, May 2008, every last belief the couple had in the House of Prayer was well and truly shattered. In their own words, they could now see clearly that it was nothing more than a 'money-making racket.' Shaking her head bitterly, Betty said back then: 'We think it is the greatest fraud. I mean preying on people's religious beliefs – how low can you get? They deliberately targeted old people, because the older you get the more worried you are about the next life. When you are young you are only living for the next day. But when you are getting old you worry about what your chances are in the afterlife.'

She and her husband had no doubts that they had been an active part of a cult, until they finally saw through it and got out. 'The people who go there are brainwashed. We can stand back from it now and see that. But whatever is said, people will believe what Fr McGinnity tells them. They are not open to argument. It is the saddest thing.'

Betty said that of all the scandals she read about the House of Prayer, the one that sickened her most was the *Sunday World* story about Tim McCarry. McCarry was an 89-year-old devotee of Christina Gallagher, who gave the self-proclaimed visionary his life savings of €70,000 before he died in December 2007. Tim's daughter Bernadette Rees told the newspaper in March 2008 that she felt her dad had been robbed.

The story shocked Betty and Michael Morrissey to the core. 'It horrified so many people, above every other article,' said Betty.

The Morrisseys knew of Tim McCarry, because one of their friends in the House of Prayer used to help him out while she was working there, before she herself was dismissed after crossing Christina Gallagher. The woman used to clean out his mobile home that he had in the grounds of the House. When she was baking scones for the café, she would always bring him some. She and another friend of the Morrisseys, who worked in a clothes shop in Achill, were able to vouch for just how poor Tim McCarry was towards the end.

The shopkeeper told them that McCarry came into the store one day and wanted to buy a couple of vests, but he only had a few euro. He said he had given all his money to the House of Prayer. The woman felt so sorry for him that she took the money out of her own handbag and paid for the clothes, knowing that the old man was living in a mobile home.

The Morrisseys themselves were left short of money after giving away so much of their own savings to the House of Prayer. With just a bit of their savings left in the bank, they were suddenly hit with bills that they had never planned for. The couple live in an old house and their heating system broke down and needed replacing. There is no water mains in the area – the locals rely on private supplies – but the Morrisseys' well dried up.

'That was something you would never ever anticipate. We have no water now only for the goodness of our neighbour who has allowed us to tap into his supply. Our ambition is to bore a well. It is very embarrassing. We would like to have our own independent water supply. Our neighbour has been so good to us.'

Before they got their money back in August 2008, following legal action against the House of Prayer, they had to watch everything they spent. Their generosity in giving away most of their savings would be regarded by many people as absolutely extraordinary or even foolish. Money became a large concern. The couple receive an old age pension and a number of ESB units, but they use up a lot of electricity on heating. Michael has a heart condition and one of the side effects of his medication is that he feels the cold. To get away for a weekend, the couple had to rely on supermarket tokens. 'But we thought we were giving our money to a good cause,' said Betty.

Even attending the regular House of Prayer sessions on Saturday afternoons was a costly business for the couple, because of the huge distance they had to travel from their home. B&B costs had to be added to petrol and meals. When they started a novena – a devotion which meant attending the House of Prayer on nine consecutive Saturdays – it meant even more financial hardship. Betty said they could only afford to have one proper meal a day.

Despite the hardship, the couple managed to keep up the nine weekends of the novena. Betty recalls on the very last Saturday, that Christina Gallagher came out and said Our Lady had appeared to her and she had made an urgent request for the novena to continue until Christmas. That meant two more sessions of nine: a total of 27 successive Saturdays in all.

'Well, everyone cheered and clapped, and here was I nearly crying, my heart was after sinking down to my shoes,' recalled Betty. 'How were we going to continue? So we said we would try to do it on a weekly basis, until we couldn't do it any more. We struggled on and on.'

The journey to Achill was a major ordeal for the couple, and meant Betty getting up at 3.00am on the Saturday to organise their dogs before setting off. Towards the end Betty did not want Michael to go at all, because he did not believe in it at that stage. But he insisted on travelling, because he said his wife would only fall asleep at the wheel on the way up. Betty admitted that she could never make the whole journey without falling asleep.

Michael said: 'We would get home Sunday evening and then it was back to work on Monday morning. It was very tough. We didn't know anyone else from this area who went to the House of Prayer so we went on our own.'

But the Morrisseys were not the only ones who made huge sacrifices to get to and from Achill Island. Close friends of theirs in Cork, a married couple, who were huge fundraisers for Christina Gallagher, also went to extraordinary lengths to get to the regular Saturday afternoon prayer meetings. The Cork man used to travel all the way to Achill and back the same day, because he could not afford to stay in a B&B. And he would bring up large amounts of cash collected from one of the poorest parts of Cork. On one occasion he was stunned when he handed the money to Christina Gallagher, and she simply slid it into one of the high boots she was wearing with hardly a word of thanks. 'He couldn't stop talking about it. But he still believed in her,' said Betty.

The man has since died, and his widow has turned against the House of Prayer. She adamantly refuses to go public. She now feels terrible because they collected so much money from a very poor part of town. As Michael says, she was collecting money from people who could not afford to give it, and was still getting hassle from people now. When articles appeared in the paper, people said to her, 'Where were you leading us?' But the woman believed back then. Betty said that when the husband died, the woman could never get over the fact that she had been promoting a false visionary. She had seen the cracks all the way through but was covering up for Christina Gallagher's deception. She could not admit to herself that she was wrong but she knows now.

'Your stories were a bombshell to so many people. But Christina Gallagher did not put a gun to people's heads. They gave money willingly. But my instant reaction after reading the stories was that she should be exposed whatever the cost to other people. I wanted her named by the Revenue Commissioners and targeted by the authorities.'

Betty became so fired up that she even turned detective herself at one point, driving to Gallagher's homeland around Knockmore, near Ballina, to see the €1 million house that Gallagher had bought for her daughter. She also visited a Co. Mayo priest, who knew Gallagher from years before who told her Gallagher was so money-hungry she would 'skin you' for a shilling. The priest knew the man who sold his house to her for her daughter. Her daughter has since spent a fortune doing it up.

Today Betty and Michael Morrissey have one reminder of Christina Gallagher they can never forget – old House of Prayer stain glass windows they bought for their own home. The windows were in the original convent, before it was bought and turned into the House of Prayer in 1993. They were eventually replaced after a fundraising drive. 'What good were the old ones to them when they could make money by fundraising for new ones?' said Betty bitterly. 'Christina said that Our Lady had requested the new windows and everyone believed her. There was a big fund raising appeal.'

Apparently, Gallagher's supporters didn't think that the Virgin Mary might have more important things to worry about than the colour of the House of Prayer windows. But back then Betty was one of those who believed everything Gallagher said. When she saw the old frames advertised in the shop window at the House of Prayer around 2003, she begged Michael to buy them. She and her husband were building a little annex in their house, which was going to be a sun room but could double up as a prayer room. The couple were holding a prayer meeting once a week, and Betty wanted to incorporate the windows into the new extension.

When they finally saw the frames and glass, Michael was shocked at the poor state of them and didn't want to go ahead. He said they were falling to bits and that all the lead was gone. But Betty was determined to have them because of their significance – having come from what she believed at the time was such a holy house. To her, they were from a special place where Our Lady regularly appeared. The couple ended up paying €1,500 for the two windows, and more still doing them up.

Today the couple feel that the whole window appeal was just one more money-making exercise. Nobody knows for sure what it brought in, but Betty heard that one person donated €10,000. She also felt that American donors would have been very generous because this was supposed to be Our Lady's appeal. 'People were

coming in asking if their names would be put on the
windows if they contributed. There was a very big time
lapse from when the windows were taken out until the
new ones were put in. But that was deliberate to collect
more and more money,' said Betty.

The old frames still sit in the Morrisseys' home.
A prayer room might seem an odd feature in today's
largely secular Ireland, but the Morrisseys are a devout
couple without ever being preachy about their faith.
They would laugh at the suggestion that they were
over-religious and would certainly not take themselves
too seriously but, nevertheless, they remain devoted to
the Catholic faith. 'We are devout Catholics. Michael
says his prayers anyway,' says Betty laughing. Their
deep faith makes the hypocrisy of the House of Prayer
all the harder to bear.

But back in the days when they were still travelling
to Achill Island, Betty was thrilled with her new
acquisition which was her pride and joy and took centre
stage in her prayer room: 'I would be standing in there
looking at them and I thought I was so privileged to
have those windows.' Betty was so proud of them, in
fact, that she even took photographs which she brought
to the House of Prayer to show Christina Gallagher.
She recalls that the House of Prayer was appealing
for money at the time, which was normal. She said
that almost every Saturday they were in Achill, Fr
McGinnity would ask people, if there's any way you
can help with Our Lady's project, could you come and
talk to me afterwards. 'And this is the man who says he
wasn't involved in fundraising!' says Betty.

As a result of the appeal, Betty went to see Gallagher
and was keen to show her the photographs of her
new prayer room. But she was disappointed by the
visionary's obvious lack of interest. 'She couldn't have

cared less. I thought she would be delighted. I said we felt so privileged to have the windows and that they were the focal point of our little prayer room, and everybody coming to the prayer room felt privileged to be in this room where the windows were where Our Lady had appeared to her so many times. Oh my God, when I think of it all!' said Betty, shaking her head.

Betty told Gallagher that her finances were limited, but that she could afford a small donation for the latest appeal. Fr McGinnity, who was at her side, said straight away: 'There is a problem with the Revenue Commissioners at the moment. It's in the process of being ironed out so if you could make the cheque payable to myself personally I'd appreciate it.'

Betty subsequently handed over a cheque signed to Fr McGinnity for €5,000 from her own personal account. This was in May 2005, just prior to the Rooney meeting where she and her husband were bullied into pledging €100,000. 'And that, of course, was why I was invited to the Rooney meeting. They felt I had a lot more to give,' said Betty.

Today, more than a year and a half after going public, the Morrisseys are frustrated that the House of Prayer is still up and running, and that busloads of people are still turning up every Saturday, although numbers are well down. By speaking out, Betty hoped that she would encourage many others to do the same. But although many former devotees have fallen away, few of them are willing to accept public ridicule, by admitting they handed over land or large amounts of cash to the supposed holy woman.

An investigation into the House of Prayer by the Revenue Commissioners is still on-going, but little is heard about it. The DPP announced in March 2009 that there would be no prosecution of the House of Prayer following a garda inquiry. This was expected as the chief complainants were Betty and Michael Morrissey, and their case had effectively been resolved when they were given their money back in August 2008. Officers involved in the case rang the Morrisseys to tell them as much, after their settlement was made public. The Morrisseys were shocked and disappointed.

The Morrisseys have also been frustrated by the lack of action by the Church hierarchy. Like many other Catholics up and down the country, they are incensed that the ecclesiastic authorities have not stamped down on the House of Prayer. They accept that they might not have the power to close it down, as it is a private concern, but they believe they could at least blast it from the pulpit and cut off its lifeblood.

Now the Morrisseys fear that Christina Gallagher has got away with it. They suspect that one day she will simply disappear abroad, probably to America, without ever being brought to task over her wealth, and possibly leaving her devotees to carry the can. Like other former followers, she suspected Gallagher might have been laying the groundwork for her escape in November 2008, when she began telling supporters that she would be 'assumed' into heaven in the next six months. 'Assumed' meaning she would be raised body and soul to heaven in the same way Catholics believe the Virgin Mary was raised to heaven.

Absurd as it sounds for a roly-poly Co. Mayo housewife with a taste for jewellery and fast cars to claim she was going to be lifted through the clouds by God, it was nonetheless lapped up by her followers. Months earlier Betty had by chance bumped into the former nun Treasa, Gallagher's constant companion, while Betty herself was on a trip to Achill to visit a friend. The 71-

year-old former sister, who had given up her vows to join Gallagher, burst into tears and said Gallagher was not long for this world. She said the visionary's suffering was so great that Our Lady was going to take her out of this world and she cried: 'How are we going to live without Christina?' Betty's reaction was that Christina was preparing people for a quick exit. Betty was also surprised by Treasa's appearance, as she was dressed 'like a duchess' and not in the old clothes she used to wear. 'She had on a magnificent gown and looked ten years younger. Her image had completely changed and all her wrinkles had gone, although she is 71.'

Fr McGinnity had also been telling worshippers that his mentor had done enough work in this life and would soon be called to heaven. Many more months on, Gallagher is still very much in our midst. But the Morrisseys, like many others, feel it might only be a matter of time before she does disappear. Except, of course, it is very unlikely it will be to heaven.

CHAPTER SIX

The Whistle-blower

'This woman has pulled off the greatest scam in Irish Church history…They have been lying to us for years. She is a charlatan, and he is a hypocrite and a gold-digger.'

Mike McCrory couldn't believe his ears. He had just come in to see Christina Gallagher, a woman to whom he had devoted the last four years of his life, with some shocking news. It involved a regular at the House of Prayer.

Just hours earlier, a young volunteer at the House had told McCrory and three other followers that someone at the centre had made sexual advances on him. The young man was appalled and frightened by this unwanted attention from the man and didn't know what to do about it.

But McCrory knew instantly what had to be done. Christina and her spiritual director, Fr McGinnity, had to be told. A homosexual preying on younger members of the community could not possibly be allowed to continue. As a devout Catholic, McCrory had strong views about homosexuality. He says: 'If someone is a homosexual it is not their fault. If he does nothing about it, he is doing no wrong. But if he practises his homosexuality then he is going against the teachings of the Church.' McCrory believed that for anyone attending the House of Prayer to be living a secret homosexual lifestyle was bad enough, but for a supposedly devout man to sexually harass a young male half his age was simply unforgivable.

McCrory thought the news he was bringing to Gallagher and Fr McGinnity would horrify them. He expected them to be deeply upset by what he himself saw as a huge betrayal of trust. But he could not have been more wrong. The two couldn't have been less interested. McCrory was stunned that they, in his words, just seemed to 'laugh it off.'

Later, they told McCrory that they had called in the two men to discuss the matter and they were now satisfied it was all a mistake. The older man had simply put his arm around the young man and the latter had misinterpreted his move. They seemed happy with this explanation – even though McCrory said the incident was far more serious. He had since discovered that other House of Prayer members had previously reported the same man for inappropriate behaviour.

'I named three people whom the young man talked to about the incident, but they didn't go near any of them. There was no investigation,' said McCrory. The two House of Prayer leaders then went off on a trip to the US, but when they returned McCrory raised the subject again. He said he had a lot more evidence, but they still never followed it up. McCrory said another follower, a woman, brought up another incident concerning the same man. She had caught him in a dark room with another man in suspicious circumstances, and McCrory reminded Gallagher of this. But again the visionary laughed it off saying, 'the past is the past'.

McCrory was adamant that if it happened years ago and was happening again now, they should look into it. But rather than carrying out any kind of inquiry, he said the two House of Prayer leaders tried to silence him. He noticed a wave of fear sweeping through the house and saw that people no longer wanted to talk.

Witnesses started to back off. 'For the first time I started to use the word "cult",' McCrory recalled.

Still intent on getting satisfaction, he then wrote to Fr McGinnity and gave him the names of the witnesses. But the priest did not reply to his letter or his follow-up calls. Then came the final blow that was to make McCrory finally cut all links with the controversial centre to which, not only had he been devoted, but had been one of its mainstays.

After the usual Saturday afternoon novena at the House, the priest suddenly attacked McCrory from the pulpit. Without naming him he said: 'Christina has asked me to pass on this message. There are people here today who talk about people and disparage people.' He went so far as to say an 'agent of the Devil' was at work in the House of Prayer.

It was a shocking accusation, particularly in reference to a man who had devoted his life to his faith, but it was not entirely unfamiliar to Mike McCrory. At the House of Prayer the term 'agent of the Devil' was commonly used to describe those who questioned Gallagher's authority or who cast doubt on her work. Nevertheless, this very public rebuke in front of the entire congregation still cut McCrory to the heart, particularly as it came from a man, a priest, whom he had previously revered.

'I could not believe it. He didn't actually name me, but everyone knew who he was talking about,' says McCrory. 'That's what they did when you fell out with them. They would bully you from the pulpit.'

McCrory was so outraged that he demanded to see the priest. He told Fr McGinnity that when there was a homosexual in Our Lady's House who was openly hitting on young men, he had no choice but to speak up. McCrory told him that there were many people sacked from the House of Prayer for far less than that, and that he could not understand why this man was being protected.

'One of the staff said to me that he must have made a big donation to the House. But I think now that he probably knew too much about what was going on, and that they could never get rid of him,' says McCrory. The next time he saw Gallagher, she too tore into him. McCrory said the visionary was furious at him for not dropping the subject. 'She was losing it and was swearing and berating me.'

Gallagher, he said, was a woman who never liked to be contradicted and was certainly not used to being questioned so vigorously by any of her followers. In the House of Prayer her rule was absolute and she would explode in a rage if anyone questioned her authority. She banned McCrory from the House, saying he was nothing but trouble. This was something else she was prone to doing: banning someone for a month and then inviting them back. 'I told her she couldn't ban me because the house was not hers, that it was owned by a trust. But Fr McGinnity said, "She can ban you. It's her personal house." He had obviously changed his tune because he had always told us the house was in a trust and Christina had no connection to it. But it definitely never stopped her acting like the owner.'

Nothing was ever done about the alleged sexual aggressor, and the man is still a regular at the House of Prayer. But for Mike McCrory, it was the end of his devotion – some would call it obsession – to Gallagher, McGinnity and the House of Prayer. He was invited back weeks later, but McCrory refused to return. He had seen a side of the supposedly religious movement that he didn't like. He was convinced their invitation to him to return was simply to get him back onside, to keep him quiet.

Mike McCrory certainly doesn't look like a rebel. Grey-haired and quietly spoken, this 64-year-old man who goes to Mass every day and says he would die for his faith, had moved to Achill four years previously just to be near the House of Prayer, after spending nearly 30 years living in the US. He and his wife, Marie, had left their life and family behind in California, because of his admiration for Christina Gallagher, and her mission to spread faith and prayer in an Ireland that was rapidly becoming more secular.

A former theology student himself, he felt much of the doctrine of his beloved Catholic Church had been watered down in recent years, and had welcomed the no-nonsense approach of this self-proclaimed visionary.

But McCrory's life was not all religion. The Northern Irish man was once a very promising sportsman who played GAA for Antrim. He also had a trial for London soccer club Tottenham Hotspurs, and won a soccer scholarship to the US, as well as being a champion high jumper in Northern Ireland. He was also very much the family man, with five children. Both he and his wife were from families of eight, so big families were important to him. His own mother was one of 12.

McCrory was born in Andersontown, Belfast, in the heartland of much of the Troubles. When he was young, the IRA were always calling at his family's door collecting money and 'you could not say no'. He and Marie were determined not to raise their own children in that atmosphere and they moved to England. 'We were married in London and my oldest son, Thomas Moore McCrory, was born in Hackney and my oldest daughter Tanya was born in Maidstone.'

While in England, McCrory, had a trial with Spurs and played alongside Tottenham and England legends Jimmy Greaves and Alan Mullery in a pre-season warm up match. 'I was marked by Phil Beal but I still managed to score against Pat Jennings,' he recalls. 'But Jimmy Greaves ruined my trial because he was showing off and kept the ball. He wouldn't pass it. I always had great anticipation on the pitch and knew where to go.'

He played for Enfield, including a game against Chelsea reserves, before heading off to San Francisco where he had won a soccer scholarship. This was to change his life. He travelled to America on a student visa but outstayed his welcome by many years, like many other Irish men and women at a time when there were very few prospects at home. The US authorities tried to deport him for overstaying his visa, but by then the rest of his children had been born in the US and were American citizens. After 13 years the immigration department gave up trying to send him home, when a judge ruled that it would not be fair to send American citizens to live in the middle of the Troubles. McCrory was free to stay.

'My kids still thank me for getting them out of the Troubles and raising them in California. I got great enjoyment out of my children and they used to go everywhere with me,' he says. One of his daughters now lives in Galway, but the rest of the family are in the US. As for his sporting days, they are long gone. He has two artificial hips and is almost blind in one eye after a car battery blew up in his face in San Francisco. He needed eight internal stitches.

McCrory was always an extremely religious man who, as well as going to Mass every day, says 15 decades of the rosary, and spends an hour in prayer. When he says the Stations of the Cross, he does so on his knees. 'I know I am weak. I know I need God, which is why I pray as much as I do,' he says. 'People call me holy but I know how weak I am. I am always trying to be a saint before I die.'

He first heard about Christina Gallagher in the 1990s when, he says, 'visionaries seemed to be popping up all over the place.' He was visiting another shrine in Denver, Colorado, when someone started talking about 'this woman in Ireland who seemed very down to earth.' He began to read any available information about her and the House of Prayer, and, although sceptical at first, found himself fascinated by her story. But what really got him going was a meeting in Belfast with a former IRA man who told him that he had turned his life around after a religious conversion in Waterford. 'I believed him and the story was all over Andersonstown, where my parents were living. He had gone to the IRA and said there would be no more killing.'

This man had recently met Fr McGinnity and was singing his praises. He spoke of the priest's beautiful Masses, which he did not rush through, and of his homilies. He also spoke of the priest's charisma, and when he told McCrory that the priest was the spiritual director for Christina Gallagher, the Belfast man was intrigued even further. McCrory and his wife travelled to Achill to see the House of Prayer for themselves. He recalls that it was a less than auspicious start when he first met Gallagher. In fact they had a row.

'She was doing a questions and answers session with some American tourists in a hotel in Achill,' McCrory recalls. 'It's a treat for the Americans and she often meets them when they come over. About six times a year they arrive by the coach load. Christina would meet them, while she would not make herself available to the people who came every weekend. She would meet the Americans, I now know, because that is where the money was.'

He said that he listened as Fr McGinnity sang her praises before the assembled crowd. Just as he did everywhere, the priest was telling everyone how holy she was, how good she was, and how she suffered battling the Devil. McCrory was surprised that he was so over the top, while she was sitting there right in front of him listening to it all. 'There was no humility there at all,' thought McCrory. 'People who are called by God do not go broadcasting themselves.' He then said as much to Fr McGinnity, telling him that he could see why he had to praise Gallagher if she was under attack, but that people might assume she was a saint the way he went on about her.

'Christina just tore into me. She was furious,' recalls McCrory. 'But then a woman sitting next to me said to her that she seemed to have a lot of anger. Christina immediately went all sweetness and light, saying it was not anger but hurt.'

Despite this unpromising start, McCrory was to become a huge follower of Christina Gallagher and was to devote the next four years of his life to her. He never really warmed to her as a person, because of her severe personality and the fact that he could see no joy in her. She was also prone to temper tantrums. But he greatly admired what she was doing.

The couple made the momentous decision to quit their home in California and move to Achill so that they could be closer to this woman they so admired. They rented a house directly behind the House of Prayer, so he could spend much of his time there. The couple would visit the House every day to pray and then began attending twice a day. Soon they were spending nearly all their time there and he would help out wherever he could. Marie became almost a full-time helper, putting in hours of unpaid work most days. They found the services at the centre to be quite mesmerising. There was an excitement about the place on big celebration days, when thousands of people would show up, arriving in dozens of buses.

'You felt part of something great and it was quite exhilarating at the time,' said McCrory. He loved the involvement and the participation of the congregation that was in stark contrast to the emotionless reaction in most churches at regular services. 'It was easy to see why people loved going there.'

When he first arrived in Achill he was shocked at the local people's apathy towards Gallagher and the House of Prayer. He said some locals warned him about her activities, but he was too blinded by his devotion to Gallagher to listen. He became such a fanatical devotee of the House and Gallagher, and was so knowledgeable about theology, that he was regularly wheeled out to hit back whenever anyone, including the press, criticised his beloved leader. One local priest later told me that he was the bane of their lives, calling them up and telling them that they should be backing the House of Prayer and its work. He would berate them if they said anything against Gallagher from their pulpits, or if they showed anything less than 100 per cent support for her mission.

'My role was to go on air and defend her. But she still kept me at a distance,' said McCrory, who had a religious programme on KFRC, Castlebar Community radio. He regularly talked about Gallagher and her work on the radio. He told his audience that Gallagher was the most unappreciated visionary in history. She would call him occasionally and ask him to speak about specific things that promoted herself or her movement. Once she got him to talk about how unfair it was that Bishop Eamonn Casey seemed to have been forgiven for having a grown-up son with a divorced woman, while Fr McGinnity, who was bishop material and who was a doctor of theology and a former dean of a seminary, was left out in the cold.

McCrory says he had a steady working relationship with Gallagher during this time, although it was never a particularly easy one. Strong willed and opinionated himself, he was not one to stand down on a theological point. But they got on okay, probably because they saw so little of each other. The truce held until McCrory went to see them over the sexual harassment case.

'I was so committed to the House of Prayer that I would go over and talk to anyone I saw arriving in the car park. I made it fun for them with a few jokes, while others were very serious. Everyone knew me... I was always promoting the House of Prayer. After I left they claimed I was not important and was never in the inner circle, but then why did they always call on me to go on radio or to speak on their behalf? I was their main PR.'

Despite this dedication, and despite the huge sacrifice of quitting his comfortable life in the US to move to Ireland, it was not long before McCrory began to sense that everything was not quite right about the House of Prayer. Although it was in a serene location on the edge of the beautiful but rugged island of Achill, he noticed that it was not a place of peace and joy, as one might expect. 'There was no tranquility there. People who worked in the house were watching each other and spying on each other and vying for position with Christina. There was a lot of envy and jealousy,' he says.

Gallagher and Fr McGinnity were never really around to see this, except at weekends, but people were fighting to be in their good books. When the House of Prayer offered his wife a full-time paid job, he knew instinctively it would be a bad move. It was one thing having her work long hours for nothing, but if they were paying her she could be dragged into this same negative world of jealousy and spying. 'It was not a good feeling in the place and we turned them down.'

The first seeds of doubt had been sown. Others quickly followed. One thing that did not sit easily with McCrory was Gallagher's apparent wealthy lifestyle.

'She always seemed to have the best of everything and would always be driving a new car,' says McCrory. 'She wore designer clothes and always had a lot of jewellery. She would tell us that money didn't mean anything to her but [she] had this great lifestyle. You had to wonder where the money was coming from.'

He said that if he ever said anything to Fr McGinnity, the priest would reply that she deserved some comforts because the life of a visionary was not easy. The cleric would claim that she was often sick or exhausted from battling the Devil or from the enormity of the visions shown to her by Our Lady. The priest was regarded as such a holy man that McCrory was happy to believe him at the start.

He also noticed that Gallagher was obsessive about control and made every decision about the House of Prayer. Rather than spend her time in prayer, she obsessed about every detail of the House of Prayer, down to the furniture and chandeliers. He said she was a woman who micro-manages.

'You couldn't put up a pair of curtains without asking her first,' he said. 'Visionaries are supposed to be humble people who devote their lives to prayer. But with Christina we didn't see much evidence of this. I don't think I ever saw her praying on her own in the chapel.'

Gradually McCrory began to get more and more uneasy about the woman he was following. At the start he believed in her and did not need proof. As he said, 'For those who believe no proof is necessary and for those who do not believe no proof is possible.' He was one of the former. His children were suspicious of Gallagher right from the start, and did not like her. But even this did not hold him back at the beginning. The first time his daughter, Tanya, met Gallagher she turned to her father and said: 'Dad, she's a phoney.'

As McCrory says, 'When the evidence said I should not believe – I always had excuses to explain away her behaviour. If she was angry, I would think, "Maybe she was suffering, maybe the Devil was attacking her. She did not really mean what she said."' And Fr McGinnity was always there to ease away any doubts. But McCrory was still surprised at how little Gallagher actually attended the House of Prayer, as she would only show up about 20 times a year. 'And then she would only appear before her supporters for a few minutes on the Saturday afternoon and rarely stayed for a full prayer session. And she never did the overnight vigils that she expected her supporters to do.'

Fr McGinnity would explain away her absences, by claiming she was exhausted from the visions or was suffering from bad health. But nobody ever explained what was supposed to be wrong with her. McCrory says today that they were all complete mugs for believing these stories.

Another clue, that should have warned him that she was not all that she appeared to be, was her drinking. He travelled with her by plane once and was shocked at the way she knocked back the alcohol. 'She was spending up a storm and I excused it at the time because of her "suffering". The drinks trolley would come along and she would be buying up the stuff. I was embarrassed for her. I had heard she liked to drink but I had never seen evidence until I saw her on the plane. Other people had told me she drank a lot.'

She was spotted in Dunnes Stores in Castlebar

buying two big boxes of booze and paying for it with a House of Prayer cheque. 'Why is a visionary buying cartloads of alcohol and gifts? All this stuff must have gone to her home, because there is no alcohol in the House of Prayer,' he said.

By this stage he was also handing over money to the House of Prayer, and he had very little to give as he was not working. He estimates that he gave one third of everything he owned to Gallagher and her cause, something in the region of €3,000. He gave the first €1,000 while he still lived in California. He said requests for money were made very subtly, because they would never come right out and ask for cash. Instead, Fr McGinnity would say that they needed help with a certain project and asked if there was any way he could help. The priest would rarely give any specifics about where the money was actually going to go. He kept it vague, sometimes suggesting it was to help build the Houses of Prayer in America.

But one cheque McCrory did sign for a specific cause was for €1,000 on 8 August 2006 to the Blue Ivory Trust. Like the Morrisseys, McCrory was told that Gallagher had to sell the Newport house she lived in, because she was getting hassle from the neighbours, and it was too big for her needs. She could not afford it, and the big house was being used as a stick to beat her with. At the time, McCrory was only too happy to help and he heard that the fund raised between €600,000 and €1 million. Imagine his shock a year later, after he had left the House of Prayer, when he discovered that Gallagher had bought a far bigger house for nearly €1 million, not far from her native Knockmore. She handed it over to her separated daughter

If Mike McCrory was happy to make excuses for the 'humble housewife' at the beginning of his devotion, he could not argue away Gallagher and McGinnity's lack of action when they heard of the sexual harassment in their holy house. Their failure to follow up this complaint was possibly their biggest mistake in 15 years, because it was to set in motion a chain of events that would ultimately destroy the reputations of both Gallagher and McGinnity and the House of Prayer itself.

It was McCrory who chipped away the first stones of the edifice by speaking out about his suspicions. Months later, after a major investigation, the first stories appeared of Gallagher's vast wealth and the walls of the House of Prayer and its 'prophet' began to come tumbling down.

McCrory said that after leaving the House of Prayer he became aware of all sorts of financial irregularities that had been going on there. Former insiders, who had left the organisation but who would not open up to him while he was still close to Gallagher, were now happy to talk. He said he received regular phone calls from one follower who was desperately worried after she collected €50,000 for the House of Prayer, and was asked by Fr McGinnity to keep it in her own bank account. Her husband was an ex-guard and she was terrified that they might become targets of the Revenue Commissioners, who would assume the money was theirs. The money was raised from collections among the buses of pilgrims that travelled to Achill every Saturday. 'She no longer goes to the House of Prayer, because she is too terrified,' said McCrory. He also said another female volunteer told him she used to do the books at the centre, but stopped when she realised there were problems with them.

McCrory also heard how one day Gallagher called in the coach owners and told them that one of her loyal supporters car had been stolen, and that she wanted them to have a whip-round to raise €16,000 to buy her a new one. The drivers felt duty bound to chip in or they might lose their valuable trips to the House of Prayer. Another former member told me that the €16,000 was actually for Gallagher, as she was selling her loyal supporter one of her old cars.

McCrory's new attitude to Christina Gallagher was summed up in a letter he wrote to *The Irish Catholic* newspaper in March 2008. He asked the very pertinent question: 'How did Christina Gallagher, who claims to be "a simple country woman who has never read a book in her life," acquire such tremendous wealth in such a short period of time?' The letter went on:

> *We are talking about millions. I do not include here her seven Houses of Prayer worldwide; I refer only to her own personal wealth and that of her family. Recall that she started all this with practically nothing. And why is it that ANYONE who questions her in ANY way is immediately fired or banned and their reputations defamed? I have spoken with many one time believers who have experienced this bizarre banning, expulsion and subsequent assassination of character. Their mindset is such: If you disagree with us it is because you are wrong, and an agent of Satan, for we are the chosen ones.' Does this sound like a genuine religious movement to you? Rather it is more that of a cult. Many who attend there are elderly and vulnerable; it is for them that I continue to investigate such strange and uncharitable behaviour – as well as this mysterious acquisition of wealth.*
>
> *I can assure you there are many other ways I would like to spend my time besides putting myself in the firing line of this unfolding tragedy of faith. I am blessed to have a loving wife and five wonderful children and I hope for their sake as well as for all families across Ireland that the truth of this*

situation will soon be fully revealed and put to rest once and for all.

Sincerely, Michael P. McCrory.

McCrory believes that every idea that Gallagher came up with at the House of Prayer was to make money. People were asked to pay €50 for a bead or to sponsor a bench for €650. 'I paid €350 myself, and a friend another €300. I was their biggest supporter.' In his latter days there, and in the months after he left, he heard rumours that Gallagher owned properties around the country, but he had no evidence. Of course, he knew about the luxury home outside Newport, Co. Mayo – he contributed €1,000 to help buy it off her through the Blue Ivory Trust. He had heard about the luxury furnishings, but he was never invited inside to see for himself. Only a chosen few were ever allowed through the front door of that house, which sat behind huge walls and had a security camera, on the road to Castlebar. Christina Gallagher was never likely to invite a man of independent thinking like Mike McCroy, who would have been shocked by the opulence of the place. Those who did get through the electronic gate were usually of a more submissive nature, people she could control, like Fr McGinnity himself, who had his own room there.

McCrory said that Gallagher was rumoured to own a fabulous home in Dublin somewhere, but nobody knew where it was or knew anything about it. A few months later this fact was confirmed.

Today, back home in California where he returned with his wife in 2008, McCrory says that there is no doubt in his mind that the House of Prayer is a cult, and that Fr McGinnity has been completely duped by a devious and avaricious fraudster. 'I believe he has been completely taken in by her. He was always naïve and gullible, even though he was very smart. He had a reputation for running after every visionary he heard about.'

Nobody was drawn to her personality or her holiness and she was hidden away most of the time. It was the priest's presence that made Christina Gallagher what she is today, he said. The very success of the House of Prayer was down to him and his blind support. When the first stories began to emerge about her wealthy lifestyle, many of her followers would not believe them, simply because he was involved. 'The first thing people say is, "Why would Fr McGinnity be involved if it's all a fraud? How could she be a phoney if he is there behind her?" Fr McGinnity is 95 per cent of the House of Prayer.'

The people who saw more of Gallagher, often saw a vindictiveness and ruthlessness which was frightening, said McCrory. She would use people and then discard them. 'Nobody with any close connection to her has not experienced the whip of her tongue. "Don't wait for her to apologise because you will not get it," one of the House staff used to say. Most people leave and say nothing in fear of the wrath of God. They are frightened she could be holy, and they don't want to criticise her. A long, long list of people who have devoted time and talent and money have all been dispatched summarily for the flimsiest of reasons. They have all experienced her wrath.'

One of the many things McCrory held against her was her threats over many years to write a book about everyone who had caused her problems. 'She said that Our Lady had told her to write it, which is a truly terrible thing to say, that Our Lady would encourage something so vindictive. That has got to be heretical. She was always saying it, claiming Our Lady was upset with her because she had not written that book yet.'

The Belfast man said he had seen Gallagher's famous

temper three times at close quarters – twice directed at him and once at a workman in the House of Prayer grounds. He said she was 'more like a washer woman than a visionary'.

People who still support Gallagher today, he said, had a very simple choice. They could either claim they were loyal Catholics and follow the established Church, or they could go against the bishops and follow Christina Gallagher. 'You cannot have it both ways. People need to make a decision. Only the bishops can say messages are from heaven and they have said they have found no evidence of supernatural happenings,' he said. 'For myself, faced with Fr McGinnity and Christina Gallagher... I, thankfully, chose Christ and His Church, and I am so much happier for it.'

This was a point he hammered home as far back as December 2007, before the House of Prayer scandal even broke in the press. McCrory wrote another letter to *The Irish Catholic* pointing out that Pope Benedict XVI had recently warned Catholics worldwide of the danger to their faith and to Church unity posed by the following of Charismatic figures, who operate without the approval of the local bishop.

'Christina Gallagher has "no approval whatever" from local Bishop Michael Neary and operates anyway,' wrote McCrory. 'The Bishop has repeatedly stated this. Short of denouncing her outright, how much clearer can it get?' he asked.

Nearly two years on from that letter, he says it simply 'beggars belief' what the two House of Prayer leaders have got away with for the past two decades. 'This woman has pulled off the greatest scam in Irish Church history, aided and abetted by a priest in good standing. They have been lying to us for years. She is a charlatan and he is a hypocrite and a gold-digger.'

CHAPTER SEVEN

The Investigations Begin

'There is such a thing as a cult mentality, and there are people who fall into it easily. If you question some of her supporters they just explode'.

So how did the investigation into Christina Gallagher begin? It all started with a phone call in March 2007.

A woman, who would only give her first name, rang me to say a group of people, all former devotees of the House of Prayer on Achill Island, wanted to talk to a reporter. She said they were very disturbed about what was going on at the prayer centre and that they had all recently distanced themselves from it. The woman said they had lost faith in the founder, Christina Gallagher, who appeared to be living well beyond her means.

The group wanted to meet discreetly, not in Achill where they might be seen. I arranged to drive over to the West, and meet them in the newly refurbished Park Inn in Mulranny, a few kilometres before Achill Sound. Being a newspaper reporter, I had obviously heard about the House of Prayer, but did not know very much about it. I knew vaguely that the Church did not approve of it, and that Gallagher claimed to have carried out miracle cures. It sounded like an interesting story, particularly as those who wanted to talk were all former followers.

The meeting was arranged for 8pm on 26 March 2007. I met the woman I had spoken to on the phone, an hour earlier than the rest of the group. She then left, because she felt that some of the others might not feel confident talking in front of her, as some of them did

not know her. It was long after 8pm when they finally
arrived. One man introduced himself as Mike McCrory,
but said that at this stage he did not want his name
published. There was also a middle-aged couple, but
they were so wary they wouldn't say their names. A
fourth expected person did not show up. For the next
three hours these two men and one woman, all devout
Catholics, spoke about how they had all been drawn
into the House of Prayer, but now thought it had gone
terribly wrong.

Mike McCrory, clearly a deeply religious man, did
most of the talking, telling me how he had once been so
devoted to Christina Gallagher that he and his wife left
their home in the US, to live next to the House of Prayer.
In recent months he had become very suspicious about
Gallagher's lifestyle, and also felt disquiet at the climate
of fear and mistrust that pervaded the supposedly
holy house.

The other couple were not so concerned about
Gallagher's apparent material wealth, but by what they
saw as her increasingly heretical views. Traditional
Catholics, they were shocked by Gallagher's message
that anyone who supported her Houses of Prayer in
Ireland and America would be saved in the next life.
This was against all the teachings of the Church, they
said, which preached the importance of prayer and good
works to earn a place in heaven. Gallagher also claimed
that anyone wearing her Matrix medal would be saved
when Judgement Day came. The couple thought this
was absurd.

It then emerged that the group did not want a story
written about what was discussed at the meeting, but
were keen for the newspaper to do its own investigation.
I pointed out that any investigation would have to rely on
insiders, like themselves, providing information, because

they were obviously the only ones who knew what went on in the House. But the couple were adamant that they did not want to be quoted, even off the record. McCrory, on the other hand, said he might go public at some point, but it would serve no purpose at that time. We parted, promising to stay in touch. McCrory and I were in regular contact over the next few months, as we both gathered information about Gallagher and her close circle of devoted – some would say brainwashed – followers.

Then, finally, towards the end of 2007, the first big break came when McCrory discovered that Gallagher had bought a massive new house in Corroy, outside Ballina. McCrory was horrified by the purchase, especially since he had paid money into the Blue Ivory Trust to buy her previous home, because it was allegedly too big and too expensive to run.

He had contributed €1,000 to the fund even though he had little money to spare. He paid by a Bank of Ireland cheque and signed it to the Blue Ivory Trust. He had not seen anything suspicious in Gallagher's plan for a shrine to herself while she was still very much alive. McCrory was one of Gallagher's staunchest defenders at the time and was happy to help.

Now, a year later, he had learnt that Gallagher had bought a far bigger home than the one she supposedly could not afford. He was in utter disbelief. In fact, he was so shocked that he decided to turn detective himself, and track down the house. He drove to the remote area and ended up talking to a member of the family who sold the property to Gallagher. He was told that Gallagher paid nearly €850,000 for the mansion, complete with electronic gates and driveway, but had since spent a fortune refurbishing it. The woman he met told him how all the locals were wondering what the house was going to be used for. Workers were not being paid by cheque or through contractors, but were being paid in cash.

Our own inquiries revealed that Gallagher had bought the house for her separated daughter, Mary, whose married name was Gorman but who had since taken to using her maiden name. Mary Gallagher worked part-time at the House of Prayer, and looking after the finances was one of her duties. A separated mother of two, Mary had one child from a previous relationship before she married her husband. Then she had another child with her husband. She is now separated and in a new relationship. Gallagher bought the new three-storey house, which dominates the local landscape, in May 2007 when average family houses in the area were €200,000 to €300,000. The house is by far the biggest in the area and sits near Lough Conn, a name which many locals now feel has a certain irony. The house is a beautiful modern building with new trees planted all around it and a private driveway leading up to it.

The *Sunday World* decided to go with the story that the supposed visionary had bought this extensive property, as Gallagher had no job and no visible means of income to pay for it. We had also come across a remarkable document from the US, in which a fundraising priest for the House of Prayer warned donors in the US that Gallagher wanted cash only from now on and 'no checks'.

Written by Fr Robert Burns, of Omaha, Nebraska, the fundraising letter was addressed to the 'recipients of my 5 March 2003 letter,' and was entitled, 'Christina Requests A Major Correction.' The correction was that Gallagher wanted donors to send money direct to her own house from now on because 'Christina wishes to answer you immediately'.

The letter then gave an astonishing series of instructions to anyone planning to send money.

The letter said:

Some of us can only help Christina by our daily prayer for her; but if any of us can help her financially, please follow these guidelines ABSOLUTELY:

1. *Put cash – NOT a check – in an envelope and seal the envelope; then scotch tape over the seal;*
    - *It will be opened only by Christina.*
    - *Do not let the envelope be bulky with written pages.*
2. *Clearly print your name and address on the sealed envelope.*
3. *Go to the post office and get a 'Global Priority Mail' envelope (this is an international express priority service)*
    - *Put your sealed envelope in the Global Priority Mail envelope;*
    - *If this total package weighs more than 1 pound, you will have to fill out the proper customs declaration form and affix it to this envelope – WHICH YOU DO NOT WANT TO HAVE TO DO;*
    - *THEREFORE: be absolutely certain that the Global Priority Mail envelope AND its contents do not WEIGH a pound.*
    - *Put your return address in its proper place*
    - *Put Christina's address in its proper place:*
    Mrs Christina Gallagher
    Cortoon, Culmore
    Westport
    Co Mayo
    IRELAND
4. *Have the post-office clerk affix the proper postage*
5. *Mail it.*
Christina will immediately write you.

In the Immaculate Heart of Our Lady Queen of Peace,
Robert Mary Xavier Burns S.J.

This indeed was an incredible piece of evidence that things might not be what they seemed at the House of Prayer. At the very least, it placed a huge question mark over the validity of Christina Gallagher's fundraising techniques and the honesty of her cause. At worst, it suggested out and out corruption. You could just imagine the uproar if the chief executives of Ireland's best-known charities suddenly announced that all money from now on was to go to their home addresses – and cash only please.

Fr Burns' request seemed even more suspect, when other former supporters revealed that Gallagher rarely thanked anyone for donations and was highly unlikely to 'immediately write back,' as was promised in the letter. One ex-devotee who used to work in the House of Prayer told this author: 'Christina never thanks people but just expects people to do as she says. There is no way of telling how much money she was sent.' Another woman revealed how she once saw Gallagher kissing letters containing cash and tossing others to the side.

By this stage I had also tracked down a former fundraiser for Christina Gallagher in America, Christine Adler, who had stopped supporting the Mayo woman years before, after realising that she was a false prophet. Adler said that she was turned off by the violence of Gallagher's so-called messages from the Virgin Mary. A devout convert to Catholicism who lives in Los Angeles, Adler said that she had collected a lot of money for Gallagher in the early days, but would not say how much. She had stopped fundraising after realising that the prophecies Gallagher claimed to get direct from heaven could not possibly be true. She said real messages from God would never be threatening or frightening like those of Christina Gallagher. God wanted people to love each other, but you couldn't grow in love if you were full of fear, she said. To Adler this was far more important than any questions about money. Gallagher was frightening people. 'There is such a thing as a cult mentality and there are people who fall into it easily. If you question some of her supporters they just explode. They are not reasonable, they can't have a discussion, and that is not of God.'

Adler said she was present at the opening of the House of Prayer in 1993, and also brought Gallagher to the US in the 1990s. Gallagher even stayed in her home. But Adler no longer backed her or had respect for her. 'Love was not there and humility was not there. There was no joy in what she was preaching and that is the most important thing.' She was also aware that Gallagher had a ferocious temper, which she turned on people. And she certainly didn't welcome Gallagher's claims that if people did not go to the House of Prayer, they would not be saved. Adler thought this was abhorrent. 'That is not God's word. Even the Pope doesn't say everyone has to go the Vatican to be saved. They are the words of a false prophet and it is very frightening.'

Adler was also uncomfortable with the way Gallagher sometimes handled herself when they were travelling abroad together. Not only did she not show gratitude to people who helped her but occasionally her behaviour was even unsavoury. The visionary is known to like a drink, but when Adler saw her flirtatiously riding on the shoulders of a man while on one of their trips abroad, she was shocked. This was hardly the sort of behavior she expected from a self-proclaimed holy woman, someone who claimed to have regular contact with the Virgin Mary and Christ himself.

Adler also resented the way Gallagher would dump loyal supporters instantly if they ever questioned her. One such victim was the late nun, Sister Monica

Cavanagh, who worked very hard for the House of Prayer. She was very kind to Gallagher but was dismissed after a row, said Adler. 'She lets go of so many people when they know too much. When she got rid of Sister Monica, I decided then never to go back. There is a total lack of holiness there,' said Adler. The American woman said she had had no contact with Gallagher for over a decade, but had heard how her lifestyle had completely changed.

'When I first met Christina she was married and living in Foxford. She had nothing. I paid to take her to Fatima and to America. People who serve God do not live in luxury. They are supposed to show that material things are just temporary,' she said. 'I would like to see Ireland saved from this. A lot of innocent people are blind to what is going on.'

Adler was not the only American to change their mind about Christina Gallagher. Others, too, were disturbed by the violence of the self-proclaimed visionary's messages. In July 2006 Gallagher caused outrage in Catholic circles with an apocalyptic message that seemed to threaten millions of deaths in the US. She warned: 'If the House of Prayer in Texas is not free of debt in the ninth month of this year, it is to be dissolved…the greater part of that state will be levelled and torn to shreds.' Many who heard this message thought it was ridiculous – and needless to say, Texas survived.

But disquiet was also growing at home and on 15 November 2007 *The Irish Catholic* newspaper joined the clamour against the House of Prayer. An article by JP Weir stated: 'Far from being filled with a sense of peace, calm and joy, the diatribes of the House of Prayer leave one nauseous, fearful and full of anxiety for the future. Surely this bullying and threatening depiction of Christ is a complete fabrication.' The religious paper said Gallagher's claims that eternal life would be given automatically to those who made pilgrimages to the House of Prayer were heretical and contrary to all Church teaching. So too was her claim that anyone wearing a 'Matrix' medal bought in the House would be saved when the end of the world came.

By the end of 2007, the *Sunday World*, had more than enough evidence for a hard-hitting article on the House of Prayer. It appeared on 6 January 2008 under the headline, '€1m Room With a Pew.' The story told of 'the cash secrets' of the religious icon Christina Gallagher and how the secretive founder of the House of Prayer had splashed out €1 million on a stunning new mansion. 'We can also reveal the woman who claims to suffer the unexplained stigmata wounds of Christ and receive regular messages from the Virgin Mary, has become so obsessed with money and wealth that it has outraged some of her own supporters,' said the paper, which carried recent House of Prayer accounts showing it had accumulated profits of over €2 million.

'Today, for the first time, some of her former followers turn whistle-blowers to reveal the truth about Ireland's most enigmatic visionary and the reality of life in the House of Prayer,' it said. The story told how Gallagher's disciples were encouraged to sell their own homes to fund the House of Prayer, and how vast sums of cash were donated over the years. It revealed how some followers were growing increasingly disturbed that Gallagher's 'messages' from Our Lady were becoming ever more terrifying and threatening towards those who did not support her.

The article reminded readers that Gallagher was a humble housewife 20 years before, when she claimed she had her first visitation from Our Lady. And while she told her supporters that she had no interest in material things, the *Sunday World* investigation revealed a huge accumulation of wealth and property. The article explained how some of her supporters had quit the House of Prayer after becoming deeply suspicious about its finances and that Gallagher was coming under increasing pressure to explain where she got her money from.

Mike McCrory, who was now willing to be quoted but not identified, said: 'People who worked in the House of Prayer voluntarily were told that if they owned their own house they should sell it and give the money to the House of Prayer to help Christina Gallagher's work. Others were asked to will their homes, money and land to the cause, while she herself seems to have the best of everything. I don't know how many people did, but it could have been hundreds.'

He revealed that a woman volunteer he knew well, who worked in the House of Prayer for years, was suddenly sacked when she admitted to another volunteer that she had a house but had no intention of selling it. 'The woman told Christina and she was fired,' he said. McCrory told how he himself persuaded two wealthy Catholics to donate between €50,000 and €100,000 to the House of Prayer, which he now regretted every day. The 6 January article then went into detail about Fr Robert Burns' extraordinary letter asking for 'cash only' and no cheques.

Before publication of the article, I had rung the House of Prayer and asked for an interview with Christina Gallagher but was turned down. The Catholic Church was a little more forthcoming. The archdiocese's official spokesman, Fr Fintan Monahan, secretary for the Tuam Diocese and a spokesman for Archbishop Michael Neary, said: 'The House of Prayer does not have the support of the Archdiocese. As far as we are concerned it is officially closed. We tried to integrate it into the archdiocese but it didn't happen. We asked to see their accounts in 1998, but we have had no real communication with them since then. As they are a private body and do not have our support, any money matters are a concern for the Revenue Commissioners rather than the archdiocese.'

Another source confirmed to me that the Archdiocese had never seen full accounts from the House of Prayer: 'We stopped pushing for them because we knew it was a cash-only business up there and the accounts wouldn't mean much'.

The House of Prayer was still claiming on its website that it had charity status, but in reality this was taken away two years previously, following a lengthy review. The House of Prayer has never revealed why. Official records show that annual profits from donations and sales of merchandise as far back as 1996 and 1997 were already reaching a princely IR£300,000 a year. But this was only what they were admitting to, and critics believe donations were in excess of this.

In January 2008, Mike McCrory still believed that Christina Gallagher might have been genuine at the start but was ultimately corrupted by money. This was a charitable view he was later to change, as more and more secrets about her life emerged. But back then he said: 'Whether or not she is a charlatan or a genuine messenger of God, she owes it to her followers to explain how she has become a wealthy woman when she started out a poor one, i.e. before her alleged visions. To any objective observer it looks very suspicious. Why the silence? Why doesn't she just tell us what she owns and where the money came from?'

McCrory and others inside the House of Prayer had heard rumours that Gallagher owned a big house in Dublin and that she had also paid for separate houses for her children near Ballina. Finding those properties was going to be the next challenge. And the 'big house' in Dublin turned out to be far more than a rumour.

It was real all right, and was in fact one of the most magnificent piles in the capital. We found it within a week of the first newspaper article. Days later we followed Gallagher herself, as she left the fabulous house on a private estate in Malahide to go on a shopping spree. We snatched photographs of her with her bodyguard and gofer Tony Fitzpatrick and the former nun, Treasa, who usually followed Gallagher everywhere and who lived with her. The pictures were the first new photos of the House of Prayer leader published in the mainstream press for nearly ten years.

But before that edition hit the streets, the *Sunday World* had to deal with the threat of a lawsuit. Five days after the publication of the story about Gallagher buying a €1 million mansion outside Ballina for her daughter, a legal letter arrived at the newspaper from the House of Prayer. Not just any legal letter, but one filled with vitriol and abuse. It was also laughably amateurish. The letter was from the House of Prayer's solicitor, Donal J. Corrigan & Co, Dublin. The most noticeable thing about it was the crossings-out at the top of the first page. A previous telephone number had been blacked out and a new number typed in above the smudge on an old-style typewriter. A fax number had also been typed with a different typewriter, what appeared to be a portable one. In these days of immaculate computer printouts, the letter seemed to be from a different era. Christina Gallagher was obviously not employing the country's top legal mind.

In the letter, entitled Christina Gallagher v Jim Gallagher and The Editor, *Sunday World*, Corrigan said he was acting for the founder of the House of Prayer.

He said the previous week's article was 'completely untrue, incorrect, inaccurate, misleading and libellous. It is false, without foundation and grossly defamatory and clearly injures our client's reputation and character and also damages The House of Prayer.' He stated that the article was 'poorly researched' and relied largely on unnamed sources, rumour and innuendo.

Then in an astonishing personal attack on the author, he ranted (his grammatical errors have been left in): 'This is gutter journalism. Who is Jim Gallagher?, and what qualification has he to write about the House of Prayer. How many times has he visited it? It is clear that Page 11 of the *Sunday World* is his journalistic level and there he will remain. The *Sunday World* is a Secular Newspaper and it is apparent that its sole motive is to greatly damage the reputation of Mrs Gallagher in the eyes of the public.'

The letter went on: 'The comment made regarding "estranged husband" is untrue and incorrect. Christina Gallagher and Patrick Gallagher are not estranged and this defamatory statement has been referred to Senior Counsel to issue separate proceedings against you.'

Corrigan said Gallagher was 'not the legal owner' of the Ballina house. 'The sub standard gutter level of the article is shown by quoting a Ms Christine Adler who has no contact with Christina Gallagher since or about 1994 and yet Jim Gallagher considers it appropriate to quote her.' He then ended with this demand: 'We now formally call upon you to withdraw the damaging content of the said article and to immediately apologise to our client. We require that you publish this letter in full and that your apology be published forthwith in a prominent position of Page One of your Tabloid Newspaper. Furthermore, we require you to contact us in advance of the proposed apology to enable the format be discussed and agreed. Please note and be fully aware that unless we receive an apology forthwith which is to our client's satisfaction, High Court Proceedings will be issued against you without further notice.'

To anyone reading the letter, the over-riding impression it left was that Christina Gallagher must have been sitting at her lawyer's side when he wrote it. Surely they were her words rather than his? The bullying style and personal insults were far removed from a normal legal letter.

But the letter was, of course, expected. Anyone who had ever questioned Christina Gallagher automatically got one, which was why for 15 years she had been able to get away with what she was doing at the House of Prayer. She scared off any possible opponents or potential whistle-blowers with the threat of litigation. Even a priest who spoke out against her from his pulpit in Co. Mayo got a legal letter ordering him to desist. Former follower Mike McCrory got one too, after he turned against her. But he called her bluff by ringing up the House of Prayer and saying he looked forward to seeing them in court. He never heard from them again.

The Irish Catholic newspaper also got a threatening letter from the House of Prayer following the first *Sunday World* stories. Why? It was an obvious attempt to frighten them away from following up any of the revelations. Sent by email on 21 January 2008, and simply signed 'Our Lady Queen of Peace House of Prayer,' the letter to the weekly Catholic paper said that a strong letter of response and rebuttal had been sent to the *Sunday World* claiming their first two articles were grossly defamatory and demanding an apology.

'In the event that an apology was not forthcoming, High Court Proceedings will now be commenced against the *Sunday World*. No further statement will be issued pending the Hearing of the High Court Action,' said the House of Prayer.

Only no High Court action was ever taken. This was just a blatant attempt to stop further bad publicity getting out. The *Sunday World* never retracted a word and never apologised. Far from an apology appearing on Page One the following week, as Corrigan demanded, the newspaper instead carried pictures of Gallagher's fabulous Malahide mansion on the front page.

As well as the exposé on Gallagher's amazing millionaire lifestyle, the next article also carried some interesting news about the lawyer Donal Corrigan himself. Checks revealed that he was in fact one of four directors of the Our Lady Queen of Peace House of Prayer (Achill) Ltd. It was not a good year for Donal J. Corrigan. Months later he was back in the news because of his connection to a rogue lawyer, Thomas Byrne, who had disappeared with debts of €9 million. In July 2008 Corrigan disputed the IIB Bank's claim for possession of a €1 million building which housed his own office. The IIB was claiming the property as it had been advanced by Byrne as part security, along with several other buildings, for a €9 million loan he had obtained the previous year. Corrigan claimed in court that he had a prior claim over the premises in Crumlin Village, Dublin, because he had sold it to Byrne for €800,000 in September 2007 but the cheque had bounced. Byrne had told the bank he owned the building and had leased it to Corrigan. But Corrigan claimed his signature had been forged on the lease documents. Byrne had defaulted on the loan and was struck off by the Law Society in June 2008 and fined €1 million. The legal battle was covered in all of Ireland's national daily newspapers. It was also interesting to see that Corrigan's address in court was

given as 'The Matrix', Dublin. This obsessed follower of
Christina Gallagher had even called his home after the
money-making medal she had created.

The *Sunday World* never heard from Christina
Gallagher or Donal Corrigan ever again, even though
it published a whole series of hard-hitting articles about
her greed, her ruthlessness and her lies. The threatened
High Court action never took place. Nor did the 'separate
proceedings' over her marital status. Gallagher and her
husband Paddy had been living apart for over a decade.
And all those who worked at the House of Prayer were
well aware of the fact. As Mike McCrory said, Gallagher
spent 20 times more time with her manager, Noel Guinan,
than she ever did with her husband. But Gallagher was
keen to put on the façade of being a happily married
family woman; So much so that she wheeled out Paddy
and their children, Brendan and Mary, and even her
grandchildren, at the House of Prayer the very first
Saturday after the initial *Sunday World* story. It was a
rare appearance indeed for Paddy Gallagher, a plumber
by trade, who got a lot of work from his estranged wife
in the numerous properties she controlled and owned,
according to House of Prayer insiders.

The unveiling of Gallagher's Malahide mansion
attracted much attention around the country. Other
national and local newspapers immediately followed
up the story. Former victims of the House of Prayer
and their families rang radio presenter Joe Duffy on
RTÉ's *Liveline* programme to vent their anger. Fr Gerard
McGinnity went on air in a desperate bid to defend his
mentor but failed dismally. This was the first and last
time since the scandal broke that he publicly spoke
about Gallagher away from the safety of his own House
of Prayer pulpit where he was free to rant as he liked.
Over the next few weeks he continued to call this author

'the agent of the Devil,' an obvious slander in itself.

Finding the Malahide mansion had been key to the whole Christina Gallagher investigation, and it came about, courtesy of the *Sunday World*'s very own 'deep throat'. After the first House of Prayer story was published, a woman sent an email claiming she knew where Gallagher lived in Dublin. She gave a false name and set up a new email account just for the purposes of our dialogue, so that she could not be traced. The woman was adamant that she would never be identified. All she said was that she was a former follower, who had become utterly disillusioned and quit. She said she was one of just a handful of people in the country who knew where Gallagher lived, because the so-called visionary kept it a closely guarded secret.

The woman agreed to show me the house and we met the following day in a Dublin hotel. We travelled by car, but the woman was so scared of being seen by Christina Gallagher that she donned a baseball cap to ensure she would not be recognised. She didn't give the address, just the directions on how to get there. We headed for Malahide on her instructions, which was a surprise in itself. The North Co. Dublin seaside town is known as one of the most expensive places to live in the whole of Ireland. We drove up the Dublin Road to the edge of Malahide, turned left onto Swords Road and then left again into the exclusive Abington Estate. This was another huge surprise. Just what kind of house was Gallagher living in? I had been here years before looking for popstar Nicky Byrne, who lives on the estate, while covering a Westlife story. Ronan Keating, the millionaire singer and frontman of Boyzone, also lived in this development. Surely, the leader of a prayer organisation in rural West of Ireland could not live on this millionaire's row, rubbing shoulders with the rich and famous?

We passed a whole series of expensive homes, as we drove to the very end of a narrow lane, which opened up into a circle for turning at the dead end. My passenger pointed to this fabulous Italian-style villa and said: 'That's it.'

There in front of me was one of the most stunning homes I had ever seen in Dublin. I could hardly believe my eyes. The house was simply magnificent. The cast-iron gates were closed, but you could see a long drive leading up to the mansion, with manicured lawns on either side. Young, freshly planted trees and ornate lampposts lined the driveway, and I caught a glimpse of sculptures in the distance. The house itself was enormous and three-storeys high. It looked like something you might see on the Italian Riviera.

'Are you sure she lives here?' I asked incredulously. 'I absolutely know she lives here,' was the reply. We did not hang about, as we did not want to be seen at this point. Getting photographs of Gallagher using the mansion would be the next priority, and surprise was of the essence. The newspaper's veteran photographer Liam O'Connor was put on the case. And three days later he came up trumps. The house itself was almost impossible to 'doorstep', as anyone standing outside or sitting in a car could be seen from the house. There was also a security camera in the gate's intercom system. As the road was a dead end there was no excuse for anyone to just be sitting there.

Photographer O'Connor had to sit some distance away, but he eventually hit the jackpot when a beautiful, top of the range 7 series BMW came out of the driveway of the Abington home and headed for the shops. The exclusive car – prices began at €110,000 at the time for a basic model – drove to a local Woodies DIY store. Liam watched as Gallagher, her bodyguard-come-handyman,

Tony Fitzpatrick, and the former Dominican nun, Sister Treasa, who left her order to follow Gallagher, went into the shop.

When they came out later, carrying pictures and pushing a trolley filled with goods, O'Connor was ready. He captured Gallagher leading her little posse back to the car, car keys in hand, without any of them ever realising what was going on. Gallagher looked like any other shopper out running errands on a normal weekday afternoon – except of course most people don't have the privilege of doing it in a €110,000-plus car. And funnily enough, there were no signs of the stigmata, which she claims to have on her head and hands. Gallagher herself bore little resemblance to the few photographs that were available of her, having put on a huge amount of weight over the years.

On the Friday I called to the house with another photographer, Val Sheehan, to try to get an interview with the reclusive Gallagher, ringing the intercom bell at the gate several times. Nobody answered. Sheehan then started taking photographs of the house from the closed gate, as I rang the neighbours' intercom to see if they knew who lived next to them. The woman who answered said they didn't know anything about them. As we got back in our car and were just beginning to drive away, I saw a woman walking down the driveway from Gallagher's house towards us, talking into a mobile phone. She had seen the photographer taking pictures and had come out to investigate. I recognised her straight away as the former nun Treasa, who we had photographed with Gallagher 48 hours earlier. She follows Gallagher everywhere and, I was told by former House of Prayer insiders, actually lived with Gallagher.

'What do you want?' she asked, after I got out of the car. I said I wanted to talk to Christina but she said no Christina lived there. Looking embarrassed, she said she did not know any Christina Gallagher when I persisted. She admitted living in the house herself, but said she was looking after it for the owners. She refused to say who they were, and then told us to go away, that we had what we wanted. All the time the elderly woman spoke to us through the electronic gate she was on a mobile phone talking to someone, whom we suspected was Gallagher herself, and who was possibly inside the house.

Our photographs of Treasa walking dutifully behind her mentor outside Woodies, two days earlier proved that she did know Christina Gallagher. Why would she lie if there was nothing to hide? And why would a former religious sister, in particular, lie about such a thing? She was presumably under strict orders from her boss to say nothing. And if not, she must have been aware that the general public might find it a little difficult to understand why a self-proclaimed visionary was living in such splendour.

When we arrived back in the office with the photographs of the mansion, it caused a sensation. Once they were downloaded to a computer, one of the journalists looking at the pictures shouted out, 'Holy God!' There was a stampede towards the picture desk by staff wanting a look, as Managing Editor Neil Leslie, calmly said: 'That's the headline – Holy God!'

And sure enough, two days later, on 20 January, it was indeed the headline splashed across the front page. A secondary headline read: 'House of Prayer Visionary's €4m Secret Home is a Paradise on Earth.' Two pages followed inside under the heading '€4m Kingdom of Heaven'. An estate agent's website had details of the house from when it was first put on the market, nearly three years before, and these details were included in the article. The mansion was set in a stunning 17-hectare (42-acre) wooded development. It had five en-suite bedrooms with space on the third floor to convert into three or even four more rooms. The house came with a double-height entrance hall, a solid oak staircase leading to a gallery landing, and five reception rooms. There was a detached coach-house with garaging for three cars and a loft that could be used as an office or gym. The builders had left space for a swimming pool and tennis court, if the new owner wanted them. The millionaire's row home was on the market for €3.5 million in 2005 but was now, three years later, believed to be worth €4 million. It was the second biggest house on the development.

The *Sunday World* article said: 'This is the secret €4 million paradise that is home to self-proclaimed visionary Christina Gallagher. The publicity-shy founder of the controversial House of Prayer, photographed publicly here for the first time in more than 10 years, is living in palatial luxury in a private estate where her neighbours include pop star Ronan Keating and Westlife's Nicky Byrne.' It went on: 'The woman, who claims she has no interest in material things and says she receives regular messages from the Virgin Mary, quietly moved into this beautiful Italian style mansion set on 1.2 acres nearly two years ago. Only a handful of her followers know she lives in such splendour, but the *Sunday World* this week tracked down the roly-poly religious icon and her amazing house.'

The paper reminded readers how Gallagher had splashed out €1 million on another mansion for her daughter. It also stated that she was now going to come under even more pressure to explain her apparent wealth. The paper said: 'We have a simple question for the supposed holy woman: Just who is paying for this amazing lifestyle when hard-up pensioners around the country have been giving their life-savings to the House of Prayer?' While she lived like a princess, her House of Prayer organisation was continually begging for money. The prayer centre's website still claimed that 'funds are urgently needed' to complete the work of the House of Prayer and its six sister Houses in the US and Mexico. It listed addresses where believers should send their 'donations and contributions.'

News that the once humble housewife was living in such opulence launched a national debate, played out partly on the *Liveline* show. But callers to the popular RTÉ radio afternoon programme were warned to watch what they said on air, because of Gallagher's well-known history of making legal threats. On Wednesday 23 January the national broadcaster denied claims that a legal gagging order had been placed on the show. The *Irish Independent* reported the following day: 'Callers were warned to tone it down on the popular phone-in programme on RTÉ radio yesterday after they spoke out against the woman [Gallagher], who claims to suffer stigmata, and her self-styled House of Prayer. *Liveline* host Joe Duffy said callers would have to be careful what they said or risk being the subject of a lawsuit, after several people rang the programme yesterday and spoke of their personal experiences with the self-styled prophet.'

The *Irish Independent* article went on: 'Several callers, including those who support Mrs Gallagher, were responding to claims made in a Sunday newspaper at the weekend concerning the apparent wealth of the self-proclaimed "visionary" who claims to receive messages from the Virgin Mary. The two-page newspaper feature, complete with photographs of a BMW, a sprawling mansion and pictures showing Ms Gallagher leaving a local DIY shop with a trolley full of household goods, claims she is living a life of luxury with a multi-million euro property portfolio and top-of-the-range luxury cars, despite not having any visible means of support or income.'

The *Irish Independent* said it had tried to contact the House of Prayer lawyer, Donal Corrigan, but he was not available for comment 'and did not return phone calls when contacted by the *Irish Independent* at his office yesterday'. The newspaper quoted Fr Gerard McGinnity claiming Gallagher did not own the mansion but was staying there as a guest 'to get away from it all'.

Despite denying that it had gagged callers, *Liveline* did not follow up the subject the following day, as it had promised.

When Mike McCrory saw pictures of the Malahide mansion he was horrified. 'This is simply shocking. How can she explain away all this wealth?' he asked. 'Her followers did not know about these houses and Christina Gallagher has to come forward and explain where all this money is coming from. They have always fawned over people with money while treating some of their loyal staff like dirt. It's like a cult.'

CHAPTER EIGHT

Christina's Property Empire

'… that is their religion now, not the Catholic religion.
It is a cult. I want my family back.'

The revelation that Christina Gallagher lived in a €4 million mansion on a private estate caused a sensation. But there were more revelations to come. Former followers of the House of Prayer leader, who had been reluctant to talk previously, were now so appalled at the scale of Gallagher's duplicity that they began to open up. Phone calls were now being returned, and letters and emails began to pour in, often anonymously.

The problem for many of Gallagher's devotees was that they had invested so much time, energy and hope in her that they found it hard to accept that the whole thing was a fraud. It is very difficult to acknowledge that you have spent years following a charlatan. It shakes your entire belief system, especially if you have given your time emotionally, and contributed financially to a cause which turns out to be a scam. Though a number of people were shocked by what they had read in the newspaper, there was always a slight possibility in their minds that the woman might be genuine. These were deeply religious people and they did not want to question a real visionary from God. Nobody wanted to bring down a true prophet, and risk what they believed would be eternal damnation. These were all devout Catholics, and some had invested a huge part of their lives in the House of Prayer.

Even whistle-blower Mike McCrory found it difficult to accept that Gallagher was a complete fraud. After he first turned against her, he still clung to the belief that she might have been genuine in the beginning but had been corrupted by money and wealth. This was a view that he would eventually discard, as more and more revelations came out. Former followers who now saw the light still did not want to face the embarrassment of going public. Who would want to admit to family and friends that they had given away €5,000, €10,000 or even €50,000 of their money to a con-woman: money that could have gone to their children or grandchildren? Most people preferred instead to quietly withdraw from visiting the House of Prayer, and to talk no more about it. They certainly did not want to expose their experience to a million *Sunday World* readers. Fortunately, there were certain brave souls, like Betty and Michael Morrissey, who were so outraged by Christina Gallagher's behaviour that they could not keep silent.

From the start there was a suspicion that the huge house in Malahide would not be in Christina Gallagher's name. She had kept it top secret for two years. Only a handful of people knew that she lived there, so it was highly unlikely that her name would be on the deeds of the house. That would have spelt the end of her credibility as a humble religious leader. After all, Gallagher was not even listed as a director or official of Our Lady Queen of Peace House of Prayer (Achill) Ltd which owned the prayer centre – even though she ran the whole show.

The article uncovering the Malahide house had been carefully worded, revealing that the property had been her home for two years, but nowhere did it say she was the registered owner. Days later I uncovered the land registry documents for the mansion. It turned out that the official owner, since April 2006, was a man called John Rooney. At the time nobody knew who he was, so I rang up and asked Betty Morrissey if she had ever heard of this man. Her reaction was one of stunned silence – particularly when she heard why I wanted to know. Betty was simply shell-shocked, and there and then began telling her story. Facts I had no hope of getting the day before, now came tumbling out of her mouth. Betty insisted she still did not want to be named. She told how she and countless other House of Prayer followers had been told to sign their cheques to a John Rooney. She and her husband signed one for a colossal €50,000.

Over the next few days a number of other people got in touch to tell how members of their families had been hoodwinked by the House of Prayer. The vast majority of callers, in fact, were critical of Christina Gallagher, but a handful blasted the newspaper for doing 'Satan's work' in criticising such a holy woman. One man rang to say his elderly father, who was a regular visitor to the Achill House, had been sucked into the scam and had handed over money. He explained that his mother had died from cancer, two years ago. A few months after her death, Gallagher called in the grieving widower and said she had had an apparition in which she saw his wife sitting in heaven with her in-laws.

'For my dad that news was better than winning the lottery,' said the caller. 'Gallagher just reeled him in and he swallowed it hook, line and sinker. She blatantly targeted him when he was vulnerable. She is a total fraud and someone has to stop her. My father is 72, and I am sure he is out thousands of euro, but won't tell us how much he has given her. I just hate to see him taken for a ride. My dad is down there every Saturday, and will not listen to us. She is making a fool of him. She has amassed so much wealth.'

The man said that his father used to take his wife to the House of Prayer, while she was ill with cancer, hoping for a miracle cure. The cure never happened, and she eventually passed away. Christina Gallagher was fully aware of this. He said that anyone looking in from the outside could see that Gallagher was a fraud. Gallagher had deliberately targeted his father to extract money from him, and convinced him she was genuine. The caller said: 'The things she claims are just ridiculous, and it's hard to believe that people fall for it. My dad lives in Galway, and he drives up and down every Saturday, which is a long way to go. You just hate seeing him taken for a ride. But nothing we say makes a difference.'

A Cork bus-tour operator, called Tom, told us he stopped bringing groups to the House of Prayer two years previously in 'pure anger at the way money was extorted' from people. He said he had met people who had been asked to sell their homes and give the money to the House of Prayer. And other people were asked to give their salaries or take out loans. 'I saw elderly people and relatives of my own giving money when they did not have much,' he said. 'People are told if they donate to the House of Prayer they will have eternal salvation. But those who abandon or betray Christina Gallagher will suffer eternal damnation. They extracted money from the most gullible and most vulnerable.'

He said his own uncle gave €8,000 to the Blue Ivory Trust. His 85-year-old cousin also gave €2,000. He said one couple he knew were encouraged to sell their business and come and live in the House. They refused, but did donate €15,000. Tom also revealed that the House of Prayer staff had rung bus operators, during that week, to tell them there would be a meeting soon to work out ways of getting people back to Achill. Numbers had plummeted because of the bad publicity.

A man from the midlands contacted me and said he was trying to get his parents out of what he regarded as a cult. He said Christina Gallagher had 'destroyed' his family. Neil (not his real name) said his father, in particular, was completely devoted to Gallagher and Fr McGinnity, and he had become a major player in the House of Prayer, giving away thousands of euro. But far worse than that, Neil said that they had lost years of family life together. His parents went to the House of Prayer every weekend, and now rarely visited their own grandchildren. He said his father was a devout Catholic, who believed everything Gallagher and Fr McGinnity told him. Neil was in touch with me over an 18-month period.

'I am a strong Catholic myself but this place is a cult and I think Christina Gallagher is an out and out fraud,' he said. 'I am disgusted that Archbishop Neary has not condemned her because of the heresy that comes out of the place. All this stuff about being saved if you wear her Matrix medal! She says we are damned if we do not follow her, so is the Pope damned?'

He said he could not understand why the Church authorities had stayed quiet. The House of Prayer had prospered because of this silence, he said, and because people in Ireland had become disillusioned with the Church and were looking for something different. A lot of older people in particular had latched on to Gallagher. 'I know my mum and dad have sold off land, and given her the money – because they are told they will go to heaven. She has destroyed my family. Christina Gallagher has destroyed so many lives. She should be in prison. I hope the Revenue Commissioners go after her. The people who go there every weekend – that is their religion now, not the Catholic religion. It is a cult. I want my family back.'

A cancer victim called Ann from Co. Limerick said she visited the Achill house just once, and would never go again. 'It was like travelling with a bus full of demons. The whole way up and back they were shouting out prayers, three hours up and three hours back. It was pure brainwashing.'

Ann said she had been diagnosed with breast cancer, and although she had been successfully treated, she was at a vulnerable stage. She thought the day trip would do her good and give her some peace, but she said it had the opposite effect. 'It reminded me of one of those Hitler rallies. I was scared to death. My whole body was shaking when I got home.' Although Gallagher was not present that day, Ann said a lay preacher was ranting at the congregation in the most arrogant way. Straight away, Ann thought it was a cult. 'I could not believe how Irish people were falling for it.'

The *Sunday World* was flooded with many such calls, and the newspaper recorded some of them in its next story, published on 27 January 2008, about John Rooney and the secret fundraising meetings. Under the heading, 'Immaculate Deception,' the paper told how it had uncovered 'shocking financial dealings involving 'holy' woman Christina Gallagher and her controversial House of Prayer'and how hundreds of people around the country were asked to give large donations to the House, but to sign the cheques to her American aide John Rooney. Readers were told that so secret was this mission to save millions of souls that nobody could be told what it was about in case the Church – which did not approve of the House of Prayer – stopped it. Devout Catholics, who had been called to these meetings were now left wondering what had happened to the huge sums of money they handed over.

The same day as this article appeared, the *Sunday World* also carried a two-page piece by another reporter, Geraldine Comiskey, who had been sent undercover into the House of Prayer, on the Saturday of the previous weekend. Her report told how Fr McGinnity slammed the newspaper as 'the work of demons' from the pulpit and attacked this author as 'an agent of the Devil' for daring to criticise Christina Gallagher. His remarks were made hours before the *Sunday World* hit the streets, uncovering the €4 million Malahide mansion.

Referring to the first exposé of the House of Prayer on 6 January, Fr McGinnity told the crowd that it was defamatory and that the accusations were 'not true'. He said Christina 'does not own a big house in Dublin'. Then turning his attention to the American fundraising letter in which Fr Robert Burns said Gallagher wanted cash only from now on and no cheques, Fr McGinnity admitted that a priest had indeed collected money to pay 'Christina's medical bill', but it 'caused Christina embarrassment and it stopped'.

The priest then delivered a fire and brimstone sermon to 200, mostly elderly, pilgrims about 'the fires of Hell'. Hardened reporter Comiskey was shocked. She wrote: 'It revolted me to think that these nice people were being codded, ripped-off and threatened with eternal damnation, if they did not support Christina Gallagher morally and financially. They were gambling their life's savings – and the last years of their lives – on a promise of reduced Purgatory in return for funding her cause.'

The next morning Comiskey saw House of Prayer staff buying up multiple copies of the *Sunday World*, so that locals on Achill Island could not see the first pictures of

Gallagher's fabulous Malahide home. 'In a newsagent on Achill Sound, I saw one of the women grab a bundle she could barely carry. Elsewhere on the island (population 3,000) the *Sunday World* was sold out.'

Locals told Comiskey they were not surprised by what they read. The reporter then visited the House of Prayer shop, where she was encouraged to buy a brick that you could have your name enscribed on 'and Christina will pray for you'. People generally pay €500, but Comiskey offered €100. She then described the disappointment when she said she could only afford €20, which she handed over. Other 'pay as you pray' items, she said, included €2 pens, €8.50 rosary beads, statues costing from €10 to €50, and Mass cards signed by Fr McGinnity for €5. Pieces of cloth with 'Padre Pio's blood from his wounds' were also being touted from the pulpit and cost just €5. Customers were not told how these cloths ended up on Achill Island, a thousand kilometres from the late holy man's Italian home.

Comiskey examined files that were on show in the shop and which contained letters from people supposedly cured of illnesses at the House of Prayer. But she found that the addresses were vague, or letters were signed with just initials. There was also a list of doctors who had verified so called 'miracle cures' at the House, but nobody could give Comiskey contact details for them. 'They are mostly in America,' said a woman called Eileen.

After uncovering Gallagher's house in Dublin, the big question now was where to go with the story from here? A natural place to look was the plush house outside Newport, where Gallagher had lived for a decade before moving to Malahide. This house was another gem, sitting on a hill above the main road to

Castlebar, surrounded by high walls that made it almost impossible to see from the road.

Gallagher herself had even admitted, albeit indirectly, that this was a massive house, because she complained that it was too big for her and that its size was being used by her critics to attack her.

Gallagher must have been laughing to herself the day she came up with the audacious idea of turning her own home into a shrine to herself, when she was still very much alive. The sheer arrogance of it was startling. To her, it was just one more way of making money. And it worked. Hundreds of thousands of euro were raised – Mike McCrory heard that it was between €600,000 and €1 million – and a plaque was duly placed on the front wall of the house, next to the gate saying: 'Blue Ivory Trust'. However, Christina Gallagher was still using the house, particularly at weekends when she travelled from Dublin to Achill to appear at the House of Prayer on Saturday afternoons. Certainly, nobody else was allowed to use the premises, so nothing seemed to have changed.

A suspicion began to grow. What if Gallagher still owned the house, after taking a fortune from her followers who were supposedly buying it off her? Surely even she would not be brazen enough to pocket large sums of money, and then not hand over the property that was supposedly being bought from her?

The Land Registry in Dublin is where the nation's property documentation is kept, and it can now be accessed online. City homes are easy to look up, with their street names and numbers, but houses in the countryside, with their vague addresses, are more difficult. If you don't have a property's serial number you can find it using the online maps. But to do this you have to know exactly where the property is on an Ordnance Survey map. Checking out Gallagher's house outside Newport, meant driving to Co. Mayo, finding the property and marking its exact location on a map, which could then be cross referenced with the Land Registry's online maps. Once a property has been exactly pinpointed, all the relevant information is there when the file is opened.

When the file for the Newport house was accessed, there in black and white was clear evidence of another dodgy deal: the house was still owned by Christina Gallagher, not by any Blue Ivory Trust. The government record revealed that she remained the sole owner. The house was originally listed in her name and that of her daughter, Mary Gorman, from 1998, when they were listed as 'full owners'. But in September 2004 the register was changed, and Gallagher became the sole owner. Around this time she told her inner circle of devotees that she had bought another house for her daughter in Ballina.

Further checks revealed that the Blue Ivory Trust, as well as not owning this house, regardless of the plaque on the wall, was not registered as owning any property in Mayo whatsoever. Inquiries failed to come up with any record of the trust as a charity or as a business at that time.

Did Fr McGinnity know this fact when he told his flock that Gallagher did not own any properties? Here was the proof to the contrary in the official government record.

The Land Registry records also showed that Gallagher was joint owner of the comfortable family home in Knockmore, near Foxford, where her husband Paddy still lived, and which they had bought in June 1977.

So Gallagher effectively owned three houses: one outside Newport, one in Malahide and one in Knockmore. It all added up to a lot of houses for a woman who 'had no property'. The next *Sunday World* story, published on 10 February 2008, carried copies of the Land Registry records and a photograph of the Newport house under the headline, 'House About This Christina?' A sub-heading said: 'She says she owns no property…we prove yet *another* house is hers.'

But just as scandalous as her keeping ownership of a house that her supporters had paid for, was what was inside this impressive stone building. Gallagher had decorated and furnished her home with exceptionally expensive antiques, including crystal chandeliers and a number of Jacuzzis. Pride of place in the house was a massive four-poster bed that Gallagher had specially imported from Harrods of London, the world famous department store where the late Princess Diana and numerous other members of royalty and celebrities would do their shopping. She bought the bed with two matching side tables. One friend said it wouldn't even fit in a normal size bedroom.

There were four luxury bedrooms on the ground floor alone of the house, and every one had an en-suite bathroom and TV. A living room and dining room had marble fireplaces and were furnished with expensive crystal and antiques. Chandeliers costing thousands of euro hung from the ceilings. There was a huge kitchen, a conservatory, an extensive garden with a waterfall on the back wall and a pond with tropical fish and palm trees. Steps in the garden led to a summer house.

Upstairs there were just two massive bedrooms covering the same floor area as the ground floor. One of them was Christina's. The en-suite bathrooms of these two bedrooms both had Jacuzzis. There were also pull-down seats in the showers which became private steam rooms.

Gallagher's former friend Esther recalls the opulence of the interior of the Newport house: 'When I first walked in, I nearly died, as I come from a normal background.

Christina loves showing off her things but when you ask how much they cost, she gets all coy.' Esther said that there was a walk-in wardrobe in Gallagher's room and that she 'had never seen so many clothes'. There were also drawers and suitcases filled with thousands of euro worth of jewellery – much of it still in velvet boxes.

When Gallagher bought the Newport house in 1996 it was still a humble single-storey building, but it had since changed beyond all recognition. Gallagher had spent a fortune completely transforming the home. Another woman, Margaret, a former loyal servant who was dismissed by Gallagher but who had also been in the house, said she was embarrassed when she saw the scale of the luxuries. 'She has got incredibly expensive tastes but I just don't know where she gets the money. She spends it like water.'

Margaret said: 'The House of Prayer hired girls from the Philippines to work in the Achill House, and I know two who were paid by the House of Prayer but were taken to Christina Gallagher's own house in Newport to clean it from top to bottom. One time they began at 8am and came back so exhausted they could hardly stand up. And then they were got rid of.'

Margaret said none of the House of Prayer's regular staff were allowed near the Newport house when Gallagher was packing up to leave. Gallagher was on her way to Malahide, but the move was top secret, and Gallagher did not tell her followers she was leaving. But one day Margaret was asked to drive two Philippine women to the house to do some cleaning. She was met outside the front gate by the former nun, Sister Treasa, Gallagher's right hand woman, who was waiting for her and who was blocking her way. She wouldn't let Margaret drive up to the house, but insisted she drop off the two workers at the gate. 'They did not want me to see all the packed boxes outside the house, but I saw them. Christina was obsessed with secrecy.'

Mike McCrory was angry when he was told that his one-time mentor still owned the Newport house. 'This is simply unbelievable. I didn't have a lot of money but I gave a thousand euro, because Christina said she could not afford to live there. If it can be proved that she took this money while keeping the house, she should be prosecuted for fraud. The only people who use that house are Christina and her family.'

Meanwhile, back at the House of Prayer, Gallagher was busy telling anyone who would listen that she had predicted this assault on her by the media. She told the faithful that she had a vision from 'Our Blessed Mother' weeks before the *Sunday World* began its series of revelations telling her that the 'greatest attack ever' was about to be launched against the House of Prayer, and that it therefore came as no surprise. She even called for a special novena to fight this media assault. When the so-called attack began, her followers took it as further evidence that Gallagher had a hotline to heaven.

What Gallagher failed to mention to anyone was that Mike McCrory had actually warned her that he was going to go to the press. She knew that he was talking to at least one newspaper. She hardly needed celestial intervention, therefore, to realise that the dirt was about to hit the fan.

A month after details of the Newport house were unveiled to the public, I drove to Mayo to find the home of Christina Gallagher's only son, Brendan, on a hunch that the house might have been bought by Christina. Brendan Gallagher was married with a family. His house was only a couple of kilometres from the €1 million mansion that Gallagher bought her daughter. It was duly marked on an ordnance

survey map, and once again I checked with the Land
Registry back in Dublin. The record showed that this,
too, had been bought by Gallagher, but this time with
her estranged husband. Interestingly, it was snapped up
without a mortgage. Did this mean the house was paid
for in cash? A house bought in 2001 during the height of
escalating house prices without a mortgage was quite a
feat for anyone, especially for someone without a job.
The impressive house was bought in January 2001 for
Brendan, who married in September 1998 and has two
children. The Land Registry shows that she and Paddy
remained owners of the home in Lisdavogue, near
Knockmore, Co. Mayo, until November 2006. Then they
handed ownership to their son, who was already living
in it with his family. Brendan now became the registered
'full owner', with no mention of his wife Michelle on
the public record. In fact, at the time she handed it over,
Gallagher told one supporter: 'That woman is not getting
her hands on my property!' The gift to her son, followed
by one to her daughter, meant she had given both her
children houses within six months of each other.

On 16 March 2008, the *Sunday World* announced
it had found 'another mansion belonging to self-
proclaimed visionary Christina Gallagher'. The story
put more pressure on Gallagher to explain just where
all this money was coming from.

But, as always, she and her staff remained completely
silent over the scandal, instead telling her supporters at
the House of Prayer that everything in the press was
lies. Sadly, even though the numbers attending the
Saturday prayer sessions were declining rapidly, most
of those remaining still believed every word coming
from the Galagher's mouth.

CHAPTER NINE

No Place for Old Men

*'I want to hurry up and get him away from her while
he has a chance, while he is alive.'*

The tragic story of 89-year-old Tim McCarry was one of
the saddest to come out of the House of Prayer.

Tim was so devoted to Christina Gallagher that he
moved to the House of Prayer and lived in a caravan on
the grounds of the centre.

Before he died in December 2007, the old man had
given the 'holy' woman his life savings of €70,000. His
daughter Bernadette Rees, who lives in England, was
furious at what she saw as the manipulation of an elderly
and lonely man. In a hard-hitting interview, Bernadette
said: 'I feel as if he was robbed. They preyed on the fact
he was old and vulnerable to their suggestions. He was
led to believe that money would make him a pathway
to heaven and he gave everything he had. I think he
was cheated.'

Bernadette said her beloved dad, who was from
Dunfanaghy in Co. Donegal, was a deeply religious
man, and therefore 'an easy mark'. He had lost his wife
in the eighties, and tragically his only son had committed
suicide. 'He was mentally very vulnerable and they took
advantage of him.' She said her dad originally lived
in a rented room in Achill. He prayed regularly at the
House of Prayer, but eventually moved into a caravan
in the House grounds for several years. He cooked and
looked after himself until his last few months, when he
developed cancer of the oesophagus. He ended his days
in a nursing home in Falcarragh, Co. Donegal.

'When I sent them an email saying my dad had died of cancer I didn't even get a reply. They didn't even send a sympathy card, which is incredible when you consider they are supposed to be a religious organisation. They knew he had cancer in hospital but never visited him, even though he had been with them for years and had given them all this money. I feel very bitter towards them. They took someone who was vulnerable and manipulated him.'

Bernadette said that as well as the €70,000 in savings, her dad also had an English and Irish pension. 'We don't know what happened to that,' she said. 'We never even found out what happened to his caravan. The House of Prayer has offered no information about what they did with it.'

She said her father told her a few months before he died that he had given all his money to the House of Prayer. At one stage he told her to ring a man called Noel, the accountant at the House of Prayer, as her father had given him €2,000 for his funeral. 'I had to ring a good few times before I got him, and he laughed it off saying dad was "day-dreaming", and that he had given them a small donation at the very beginning and nothing else.'

Noel Guinan was in fact Christina Gallagher's manager at the time, and was secretary of the parent company, Our Lady Queen of Peace House of Prayer (Achill) Ltd. The former Dublin taxi company boss was a close confidante of Gallagher, and was often at her side.

Bernadette's story was confirmed to me by Mike McCrory. McCrory admitted that it was he who encouraged Tim McCarry to hand over his savings to Gallagher, because he believed so strongly in her cause at the time. McCrory had also persuaded another devout Catholic, Paddy Woods, to hand over €100,000 to the supposed visionary. McCrory deeply regretted both cases. Eventually, Woods did in fact get his money back, after taking legal action against the House of Prayer. He learnt that the Morrisseys were suing Gallagher, McGinnity and John Rooney, so he hired the same lawyer. He was a beneficiary in the €250,000 out-of-court settlement made by Gallagher's organisation in August 2008.

Tim McCarry's story appeared in the *Sunday World* on 9 March 2008 under the heading: 'Dad gave all his money to the House of Prayer... they robbed an old man.' By now other Irish newspapers were keenly following up the House of Prayer story, particularly after Dr Michael Neary, the Archbishop of Tuam, issued a statement on 29 February 2008, re-emphasising once again that the prayer centre on Achill Island had 'no Church approval whatever'. The statement came in the wake of a growing clamour by the press and public for some kind of reaction from the Church to all the revelations of the previous two months.

On 2 March the *Sunday Tribune* carried a full-page article on Gallagher under the headline: 'Heavenly pursuits, earthly paradise.' The story began: 'It's all going wrong for the woman with the direct line to God.' The article said the Archbishop of Tuam, had announced that Gallagher had no Church approval, supporters were defecting from her ranks and vulnerable elderly people were finally beginning to wonder where all their cash had gone. 'Only one thing is now clear,' wrote reporter Sarah McInerney, 'self-proclaimed visionary Christina Gallagher has some serious questions to answer about the House of Prayer, her string of properties, and where the money trail leads.'

On 30 March the same newspaper carried a story declaring, 'Revenue probes House of Prayer over donations,' and carried details about how two former followers had met senior tax officials to discuss their concerns over large cheques donated to Gallagher's organisation. The newspaper didn't name them but the 'two former followers' were Betty and Michael Morrissey, and the two cheques they had signed were to John Rooney and Fr McGinnity for €50,000 and €40,000 respectively.

The *Sunday Times* carried a similar story the same day, claiming: 'Mayo mystic investigated by tax office.' So too did the *Sunday Independent* under the heading, 'We were ripped off by House of Prayer,' quoting the Morrisseys without naming them. The newspaper said: 'Elderly couple who gave €90k in life savings complain to gardaí and warn others about controversial movement.' It said that the Morrisseys were the first to make a formal complaint to the gardaí about the House of Prayer. The *Sunday World* carried the same story that day, 30 March, saying: 'We uncover dodgy links between cheques and Gallagher's house.' The newspaper published photographs of the two cheques totalling €90,000, which the Morrisseys had signed.

The momentum was building against Christina Gallagher. The following week, 6 April 2008, the *Sunday World* revealed that one of Gallagher's former fundraisers in the US, Christine Adler, had written to Cardinal Seán Brady, warning him that the supposed visionary was a fraud. The elderly American, who raised thousands of dollars for Gallagher and her House of Prayer, told the Cardinal that she now believed Gallagher was a false prophet, and her movement a cult. She explained how she spent her own money bringing Gallagher around the US, but was shocked by her temper, her lack of gratitude and the fact that she had to be the centre of attention at all times.

Adler said that when she paid for Gallagher to travel to Fatima during a Papal visit in 1991, the Mayo woman showed no interest in seeing the leader of the Catholic world, despite her claims to be a Catholic prophet. Pope John Paul II was visiting the shrine at Fatima on the tenth anniversary of an assassination attempt against him, when he was shot and seriously wounded by a Turkish gunman in St Peter's Square. The murder attempt happened on the anniversary of the day the Virgin Mary was said to have appeared to three shepherd children in the tiny Portuguese town, and the pope always credited Our Lady with saving his life. Pope John Paul II visited Fatima the year after the assassination attempt in 1982. When Christine Adler heard he was to make a second visit in May 1991, she was desperate to go. When she discovered that the last remaining of the three Fatima visionaries, Sister Lucia de Jesus dos Santos, then a Carmelite nun, was also due to make an appearance she was particularly keen to go. However, Christine Gallagher did not share her enthusiasm.

'She told me she did not like flying, so I held her hand and sang to her the whole way there,' Adler said. 'When we got there I got a wonderful place up at the front of the stage. When the Popemobile began to approach my heart just burst with love. But Christina suddenly said she felt sick. I had worked our way down through thousands and thousands of people to get up close. The Pope was coming and she said, "I feel sick, I have to go back." You do not know how long it took to get through all those people. Sister Lucia, the last of the three original Fatima visionaries, was also to make a very rare appearance. She was about to come on stage. I was desperate to see her and the Pope. I had come all this way from America and suddenly Christina is "sick".

'We got back to the hotel, and I thought she would go straight to her room to lie down, but she sat there and held court. People left the TV where they were watching the Pope and Sister Lucia, and went and sat at her feet. She sat there talking to these people. If you were sick you would go to bed, but she was not sick at all. I missed the Pope and Sister Lucia because of her. She did not want to see them. She did not want to look at them even on TV. Why? How could this be? She just wants people sitting at her feet. But I had paid for her to go there and as she was my guest; I felt I had to look after her.'

Adler said Gallagher never even thanked her for organising the trip. She said she was on a pension now, but had spent a lot of money on Gallagher over the years. But the so-called visionary never thanked people. One American woman complained to Adler that she had given Gallagher $1,500 with little thanks. The alleged visionary had promised that those who donated to her cause would have their names engraved on a plaque, but Adler said she didn't know if such a plaque even existed.

Adler explained that she first met Gallagher through her own friendship with Fr McGinnity, who Adler had known for years, long before he hooked up with Christina Gallagher. 'He was a lovely man and his sermons were exquisite. But that was before he met Christina. He used to speak about spiritual matters but now all he talks about is her. I don't know what happened to him,' she says sadly.

Adler said that the year after going to Fatima, she brought Gallagher to the US and travelled with her around Oklahoma, Texas and California, visiting different parishes and prayer groups. She also took her to the Philippines on another religious tour.

'But you could not get close to her,' she said. The following year, 1993, Adler travelled to Ireland for the opening of the House of Prayer. But gradually she began to grow weary of this woman, whose messages never seemed to be of love and hope but of death and destruction.

'She stayed with me in the 1990s and I heard so many messages. They do not make sense. They do not bring you to love and peace. What is more important than the money aspect is that you do not have to frighten and threaten people. Humility was not there. Love was not there. There is no joy. That is the most important thing, not the money.'

Adler said that if you truly had something from God, you would not go against the teachings of the Church. But what Gallagher was saying was contrary to Catholic doctrine. 'They say in the House of Prayer that Archbishop Neary is doing the Devil's work by not supporting them. But it is they who are doing the Devil's work,' she said.

Adler is a convert to Catholicism and has been to the shrine in Medjugorje a remarkable 16 times. She began to despair for her friend Fr McGinnity when she realised he was so wrapped up with Christina Gallagher. Adler saw the power the Mayo woman had over him but she still had faith in the priest. 'I know he is caught up in this. He gets angry if you question her. I helped them in every way and I brought Christina to America, and suddenly he started talking about her all the time. He used to talk about spirituality but when he started to talk about her that was the time things began to go wrong. She has some kind of power over him.'

Adler recalled going for a meal with the priest when he and Gallagher were in California. They had a wonderful time but Gallagher went into a sulk, because she felt left out. She said the priest loved the restaurant and they were laughing together when they got back home. But Gallagher was furious because she had not been involved. 'There was a real gloom about her and she always had to be the centre of attention.'

Adler said that the last time she rang her old friend, Gallagher answered the phone and refused to put her through to him. 'Here was I ringing from LA, and she put the phone down. There was no kindness, and I had done so much for her. I took her to Fatima, I was there for the opening day at Achill. I was there from the beginning.' She said she had written to Cardinal Brady to try to get him to stop Fr McGinnity going to the House of Prayer – and to stop other people being tricked by her. She said she was concerned for the soul of her friend. She still loved Fr McGinnity, and prayed for him, and she thought he had time to see the error of his ways. 'His friends are all praying for him because he is following a false visionary. This is such a sad thing. I want to hurry up and get him away from her while he has a chance, while he is alive.'

Adler said Gallagher's supporters were caught in a web and that she felt badly for those people who had handed over all their money. She said most of them were well-meaning and wanted to give but they had become blinded. 'I just want people to see the truth. I want to stop them getting hurt.'

The American woman said she had experienced Gallagher's explosive temper on several occasions. One day she said something quite innocuous to a friend and Gallagher just exploded at her for no reason. 'She accused me of something, after I had spent so much money doing what they wanted. I spent thousands on them.' She said she had heard that Gallagher was now ringing up people and calling them traitors, which she

thought was awful. 'I would like to see Ireland saved
from this. A lot of innocent people have been blinded,'
she said.

Few people saw Gallagher's temper like Anthony
Tierney, a devout 63 year-old Englishman. Tierney had
moved into the House of Prayer in December 2007, as
a full time member of staff. Tierney's story made front
page news on 1 June 2008, when he smashed his knee
after falling off a ladder, while cleaning windows at the
House of Prayer. He claimed he was left for three days
in a room with no medical help.

The furious grandfather, who was in agony, said
he was 'treated like a dog' by Gallagher and her
subordinates. He later made a formal complaint to
the gardaí. He told me how he reported for duty as
normal on the morning of Friday 4 April 2008. 'Every
morning you report to work and get allotted the work
for the day' he said. 'My job was to clean all the outside
windows of the House of Prayer that Friday. Friday is
one of the busiest days as everyone is preparing for the
big pilgrimage on the Saturday.'

Tierney said he cleaned the lower windows. Then
when he came to the tall stained-glass ones in the chapel,
he went to the supervisor and asked for help. He said
he knew there were three men who were available. 'But
I was told no way could they spare someone that day.
'You know Friday is the busiest day,' I was told. One
of the staff was ranting and raving at me as if I was a
child. She told me to get on with it. I was embarrassed
as I walked away.'

Tierney went back to the chapel and put his ladder
up against the window sill and climbed up. But as he
reached one of the top steps, he suddenly felt it begin to
move under him. The ladder began to slide across the
tarmac and fell, sending him crashing to the ground.

He felt an excruciating pain shooting through his right knee. He had also hurt his right arm in the fall. He said he was laying there in agony for several minutes before anyone found him. An odd-job man appeared, and at first thought Tierney was joking. But when he saw it was serious he ran for help and Tony Fitzpatrick arrived on the scene and got Tierney into a chair. He then went off to get a wheelchair that Christina Gallagher sometimes uses when she claims she is suffering.

They wheeled Tierney into the kitchen and to his surprise, Gallagher was sitting at the table. 'I could not believe it. It is not usual for her to be there on a Friday. It is very unusual to see her at all,' he said. 'I said "gracious me, it's you." But she did not say anything. She did not answer and stared at the floor, as if in a trance, and suddenly jumped up and left the room. That was the last I saw of her. She didn't ask me how I was or anything.'

Tierney said everyone else began fussing over him, and someone got a packet of frozen peas and put it on his knee. Tierney said he asked them to go and get his doctor in the health centre, which is just down the road, but they ignored his requests. He said they didn't know what to do with him and they decided to carry him to a room, where they just left him. 'They sat me on a bed and left me there until Monday afternoon. I kept asking for my doctor but they ignored me.'

Tierney said that when he was eventually taken to hospital on Monday, his knee was X-rayed and he was told it was completely crushed. 'The doctor said I should have been brought to hospital immediately. Why did they wait three days?' Doctors carried out an operation to try to repair the damage in Castlebar General Hospital, and then transferred Tierney to Ballina to recuperate.

He said that while in Ballina, he received hostile phone calls from Christina Gallagher and from her manager Noel Guinan. 'Christina Gallagher rang me and asked me, "What are your plans?" I said I would be going back to the House of Prayer. She said, "Oh no, you are not. That is the last place you are going." I told her I had come to Ireland to retire and that I would live on Achill Island. But she said, "You will not live on Achill Island." She told me she wanted me to go back to England and live with my daughter. But I said no way, she has a job, two kids and her house is not suitable. She didn't have the money to come over here and get me.'

Tierney said he thought Gallagher was being objectionable because she did not want any more bad publicity. 'I think she had visions of the press getting hold of me and making a story out of my injuries and bringing more disdain to the House of Prayer and her. You [this author] have really scared her. She ordered me out of the country. She said, "You are going, get your daughter to come over and pick you up." I said my daughter couldn't possibly afford it and she said, "What if I pay for it?" She said it would cost us no money and that she would pay for everything. "You must leave Ireland now and go to your daughter's. When you are better we will talk about you coming back. We will ring you and talk about you coming here."'

But Tierney told me that Ireland was now his home, that he had uprooted everything to move here and that there was nothing in England to go back to, as he and his wife had separated. He said he planned to retire here, so he was very upset by Gallagher's lack of sympathy. But because of his predicament, lying in a hospital bed, he pretended to play along just to get Gallagher off the phone. He told her: 'If you are paying for it all, for me and all my belongings to go back to England, okay, I will go.'

Tierney said: 'She was very happy. But I had no intention of going ahead with this silly plan, but it kept her off my back. That was the only time Gallagher spoke to me after my accident. I never saw her again.'

The House of Prayer boss never visited her former follower in hospital, but she did send her supervisor Eileen Blake and the former nun, Treasa, several times. Tierney said the women never once asked how he was. 'That Treasa is a right horror!'

Gallagher's plan was for one of her staff to drive Tierney to England. But when the patient told medical staff about the proposed journey, the doctor said there was no way he could travel and that his leg, which was in a cast, was in a very bad way. He forbade Tierney from making the journey. Tierney was happy, thinking at least someone was on his side.

But when it came time to discharge him, the hospital authorities wanted to know where he was going to live, as they could not put him out on the street. They asked if the House of Prayer was going to be his home. 'At first the House of Prayer wouldn't give a yes or a no, but said, "We can't have a cripple living with us as we have no facilities." But Noel Guinan eventually spoke to the chief nurse, and said they would let me back until I could find my own accommodation somewhere and the nurse accepted that.'

Tierney said that on the day he was discharged he was asleep when a nurse woke him at two in the afternoon. Then he saw Tony Fitzpatrick and Eileen Blake at his bedside. He said he panicked and asked the nurse what they were doing there, and she said they were there to collect him. Tierney said he was suddenly full of fear. 'I said I was not going back to that place, that Christina Gallagher had told me I could not live there. The nurse said, "We can't keep you here. We need the bed. These people are offering you a home."'

Tierney said he cursed Christina, saying 'that damned Gallagher woman'. He then told Fitzpatrick and Blake to go and get a letter from Gallagher confirming that he could stay at the House of Prayer, until he could find alternative accommodation. He still did not trust them.

But Fitzpatrick said that all that would be done in good time, but for the moment, they had to take him with them. 'So I went with them to the House of Prayer. I went straight up to my room and locked the door. The next day at 11.00am there was a knock on the door, and I opened it and Tony Fitzpatrick and Eileen Blake were there. He was very, very angry. He swore at me and said, "How dare you insult Christina in front of that nurse saying those things."'

'I said, "What are you going to do, break my other leg?" He punched the door, and I thought he was going to go for me. He was banging the door and screaming. Eileen Blake put her arms round him, and pushed him away. I slammed the door shut and locked it and I rang the gardaí.'

A few minutes later a local sergeant arrived at his doorstep, and asked what was going on. Tierney told him what had happened, and said he was frightened. The policeman suggested that it would be better if he moved out of the House. When Tierney said he had nowhere to go, the sergeant said there must be someone he could ring. Tierney remembered two House of Prayer devotees who had visited him in hospital, Peter and Ann, and he said he would call them. The garda sergeant said he would go downstairs and tell Fitzpatrick and Blake to keep away from Tierney, that he was busy packing and would be leaving. Peter and Ann picked him up.

'These are people who had been working six days a week for three years of their lives at the House of

Prayer. They were very loyal to it,' said Tierney.

Ann later told me she quit the House of Prayer in disgust at the way Anthony Tierney had been treated. Ann, who worked for free at the centre, said she was horrified when she heard Tierney's story. 'When he told me how they treated him, that was the deciding factor. I never went back to work the following day, and unbelievably, a month later they still hadn't rung me once to see if I was dead or sick. And that was after I worked for them full-time, six days a week as a volunteer. I am now kicking myself at being taken in by them. It was supposed to be Our Lady's house, but in the three years I was there I never saw any love or compassion. I can't believe I was led astray for three years. In hindsight, now I can see all the cracks, but I don't know why I didn't see them before. Most certainly the House of Prayer is a hoax. For the first two weeks after I left, I was in a state of shock.'

The Waterford woman said that when she first heard that Tierney had been in an accident, she struggled to get any details from the House of Prayer hierarchy. They didn't even want to tell her which hospital he was in. 'There was so much secrecy. It was such a big deal finding out where he was. The way he was treated was abominable. It is just unacceptable. I couldn't possibly lift a spoon for them now in the House of Prayer.'

The woman said she was pleased she had sold her house to family members, before moving into the House of Prayer – otherwise she would have given it to them. 'I did borrow €1,000 on my credit card to give to them.'

Ann and her friend Peter took Tierney to a former B&B outside Achill. It was 28 April 2008, and he was to live there for the next few months. He later moved to Castlebar. Tierney has still not recovered from his injuries and fears he might eventually lose his leg. He had to wear the plaster cast for over four months, because his knee was so bad. Even after that he still had to wear a support stocking and walk with crutches. He was told he would need a knee transplant, when the pain becomes too much to bear. But he said the bone that will support it was crushed, and doctors said it would be like trying to build a house on sand. 'The consultants were dropping hints that it might have to be amputated one day. They tell me a little more each time.'

Even if that does not happen, he will be using crutches and then a walking stick for the rest of his life, unless he gets the knee transplant. He said osteoarthritis in the joint would be another problem, and that it has already set in. 'It is an added burden. I know oldish people get it anyway, and I might have got it if I lived into my 70s, but now I will definitely get it in my leg and probably in my arm, which was also injured in the fall when I ripped the ligaments.'

He said the cast had made life very difficult, as it was hard to get about and he could not get into a bath. Even taking a shower was an ordeal, as it involved tying plastic bags all over the cast to stop it getting wet. Today, a year and a half after the accident, Tierney remains as angry at the House of Prayer as ever.

'My accident showed how hateful Gallagher really is. There is no love or compassion there. She is always talking of God's love, but what happened to me was the total opposite. I was so ill-treated after the accident, by her and her staff. As far as I'm concerned they put my life in danger. I was locked away in a room instead of being taken to hospital. When I told the gardaí, they could not believe it.'

Tierney said that his main concern now, being a 'hardline Catholic,' was that he could see his 'brothers and sisters' being taken away from the true faith, and getting caught up in this cult. He said he wanted to do everything he could to put it right. He said he wanted to see Gallagher taken off the scene, and would love to see her go to jail for everything she had done. So incensed was he at his own treatment, that for a while he carried out demonstrations right outside the House of Prayer gates, handing out leaflets claiming that Gallagher was a phoney. He also covered his car in the cuttings from the *Sunday World* about the House of Prayer. He even wrote to *Ireland's Eye* magazine. The magazine carries a fawning two-page plug for the House of Prayer every month written by Fr McGinnity. Tierney's letter told the magazine that Gallagher was destroying people's faith and that what she was preaching went against the teachings of the Church. The magazine's owner, Dick Hogan, is one of Gallagher's biggest fans. He was a former director of the House of Prayer for a decade. Tierney was subsequently hit with a legal letter threatening a libel suit if he did not stop his antics.

'But their threat is all bluff. They are always threatening to sue people,' said Tierney when he spoke to me. 'She fears you more than anything else. She talks about you all the time, and what she is going to do to you, how she is going to sue you. But everyone knows they are a couple of chancers, her and Fr McGinnity.'

Tierney said that he had been in the House of Prayer for four months before the accident happened, but he quickly realised it was not a happy place. From the very beginning, he said he was disturbed at some of the behaviour he saw. There was so much secrecy, and they would haul people over the coals for little things. Starting at the top, he said Christina Gallagher ruled the place like a queen in her palace giving all the orders. Everyone was frightened of her and the whole movement had gone completely away from being anything religious. It had nothing to do with the Catholic Church, but was like one of those sects you read about in America, he said. 'She is completely in control of everything but people do not see what goes on there from the outside. You have to be on the inside to see what is really happening.'

Tierney said he had handed over thousands of sterling pounds to the House of Prayer, since he first began attending in 1994 while still living in England. The pensioner said he first heard about Christina Gallagher in 1992, after someone gave him a book, called *Please Come Back to Me and My Son*. Tierney said he was interested at the time in all types of visionaries. He had read a lot about Fatima, Medjugorje and Lourdes. He confessed that he was fascinated in apocalyptic messages, and was 'a bit prone to this type of stuff. And her books are full of it.'

Tierney said he first visited another sect called The Two Patricks, based in Cookstown, Northern Ireland, but had not been impressed. 'I actually brought my wife and youngest daughter, who was eleven at the time, to that one but I did not feel any spirituality. I came to the conclusion they were false prophets, and I left after three days.'

Then in 1994 he decided to visit the House of Prayer, and was impressed with Fr McGinnity. He said that in those days everything was much more relaxed. You could take pictures, and Gallagher and McGinnity would come out into the car park to meet the people who turned up. That had all changed now, he said.

'I have to say this, if McGinnity had not been involved, I would never ever have carried on all the years I did. It was McGinnity, the holy Catholic priest, who kept me going, not Christina Gallagher. He is the one behind all the books and leaflets. She is supposed to be this prophet who takes note of the visions and he interprets them. It was him who kept me going there and he was regarded as a holy man. He has a lot to answer for! Without him Christina Gallagher would not have lasted two years.'

Tierney said he used to come every year from his home in East Anglia in England. He would usually go in July during the time of the House's anniversary. He and his wife would rent a holiday cottage in Keele. Then things began to go wrong in his life. He had open-heart surgery in 2000, following a heart attack. He had to retire from the building business, and then he and his wife split up in 2002. 'I was desperately lonely. My family was all grown up and had their own lives, and I didn't see them that much. I felt neglected and, more and more, I got this desire to live in Ireland, which I loved from all my visits.'

Tierney subscribed to a House of Prayer magazine, and the first one he received had an advert to join the 'Third Order of Our Lady's Immaculate Heart.' He rang the number and was put in touch with the House of Prayer manager Noel Guinan. He was asked to send a CV of his life and reveal everything that had happened to him, which he did. Next thing they had invited him over with the offer of a job. Today, he says the House of Prayer knew exactly what it was doing. It was pulling in another disciple, when he was at his most vulnerable, someone who could be used and manipulated. Anthony Tierney had just walked willingly into the lion's den.

In August 2009 Tierney's story took a dramatic turn when he filed a lawsuit against the House of Prayer – claiming he had been denied medical care following his accident.

Tierney, who had moved back to Peterborough, England, said he was refused access to a doctor despite his pain. His solicitors lodged a personal injuries claim in the High Court on 19 August, and started the process of serving papers on the House of Prayer.

Hardly surprisingly, the House of Prayer, yet again, refused to comment when contacted by the *Sunday Times*, who broke the story on 23 August.

CHAPTER TEN

The Plot Thickens

'It's incredible that people are still supporting her. It is so annoying, seeing such a fraudster being allowed to keep going.'

There was no doubt that that the House of Prayer was beginning to feel the heat from all the bad publicity in the press. In April 2008, the son and daughter-in-law of one of Gallagher's biggest supporters decided to turn up the temperature, by visiting the Achill centre themselves, after spending more than ten years trying to get the man's father away from what they could see clearly was a cult.

Neil and his wife's visit caused pandemonium in the centre – because they were armed with a tape recorder. They were immediately surrounded by security guards. It was Saturday, 26 April, which had been hyped as a very important day, because it was the end of a long novena stretching back to the previous year. The novena was launched to ward off 'the greatest attack ever against Christina Gallagher'. Supporters had been promised that there would be a message from Our Lady, because it was such a momentous occasion, but Our Lady didn't show. 'The first thing McGinnity announced was that the miracle that was due to happen was a media lie, an invention, that there was not going to be any miracle,' said Neil. 'He was speaking rubbish, as it was they who said there would be one in the first place. He had to say something as people were expecting a sign.'

The reason there was no message was, presumably, because Gallagher did not appear that afternoon.

Gallagher was possibly scared off by the presence of Neil and his wife, who security guards thought might be from the press. Initially, the couple thought they might not even get into the House of Prayer, as the staff seemed very wary of anyone who was not a regular. Stewards were checking cars, and one woman was noting licence plates and taking photos.

But they were not stopped. Once inside they headed for the balcony in the chapel, where they would get a good view of the expected performance by Christina Gallagher. When security men saw his wife's tape recorder, they surrounded the couple. Tony Fitzpatrick, Gallagher's bodyguard, ordered them to switch it off, as it was not allowed.

'He then went downstairs to McGinnity, who was standing at the microphone and whispered in his ear. McGinnity looked up and completely toned down his sermon. He did the very basics, but he was nervous and had to sit down for the first time. It really rattled him, as he thought the press were there. They were very worried, and he was being very cautious.'

Neil had heard that the previous Sunday the priest had told the congregation in his own parish that the allegations against him were lies, and that the cheques he had allegedly received were forgeries. 'But this day he said, "I might have received one or two cheques, but they were always lodged in the correct accounts." He was covering himself. The previous Sunday he had said he did not receive any, so that was a lie.'

The couple were certain Gallagher was at the House of Prayer that day, because of the presence of Tony Fitzpatrick, who usually travels with her. But Fr McGinnity announced she would not be appearing as 'Christina is so, so sick today.'

Neil said: 'This was supposed to be their big day, the

end of a long novena, and yet she couldn't be bothered to come out. He was covering for her. They were very rattled.' He said one security man stood next to his wife the whole time they were there, watching her. 'There were seven or eight stewards, all walking around with walkie-talkies.'

One steward asked them: 'Are you part of Mike Garde's crowd?' The steward was referring to a cult expert from Dublin, who has been campaigning against the House of Prayer for years. 'We said, "We might be – there are people everywhere in this audience." The steward said nothing. But McGinnity was shaking and had to sit down. He normally does a lot of talking about Christina, but this time he said nothing.'

Fitzpatrick asked Neil's wife, 'Have you got that attached to a listening device?' She said, 'Yes, you better be careful what you say.' He walked away immediately. 'One person and the whole place was rattled. They are a bunch of paranoid lunatics.' Neil said there were only 200 people there for this big day, when there would have been a couple of thousand a few months previously. 'The numbers have definitely gone down, and there was complete paranoia.'

Neil said the novena ended up being extended, yet again, although no end date was given. One regular, a member of the choir, later apologised to Neil's wife saying, 'I am really sorry for the hassle you got. That was ridiculous. I am really sorry.'

Neil said that Gallagher had only recently announced that her persecution by the press was over, that Our Lady had told her so. 'That was a couple of weeks before. Yet she did not have the guts to turn up. If Our Lady told her the persecution was over, why is she worried?'

Earlier that month Gallagher had also turned up at the House of Prayer with her estranged husband in tow. She called him to the front of the crowd and announced: 'He is the only man for me.' She then gave him a big hug. This was one more desperate, cynical effort to keep the myth of her happy marriage alive. Many of her supporters continued to believe that she was the perfect housewife she pretended to be.

Meanwhile, the House of Prayer drama rolled on and on. After the shocking story of how the Morrisseys were coerced into giving nearly €150,000 to Christina Gallagher appeared in the *Sunday World* on 4 May 2008, it was decided that another attempt would be made to get Fr McGinnity to talk. So far, the under-pressure cleric had said absolutely nothing, refusing to answer or return any phone calls made to his parish house. It was not just the *Sunday World* that he was ignoring but also the *Sunday Times*, the *Sunday Tribune*, the *Irish Independent* and the *Irish Mail on Sunday*, who all claimed he had failed to respond to their queries, just as Christina Gallagher and John Rooney had.

Fr McGinnity had gone on RTÉ's *Liveline* programme after the scandal of Christina Gallagher's wealth first broke. Since then, he had kept a steely silence. The crew of RTÉ's *Prime Time* programme managed to get him to answer the front door of his house. Then he dashed back inside, claiming he was on the phone, but never reappeared to answer their questions. But surely now he had to come clean and explain why he had collected so much money from two pensioners, the Morrisseys. And why had he got them to sign two of the cheques to his own name, one of them for an astonishing €40,000?

On the morning of Friday 9 May 2008 I drove from Dublin to Knockbridge with photographer Liam O'Connor. We were hoping to talk to Fr McGinnity after he said Mass in his local church. We parked behind

St Mary's Church next to a 07-registered Toyota Corolla guessing, correctly as it turned out, that it might be his.

A few minutes later, at the end of Mass, Fr McGinnity came out of the church and headed for his car. I jumped out of our vehicle, identified myself and said I wanted to talk to him about the Morrisseys and the large amounts of money he had been collecting. The priest did not speak at all. Carrying an umbrella and some papers in one hand and his car keys in the other, he looked grim-faced. He headed straight for his car and got inside, as I fired off a volley of questions. Without once opening his mouth, he switched on the engine and drove off in a hurry. He had clearly spotted the photographer taking his picture, but did not speak.

The story appeared in the *Sunday World* two days later, 11 May, under the heading 'Vow of Silence'. It told how 'the controversial priest who has raised millions of euro for fake visionary Christina Gallagher' refused to reveal where all the money had gone.

This was the same month, May 2008, that the group of eight concerned Catholics met Cardinal Seán Brady. Six of them, including Betty Morrissey, were former supporters of the House of Prayer, who had pulled away after realising it was a fraud. The other two were Neil and his wife. The group hoped to put pressure on the Cardinal to come out strongly against the House of Prayer, or at least to crack down on his priest, Fr McGinnity, and stop him travelling to Achill most Saturdays. The group was convinced that the House of Prayer would not survive without its spiritual director, as his presence drew in the crowds.

The group told the Cardinal of their common experiences at the House of Prayer, and how they thought Fr McGinnity had been led astray. Betty Morrissey showed copies of the cheques she had been asked to sign in the priest's name. While Paddy Woods, who had donated €100,000 to the House of Prayer, had a copy of a letter he had sent to Fr McGinnity. He had sent the letter two weeks previously, explaining how unhappy he was, but he had received no reply. The Cardinal was also given a copy of the explosive letter written by the former follower, solicitor John Beighton, to Gallagher and Fr McGinnity. This was the letter written in 1998 in which he expressed his concerns over the visionary's wealth and lifestyle, and over the way the House of Prayer was run with its secret cameras and its complete lack of accountability.

The Cardinal also agreed to see some of the eight individually, because they had private concerns they wanted to express to him. Cardinal Brady told one woman, Margaret, to go immediately to the Archbishop of Tuam, whose archdiocese the House of Prayer is in, after she furnished him with information about a homosexual relationship going on in the House of Prayer. This involved the same man reported by Mike McCrory to Gallagher and Fr McGinnity the previous year. It is also understood that Margaret informed the Cardinal about Gallagher's 'stigmata', and what might have caused it.

As it turned out, Cardinal Brady did little about the complaints he heard that day. He did call in Fr McGinnity for talks but, he appeared to believe everything the priest told him. Cardinal Brady accepted Fr McGinnity's claims that he was not involved in fundraising. The priest told the Cardinal that if anyone had a problem with members of their family giving money, the House of Prayer would give it back. It was neither the response nor the result the eight concerned Catholics had hoped for when they met Cardinal Brady.

Another man who supported the eight, and who helped to set up the meeting with the Cardinal, but who was not present that day, was Dr Michael Anketell. Dr Anketell was a key figure in the House of Prayer story. He was equally frustrated that the head of the Catholic Church in Ireland was not taking more drastic action. Dr Anketell had initially been a big supporter of Christina Gallagher. It was his testimony over certain 'miracles' that had given the House of Prayer a degree of credence. But like the others, he had eventually realised that he had been cynically used by Gallagher, and he became one of her biggest opponents.

When Dr Anketell first got involved, he was a huge boost to the House of Prayer. Some former members claim Christina Gallagher was at rock bottom until Dr Anketell came along. The House of Prayer had been closed for months, and people were heading to Medjugorje rather than Achill Island. Even when it did re-open, the large numbers were not turning up. As one supporter said, Gallagher was not getting the type of messages that would draw people in. But the good doctor would change all that.

Dr Anketell used to take his mother to the House of Prayer, as she was a believer at the start. Then on the big anniversary celebration of 16 July 1999 Gallagher went into one of her most dramatic trances ever, bending over backwards at a curious angle, while a film camera was recording the event. At one point she opened her mouth and there on her tongue was what looked like a communion host, which to Christians represents the body of Christ. Gallagher later claimed that the Archangel Michael gave her the Holy Communion in the middle of her ecstasy, and that it was a 'miraculous host'. The crowd, who could see this, were riveted. Even Dr Anketell, a devout Catholic who, until this point, was not convinced by the House of Prayer, was amazed by what he was looking at. Like others around him, he thought the backwards position she held was unnatural and impossible. He got to his feet and was looking to see if she was really in a trance. It was this few minutes of drama that convinced him that what he had witnessed was indeed supernatural.

I tried for many months to get an interview with Dr Anketell, but he declined. But he wrote a report about that day in 1999, which the House of Prayer used in a 16-page booklet to promote itself around the world. I picked up a copy, in one of the American Houses of Prayer, in July 2008. Even though by that stage Dr Anketell had turned against Christina Gallagher, his testimony was still being used to boost her profile and raise money for the organisation.

In the booklet, called *Four Testimonies*, Dr Anketell also gave medical evidence about four healings at the House of Prayer that defied all 'natural, medical, scientific and psychological' explanation. Christina Gallagher and Fr McGinnity claim there have been 'thousands' of such healings, but Dr Anketell found evidence for just four. In effectively authenticating these 'miracles', he became one of the most important figures in the history of the House of Prayer because he gave the place a new lease of life. His testimony was broadcast across the national media, attracting a new wave of pilgrims to Achill.

One of the miracles involved a woman called Kathleen O'Sullivan, from Co. Kerry. She claimed she was cured of inoperable pancreatic cancer after visiting the House of Prayer. She was diagnosed with the disease on St Patrick's Day in 1997. Her condition deteriorated rapidly over three months – to the point that she weighed just five stone. She was not given long to live, and when her husband heard about the House of Prayer, he drove her there on 27 June. The couple prayed and attended Mass, which was still being said at that time. Christina

Gallagher and Fr McGinnity prayed with her. On the way home the woman said she suddenly felt hungry, so they stopped in Galway. She had her first proper meal in two months. Her jaundice disappeared, and in a few days she had made a complete recovery.

Christina Gallagher uses this story on her website and in House of Prayer literature to prove that she is a genuine visionary, and that miracles take place at the House of Prayer. The O'Sullivans were in the crowd on that day in 1999 and Dr Anketell met them. He agreed to look into their story and was given permission to contact their consultants. As he reveals in the booklet, *Four Testimonies*, he also organised a private CAT scan of Mrs O'Sullivan's pancreas, which was carried out 11 days later on 27 July. The scan found no trace of a tumour. The following year, Dr Anketell's report was given to the Church authorities to make a ruling on whether it was a miracle or not. But the Church has never confirmed it, nor any other alleged miracles at the Achill centre. Last year the Archbishop of Tuam, Dr Michael Neary, was still declaring that there was no evidence of supernatural powers of any kind at the House of Prayer. How could the woman be cured? The couple themselves now credit Mrs O'Sullivan's recovery to her own strong faith and to God rather than anything Christina Gallagher did.

Even back in 1998 when she was interviewed by the *Would You Believe* programme, which was making a documentary about Christina Gallagher, Mrs O'Sullivan credited a higher authority than the visionary for her cure. Kathleen said: 'I attribute it to a miracle from the Lord above, that I got cured of my cancer. My faith comes from God. I got inner strength when I was sick. There is something out there. It came from the Lord, this inner strength. I would not let go.'

Friends claim the O'Sullivans were devastated by the revelations about Christina Gallagher over the last two years. But they had already begun to distance themselves from her before that. Mr O'Sullivan had been among those shocked by the luxurious new extension, when it went up. The couple have now cut themselves off from the House of Prayer. They have not spoken out publicly nor given their reasons. But they still firmly believe that a miracle took place on that fateful day in 1997.

The other three 'miracles' in the *Four Testimonies* booklet involved an Englishman and two American men. Englishman, John Garbutt, claimed he was cured during a Mass in the House of Prayer in 1997, of severe back and neck injuries, following a freak horse-riding accident. A 21-year-old American, Jed Michael, claimed Gallagher cured him of a rare blood-clotting disorder and speech impediment. Another American, James Hogan, said his blocked arteries were cured by the Matrix medal in 1999.

As for Dr Anketell, despite 'authenticating' all four of the 'miracle' cases, he has turned completely against the House of Prayer, and now believes Gallagher is a fraud. Fellow former supporters claim the doctor is reluctant to speak out. But he told Mike McCrory that he resented a request by Fr McGinnity to 'play up' the miracles when they were presenting their case to the Church authorities. He also kept in close contact with other former disillusioned members and encouraged them to keep up their battle to get the Church to ban Fr McGinnity from attending the Achill Island centre.

Friends said the turning point for him came one day when he heard one of Gallagher's violent messages and realised it was absurd. He could not believe it came from the mother of Christ.

By coincidence, Betty and Michael Morrissey were also in the audience that day and were coming to the same conclusion themselves. At that point they had never met the doctor and did not know anything about him. But this, too, was the day they decided enough was enough, and they walked away.

Today, according to friends, Dr Anketell believes that the day of the so-called ecstasy, which first made him believe Gallagher was genuine, was a complete set-up. So too do the Morrisseys and others. Many people had been specially invited to this meeting and there were seats reserved for them. They are convinced that Gallagher wanted to make sure all the people who mattered did not miss her performance of a lifetime. Very few of her Saturday afternoon appearances are filmed or photographed. In fact it is quite the opposite, with signs everywhere saying: 'No photos, no video, no audio'. But this day the cameras were there to capture the moment. Former followers believe that Gallagher must have been practising for months to get in the backward position she achieved. A video from that afternoon seems to show a part of the 'Communion Host' missing. Followers suspect that whatever it was, was stuck to the roof of Gallagher's mouth and then pulled down with her tongue at the appropriate moment. However, a little bit of it must have stuck to her palette.

Friends of Dr Anketell said that although he walked away from the House of Prayer in July 2006, it was not the last time he heard from Christina Gallagher. One day while he was working in his clinic in 2008, the 'holy' woman rang him and tore into him with a stream of expletives. She told him he was going to be damned to hell for all eternity for turning his back on her. This was more confirmation, if it was ever needed, that

Gallagher was not the spiritual saviour she claimed to be. Dr Anketell was so shocked and distressed by the verbal attack that he rang other opponents of the House of Prayer to tell them what the woman, who they had all once followed, had said.

As the months rolled on, other stories continued to develop. In June 2008, photographer Liam O'Connor was driving through Malahide, and decided to check if anything was going on at Christina Gallagher's luxury mansion. He was surprised to discover that the ornate electronic gates had been covered up with large black boards, so the inquisitive public could no longer stand and admire the magnificent house or its driveway and gardens. It appeared that the secretive leader of the House of Prayer had become even more paranoid and protective of her privacy.

Locals, as well as journalists and photographers from other newspapers, had been driving into the luxury Abington development to see for themselves the astonishing house that dwarfed most of those around it. It had become something of a Sunday afternoon ritual for families to check out the house where Christina Gallagher lived. People were getting out of their cars to stare and take photographs of the impressive house. Gallagher was obviously not amused.

In the same month the *Irish Mail on Sunday* revealed in a front-page story that the Irish tourist board, Fáilte Ireland, had a link to the House of Prayer on its website. The national body was effectively helping to promote the controversial centre, at the same time as it was being investigated by the Gardaí and the Revenue Commissioners. The newspaper said Christina Gallagher's centre had lost its charitable status in 2006, when the company running it posted profits of nearly €4 million. Visitors to Ireland seeking pilgrimage sites, who turned to Fáilte Ireland's website, were given details about the House of Prayer, along with established places of prayer, like Knock. Despite complaints, the tourist board said it would not be removing the link. A Fáilte Ireland spokeswoman said: 'Unless there are any criminal charges brought, we will not be removing the link from the website. It's a case of innocent until proven guilty.' The Irish tourist board later changed its mind and did remove the link.

Later that month, June 2008, I revealed how some of the four directors of the House of Prayer had quit. I had obtained a copy of a letter that director Donal Corrigan, who was also the House of Prayer solicitor, had written to the Law Society claiming he had resigned from the board, and no longer represented the organisation. Someone had complained to the Law Society about their treatment at the hands of the House of Prayer and its solicitor. Donal Corrigan was responding to that complaint.

Written on 16 June 2008, Corrigan said in the letter: 'I am not and have not been the Solicitor acting for the House of Prayer for a considerable period of time.' He then added: 'I resigned as a Director of the House of Prayer, and I understand that new Directors have been appointed.'

This seemed a sound basis for a story, as it came from the horse's mouth, as it were. There were also reports circulating that another director, retired teacher Louise Cleary, had also given up her directorship on the advice of her lawyer. Corrigan's letter had said new directors, plural, had been appointed. Calls were made to another director, Dick Hogan, to see if he too had quit. Hogan is the publishing millionaire behind the Topic group of newspapers in Co. Westmeath, including *Ireland's Eye* magazine. But he did not come to the phone and did not ring back. Likewise, Corrigan did not reply to calls made to his office.

A story appeared in the *Sunday World* on 29 June 2008 under the heading 'Crumbling House,' claiming that 'at least half the directors of the controversial House of Prayer' had resigned. It said the resignation of lawyer Donal J. Corrigan was perhaps the most surprising, as he had been Gallagher's legal enforcer for more than ten years, threatening anyone who spoke out against Gallagher with legal action. The *Sunday World*, Mike McCrory and I were among those who had received threats of lawsuits from the pugnacious lawyer.

But, as it turned out, if Corrigan had resigned as a director, as he told the Law Society, he had failed to inform the Companies Registration Office (CRO). It was several more months before that statutory body listed any official changes with the House of Payer board. That only came in December 2008, when the CRO recorded a complete change of the board at the House of Prayer. The board changes were officially logged with the CRO that month, but the resignations were made in November, according to CRO records.

The record showed that publisher Dick Hogan; Dublin lawyer Donal Corrigan; Louise Cleary, from Newbridge, Co. Kildare, and Josephine Flanagan, from Cushinstown, Co. Meath, had all resigned as directors. The record also showed that former Dublin taxi driver Noel Guinan had quit as secretary. Dick Hogan, who was 69 at the time, had served as a director for over a decade. He was appointed in October 1998, and was recognised as one of Christina Gallagher's most loyal supporters. Again he did not return calls asking about his resignation.

Donal Corrigan, who was then 60, had been the House of Prayer's lawyer and a director for well over a decade. Louise Cleary, a 77 year-old retired teacher, had also been appointed in October 1998. Fr McGinnity's 56-year-old sister, Josephine Flanagan, was the last director. She had been on the board for seven years.

The outgoing board was replaced by a panel of three little-known Gallagher supporters: Annette Casey, a 63-year-old school principal, from St Patrick's Academy, Islandeady, Castlebar, Co. Mayo; Eithne Lavery a 67-year-old retired optician from Stepaside, Dublin, and housewife Bridie Conneally, from Hazelbrook, Co. Roscommon. Casey also became company secretary. Calls were made to Casey and Lavery, and messages left on their answerphones, but the calls were never returned. It seemed like it was something of a custom by this stage.

Because nobody from the House of Prayer was willing to speak, it was not clear what lay behind the resignation of one board and the appointment of another – perhaps it was that Christina Gallagher just thought it was time for a change. Certainly, Mike McCrory could not guess. He said he was surprised by the move.

'Christina is so deceptive you wouldn't know what it is about. It can't be what it looks like, because if all these people have left the House of Prayer it would be the end of her,' he said. He guessed at the time that perhaps the outgoing directors believed she was considering leaving the country, and decided to get out first. Previously, she had told her supporters that she was going to be assumed into heaven – a statement that caused McCrory and many other former followers to believe that she was planning a getaway. McCrory said that it was possible that perhaps those who had resigned did not want to be left carrying the can. But this explanation does not really ring true, particularly as Dick Hogan, at least, continued to be as big a supporter of Gallagher as he ever was. There had been changes to the board in the past, and perhaps the latest move was just a way of bringing in new blood. Previous directors of the House of Prayer had included Gallagher herself, her devoted sidekick 73-year-old Teresa Doyle, and 69-year-old Martin Scally, of Boyle, Co. Roscommon.

In July came the front page story and pictures of Christina Gallagher and Fr McGinnity being served with writs inside the House of Prayer. *Sunday World* reporter Cathal O'Shea had gone undercover with photographers Padraig O'Reilly and Liam O'Connor to catch the historic moment. The same day as the newspaper published that report, the *Irish Mail on Sunday* carried a two-page article about life inside the House of Prayer. They had sent their own undercover reporter to a series of the Saturday prayer sessions – and he was not impressed.

He spoke of bouncers yelling into their walkie-talkies, security guards mounting road blocks and of functionaries demanding that there be 'absolutely no recordings or photographs taken'. He watched as a guard backstage punched the security code into a keypad and an electronic door swung open for 'Ireland's most controversial double act', who made their entrance on stage, all smiles and nods to their fans.

It sounded more like a pop concert in Dublin's O$_2$ but this was Achill Island on a Saturday afternoon. 'This is no Westlife concert. This is the disturbing world of Christina Gallagher and her spiritual advisor, Fr Gerard McGinnity,' wrote the undercover reporter, Warren Swords. 'For the past fifteen years, the duo have been wowing their loyal fans and bringing in millions of euro.' The journalist revealed that he had been attending meetings for two months, and heard Christina Gallagher issue ever more threatening messages of doom, allegedly direct from the mouth of the Virgin Mary. The dire warnings involved evil insects, Ireland's youth being seduced into suicide by the Devil and threats that Ireland was going to be destroyed, unless people gave more money.

An 'increasingly embittered and venomous' Christina Gallagher had lashed out at non-believers, the media and even her congregation, he said. 'She warns that the Virgin Mary will kill all who deny her, especially those who were lucky enough to have been cured of cancer', and who had since deserted the House of Prayer.

Swords watched pilgrims, mostly women in their sixties or older, stuffing €20 euro notes into the large collection boxes dotted around the House. He estimated that there were about three to four hundred people there every week, and that if they all gave €20 that would be €6,000-€8,000 every Saturday. But he saw several people donate at least €50, which would bring the tally far higher. In the shop he also saw a queue of elderly women lining up to make donations of at least €35, and their names were then recorded in a book. One former devotee told Swords that those people in the book would then be rung whenever extra cash was needed, as their generosity to the House of Prayer had now been recorded. With ten coachloads coming every week, it's a nice little earner,' noted the undercover reporter.

In the chapel, Fr McGinnity, with his 'badly dyed hair' and 'the most monotonous drone in Ireland,' tried to fire up the congregation, some of whom had fallen asleep, with warnings about this being the time of the Antichrist. The Devil was seducing more souls now than in all eternity, he said, and talked of Gallagher and her miraculous powers. When it was time for Gallagher to speak, she focused on her own troubles, telling how she was persecuted and how she had to bear the pain of her 'gift'. She spoke of lies and deceptions in the media and said: 'Every single thing and every word that

was in the paper were lies. Every single word was lies.'
She then claimed she had been warned of the media
attack by the Virgin Mary, and that when it came 'the
hand of God will be close upon the earth'. She said she
was not scare-mongering but 'you'll witness it in a very
short time'.

When she finished, she walked among her excited
fans, who reached out, desperate to touch her. One
woman asked how she was, and the visionary suddenly
grimaced and said: 'I'm struggling, I'm struggling.'
The queen of self-pity was milking the moment for all
it was worth.

The writer found that some of the staff and
volunteers at the House of Prayer were friendly and
helpful, and that the pilgrims were generally a lovely
bunch of people. He suspected that some of them did
not believe 'the hateful bile' spewed out by Gallagher
and Fr McGinnity. On the House of Prayer's fifteenth
anniversary, in July 2008, there were about 600 people in
attendance. This was double that of a normal Saturday,
but well down on the thousands who used to turn up
on this special day for the centre. Gallagher tore into
her 'persecutors' from the start, saying: 'They have
tried to destroy the house in Ohio, they've arrived in
Minnesota, and now they have arrived in Kansas.'

This was a reference to me, as I had travelled to the
US to try to talk to Gallagher's American fundraiser
John Rooney. Rather than trying 'to destroy' the house,
I simply wanted an interview with the man who had
raised a fortune for Christina Gallagher, and who
officially owned the fabulous mansion in which she
lived in Malahide. I also visited the four other sister
houses in Minnesota, Kansas, Texas and Florida to
establish that they actually existed, as so much money
had been raised in Ireland to build them.

But here was Gallagher, berating her persecutors, claiming: 'Our enemy is going from town to town. They've no problem with money, no problem with getting people to tell lies, no problem destroying people's character. I also know they got a helping hand from those you would least suspect,' she said, casting a suspicious eye over the crowd, some of whom had kept me informed of what went on there most Saturdays. Her claim that people were queuing up to 'tell lies' was comical, considering that the American houses were, in fact, so empty that there was almost nobody to talk to.

But Gallagher was in full flight, warning that the hand of God was close by, and that a vengeful Virgin Mary was angry with the people of Ireland for not doing enough for her. Fr McGinnity then stood up and announced that Our Blessed Mother had spoken to Christina, just four days previously, on Saturday 12 July, and told her: 'This is my request. Every one of you can see around you the disintegration of faith in God, and the decline of the world. I desire that you study my messages in which I foretold what will now come upon you. I desire my children to read those messages in which I tried to protect you from the dangers that now surround you. There is nothing more to be said.'

This indeed was a stark message, suggesting that Christ's mother was essentially abandoning them, that the world was about to end and that they had already been given all the warnings they needed about what they had to do to be saved. This basically meant visiting the House of Prayer, giving it lots of money and wearing one of her Matrix medals, which were on sale in the shop at €2 a pop.

Just to make sure they got the point, Fr McGinnity read out previous messages allegedly from 'Our Lady

Queen of Peace' and Christ himself. One said: 'The
justice of God is close at hand. God desires his children
to go to the House of Prayer.' Another said it would be
disastrous for the world if Christina Gallagher walked
away from the House of Prayer. 'The day is coming
faster than light when my mighty hand will crush
the world.' Another said: 'Those who desire to live
their lives primarily in sin, God will annihilate them.'
McGinnity spoke of 'evil insects' poisoning people's
bodies, and of giant birds eating dead corpses.

These apocalyptic warnings were met with unease
and silence by the crowd. But once the Gallagher and
McGinnity double act disappeared, the people's mood
picked up and good humour returned, said the reporter
Warren Swords. 'These are normal, life-loving people yet
they choose to spend their Saturdays listening to bile.'

The undercover reporter finished off by saying he had
developed a deep dislike of the 'cold and calculating'
Christina Gallagher and Fr McGinnity, who didn't mix
or chat with the pilgrims. The pair were only seen at the
House of Prayer when they were on the pulpit being
threatening and demanding. 'They have twisted an idea
as pure and holy as the Virgin Mary into a vengeful,
wrathful deity who is only too happy to destroy the
earth if the people don't cough up the cash.'

The House of Prayer saga then took a dramatic twist
in November, when a team of gardaí raided the premises.
They separated the staff and took individual statements
from all of them. The officers were investigating Anthony
Tierney's claims that he had been left in a room for three
days, with no medical help, after falling off a ladder
and shattering his leg. The 62-year-old Englishman had
made a formal complaint to the police earlier in the year,
claiming he had been treated 'like a dog'. One garda
source said that staff were taken to different rooms,

and all gave identical versions of what happened after Tierney fell off the ladder. 'They all said Tierney was offered medical help, but refused it, saying he wanted to offer up his suffering to Jesus.'

Tierney laughed at these claims when I told him what was being said. 'They are talking absolute rubbish. They have had months to get their story straight and it's all lies. I was begging them to get my doctor, who is just across the road, but they wouldn't. But it does not surprise me. They would say anything. They all went to the garda station together with their statements months ago, but were told it does not work like that. They went in bold as brass, with their stories written down.'

Meanwhile, relations between Neil and his father, who he was trying to get out of the House of Prayer, had deteriorated even more, as 2008 drew to an end. In November he told me: 'I have not spoken to my mother since May, which is ridiculous, and it's all over this rubbish. They just can't see through Christina Gallagher, and still believe in her. But the more crap she comes out with the more people will go.'

Gallagher had announced to her followers in November that she would soon be 'assumed' into heaven, because her suffering had been so great, no human being could withstand it. Fr McGinnity had been telling supporters the same thing for some time: that the visionary was not long for this world and would soon be brought home by Our Lady. Her loyal ex-nun Sister Treasa had burst into tears one day, after bumping into Betty Morrissey. The former nun said Gallagher's suffering was so great that Our Lady was going to take her out of this world, crying: 'How are we going to live without Christina?'

The *Sunday World* reported these claims on 23 November, along with the latest financial figures from the House of Prayer that showed it had received €339,283 in donations, so far that year. It also made a profit of €400,000 on religious items in the previous two years, with a mark-up of 130 per cent.

When Neil was told that Gallagher was apparently heading for heaven, he said he was not surprised by her latest claims, as she would say anything to keep the people rolling in. 'Right down through the years she has come up with some spectacular claims. She keeps making these off-the-wall outlandish statements to keep people hooked. A lot of people must be touched to continue following her. It is so unbelievable. People should be copping on. If there are 15 buses outside that place – it is 15 buses too many.'

Neil said his own father was a clever man, but his loyalty to Gallagher must come down to pride. How could he accept that he had been wrong for so long? How could he follow someone for 20 years and be wrong? He had to believe he was right. Neil, like many others, said that Fr McGinnity was the real problem, because without him Gallagher would not have the same following.

Neil and his wife had collected a huge amount of information on the House of Prayer, over the previous 15 years. They also knew past and present members. He said that Gallagher had toured the US with John Rooney on a fundraising campaign, at the end of the summer, and that they had collected a lot of money. She had told her American congregations that Our Lady was very angry with the Irish people, because they had turned their back on her. In March 2009, he confirmed that fundraising meetings were going ahead in Ireland again, including one in Multyfarnham, where supporters had pledged €1.8 million in 2005.

'One man walked out of the meeting when he heard it was about fundraising again. He said it was scandalous,' said Neil. 'The meeting was reported to have made €150,000, while another in Cashel made €100,000. They took place in the last two weeks. It's incredible that people are still supporting her. It is so annoying seeing such a fraudster being allowed to keep going.'

CHAPTER ELEVEN

The Land of Opportunity

'We don't know what they need all this property for if they are just a prayer group. But they seem to have money to burn.'

Businessman John Rooney was Christina Gallagher's right hand man in America. But just who was he, and what was his role in the organisation? And why was his name on the deeds to Gallagher's magnificent mansion in Malahide? Nobody seemed to know anything about this 64-year-old mystery man, besides the fact that he is from America's West Coast, but now lives in Steubenville, Ohio. Some people had met him briefly on his trips back to the 'old country', but nobody knew anything about his background. And the biggest question of all was crying out to be answered: was he part of the whole Christina Gallagher con-trick, or was he a naïve believer in the supposed visionary and her mission to save souls?

Phoning him got you nowhere. Calls to his home number were greeted by the answering machine. But the friendly message that greeted my first telephone call soon changed. At the beginning, a chirpy voice said it was the Rooney family home and to leave a message. Several messages were left but none were ever returned. And once the *Sunday World* story broke about Gallagher's Malahide mansion and the fact that his name was on the Land Registry records, as the owner, he was presumably inundated with calls. The perky message was replaced by an abrupt one, ordering the caller to simply leave his name and number.

One Irish journalist, who did manage to get through, got a furious Rooney shouting at him: 'How dare you ring my home.' There was no real option but to confront Rooney face to face, which entailed a trip to the US. This would also provide an opportunity to visit all five Houses of Prayer, scattered across the vast country. No journalist had ever visited these supposed places of worship, and little was known about them.

I flew out to America in July 2008. My first port of call was Ohio, the state which was home to the Rooney family, and the largest of the Houses of Prayer in America. There was a fear that if Rooney discovered that a journalist was on their way, he might go to ground, so the trip was kept secret. The nearest large airport to Steubenville is Pittsburgh, which is in the neighbouring state of Pennsylvania. To get to the Ohio town you have to drive through parts of Pennsylvania and West Virginia, before crossing the Ohio border.

The first stop was the House of Prayer itself, to see what it was like. It turned out to be a big surprise. It was not located in Steubenville itself, but was situated on the edge of a tiny town called Smithfield, which is just over 19 kilometres to the south, deep in farm country. The official address is 197 State Highway 151. The prayer centre sits on a road to the north of Smithfield, just before you enter the town. It can only be described as enormous.

A gleaming white building, brand new and shining in the hot American sun, the sheer size of the place would astound many visitors. It is the biggest building for many kilometres around, and yet it is in the middle of nowhere. Passers-by might wonder who it was supposed to cater for, because it is in such a remote location. The gates were locked and there was no sign of life. I decided to go into Smithfield to see what the locals thought of this new, giant, prayer centre on the edge of their town. Smithfield itself was little more than a one street town, and it had certainly seen better days. Every other building on the main road through town seemed to be derelict or up for rent. Other businesses advertised the fact that they were only open two or three days a week. The absence of people on the one main street added to the air of desolation. The faded grandeur of the shopfronts, which hinted that it might have been a pretty town once upon a time, was in stark contrast to the brand new, freshly-painted House of Prayer. You could see that life for residents in this outback town was worlds away from that lived by Christina Gallagher in her luxury Malahide mansion.

Few people seemed to know what the House of Prayer even was. One man cutting people's lawns thought it was a home for the elderly, but showed little interest. In small-town America, where almost every street corner has a church, prayer house or religious meeting house, the opening of a new one is hardly a huge talking point.

One shopkeeper did know about the House, because she was a Catholic and in recent years had seen the closure of the local parish church, ironically also called Our Lady Queen of Peace. She and fellow members of the congregation had hoped the House of Prayer would buy their church and keep it open, rather than build their own outside the town. 'But the Rooneys said it was too small,' she said. This woman knew John Rooney's wife, Joanne. She explained that the couple first met Christina Gallagher on a trip back to Ireland to find their roots, several years before. Being staunchly Catholic, and on the evangelical right of the Church, the Rooneys would have been delighted to come into contact with any visionary in Ireland, and would have naturally gravitated towards her. It turned out that they lived in an area outside Steubenville, which was popular with charismatic movements in the Church. The couple were apparently bowled over by this Irish prophet, and the work she was doing on Achill Island. They told her that there were many Catholics in the Steubenville area, too, and that you would often see elderly men and women walking about the streets with rosary beads in their hands. This must have sounded like manna from heaven to Christina Gallagher who, soon after, claimed that she had had a vision from Our Lady telling her to open a House of Prayer in the area. The Rooneys were put in charge of this project, and they took to the task of finding a suitable property with zeal. And, of course, the fundraising began.

It took months for Mrs Rooney to find the house, and it was much smaller then. It was the former home of an elderly couple, who used to run homes for intellectually disabled people. The house had been empty for years. The Rooneys snapped it up in late 2005, seeing its potential, with plenty of car parking space. They then began the building project in April 2006, renovating part of the present building, while erecting a huge extension. The local Heritage Society forbade them from knocking down the front of the old building, and they were forced to incorporate it into the modern structure. A large chapel was built along with guest rooms, and the work was still ongoing in 2008.

When I returned to the centre later in the day, the chains were off the gate and a car sat in the car park. A woman opened the door, mop in hand, and immediately introduced herself as Joanne Rooney. She said she was busy cleaning the toilets. Asked whether the place was open, John Rooney's wife stated, almost like a mantra: 'Christina told us to keep the place open, even when the building work is going on, otherwise the Devil would get it. I open it every day from 12 noon to 3pm to stop the Devil getting in. There is always someone here.' She then rushed off to continue to clean the toilets.

It was quite an introduction. This very intense woman obviously took it for granted that I would know who 'Christina' was. It was also funny that she was opening the door to me, as I had already been labelled 'an agent of the Devil' by both Gallagher and McGinnity. And here was John Rooney's wife showing me inside. It was a comical moment.

Just one other person was present in the Ohio house that day, an elderly woman praying at the front of the chapel. The back of the church was filled with books, DVDs, beads and pictures for sale.

Gallagher and Fr McGinnity both flew to Steubenville for the dedication of the House of Prayer in December 2006, in front of 500 worshippers, many of whom had travelled from different states. During the service Gallagher went into 'ecstasy'. She claimed she had an apparition from both Christ and Our Lady that lasted nine minutes. Jesus and his mother were seated on thrones and were 'beautifully adorned'. Gallagher also claimed that the Ohio House's patron saint, St Bernadette, also appeared. Gallagher said she was told that, 'Through this house many, many, many souls will be saved, and healings will occur at the appointed time.'

Gallagher and McGinnity were back in Ohio in June the following year, 2007, when the priest urged even greater sacrifices by people to get the House of Prayer finished. He informed those present that they had run out of time, and there would be no new Houses of Prayer, just the five already started in the US and one in Mexico. 'There is scarcely time to complete those already begun,' he told the congregation. 'Unless this is carried out quickly, their benefits will be lost.

When we think that we are half way – more than half way – through the year granted by God to bring about the completion, it is no wonder that Our Lady speaks about making haste and acting swiftly.'

Fr McGinnity said the effects would be drastic if Our Lady's special gift of protection for her children in soul and body were to be lost. 'So much hangs in the balance; the protection of millions in soul, the protection of innumerable people, even in body.' Fr McGinnity said it was impossible to understand the enormity of God's plan for the chain of houses. But those who 'sacrifice to fulfil the work' will benefit and have their lives enriched.

A pamphlet at the back of the chapel had this controversial message for worshippers: 'Christina has repeatedly confirmed that whoever donates to support the chain of Houses of Prayer will be protected in the coming times. Christina said that all those who donate, regardless of their physical location, will receive the exact same protection Our Lady has promised to give to those in or near a House of Prayer.'

It is this promise that has outraged many traditional Catholics, and forced some former devotees to leave the House of Prayer. To them, claims that people will be saved automatically on Judgement Day if they stump up cash now is absurd, not to mention heretical. It would effectively mean that everyone from murderers to rapists could enjoy the afterlife, as long as they gave Gallagher money. The Catholic Church teaches its members to build up grace through prayer, good works and the sacraments during their lifetime to guarantee eternal life. But this would all be for nothing, according to Gallagher's philosophy. All that was required was to give her the cash.

The same pamphlet urged the faithful to give 'generous donations' to ensure the House of Prayer was completed.

And it quoted a message allegedly given to Gallagher by Our Lady on 15 May 2007, in which Christ's mother supposedly gave this blood-curdling warning to the faithful: 'I call upon you to end all differences and complete the existing houses. Otherwise, all will be destroyed or the benefits removed from you. My children, if you do not swiftly respond to the gift God is offering you in the Houses of Prayer and they are permitted to be destroyed, those whom I have called will endure the consequences of their lack of response and the full impact of all that is coming.'

According to this apocalyptic 'vision', Gallagher was then shown millions of people of every race and colour, black, yellow and white, whom God wanted to save through the chain of Houses.

In another newsletter, Gallagher called for more donations saying 'only a small number' had been received that year and that 'we are forced to ask you yet again for assistance'.

There was little chance of this 'much needed' money coming from the local town of Smithfield, where locals seemed nonplussed by this prayer house that had appeared on the edge of their quiet town. One man told me: 'There was a big celebration for the opening when people came from all over America. Someone asked me if I lived here and when I said I did, they said I was very lucky because this is where it was all happening. You could have fooled me! A woman gave me some kind of medal, which I still have. But the people there don't really have anything to do with the town. They don't mix and I've never been in it.'

After visiting the House of Prayer it was time to call on John Rooney himself, a trip of some 50 kilometres. His house is on the north side of Steubenville, down a quiet country cul-de-sac, off a rural road. The first visit was fruitless as he was out. A young man, who was mowing the lawn, said Rooney had gone out for a haircut and would be back in an hour. He said he was a friend of Rooney's son, and asked if I wanted to leave a message. I didn't.

When I called back, an hour later, Rooney was waiting for me. Having obviously been informed that someone with a strange accent had called at the door, he had presumably guessed it was someone from the press. As I walked up the driveway towards his open front door, this large middle-aged man with grey hair walked towards me, beckoning me back towards the road where I was parked.

For a moment I thought he wanted to talk to me away from the ears of his son's friend, who was still cutting the grass. But this impression did not last long. Rooney pointed at my car and with a shaking voice snapped: 'Get in your car and get off my property.'

As we had been walking up his pathway, I had introduced myself, and said I wanted to talk to him about Christina Gallagher. Now he said: 'You are standing on my property. If you do not get off my property, I will call the sheriff.' Rooney was literally shaking, with what I could only assume, was rage or shock. His mouth was quivering, as he once again ordered me off his land. He seemed hardly able to talk. I said I only wanted to ask him a few questions about Christina Gallagher and find out why his name was on the deeds to her €4 million mansion.

'You mean… you just got on a plane and came to my home,' he said incredulously. 'You are standing on my land. Get in your car and get out of here right now, and if you ever come back I will call the sheriff.' I made another attempt to get him to talk. But all he said, as he looked at my press card was: 'I've read your stuff.'

Christina Gallagher secretly snapped on a shopping trip with her 'bodyguard' Tony Fitzpatrick and her devoted ex-nun sidekick, Sister Treasa.
© *Sunday World*

Gallagher's stunning 7 Series BMW which would have cost over €100,000.
© *Sunday World*

Gallagher's astonishing €4 million Malahide home, complete with manicured lawns, fountain and sculptures, on the private Abington estate.

© Sunday World

The stunning €1 million home outside Ballina that Gallagher bought for her daughter, Mary. It is the biggest house for miles around.

© Sunday World

The plush house that Gallagher bought for her son, Brendan.

© Sunday World

Gallagher's Newport home, which was filled with antiques, crystal and a massive four-poster bed imported from Harrods. The house was supposedly bought from Gallagher by the Blue Ivory Trust – but Gallagher kept the money and the house.

© Sunday World

Michael Morrissey in the prayer room of his Co. Waterford home, complete with windows bought from the House of Prayer.

© *Sunday World*

The cheques that Betty and Michael Morrissey were asked to make out to Fr Gerard McGinnity and John Rooney, rather than the House of Prayer. The sums were a colossal €40,000 and €50,000.

Tim McCarry, the 89-year-old who gave away his life savings of €70,000 to the House of Prayer before he died of cancer.

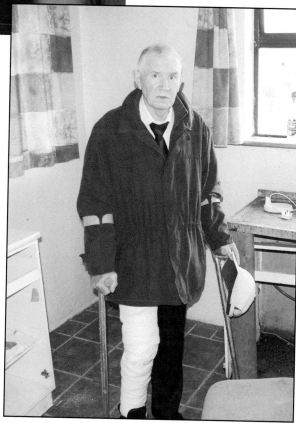

Anthony Tierney, who claims he was left in a room for three days with no medical help, after he fell off a ladder and smashed his knee at the Achill House. He has filed a lawsuit against the House of Prayer.

© *Sunday World*

The author in front of the House of Prayer in Humboldt, Kansas. Locals joked that Christina Gallagher's organisation had bought up half the town. The small town of 2,000 people already had 70 churches.

© Jim Gallagher

The sprawling newly-built House of Prayer in the village of Smithfield, near Steubenville, Ohio. Despite being thousands of kilometres away from Ireland, it was largely paid for by Irish donors.

© Jim Gallagher

The huge House of Prayer and empty car park in Leander, near Austin, Texas.

The House of Prayer deep in the farmland of Padua, Minnesota.

The House of Prayer in Lake Placid, Florida.
© Photos Jim Gallagher

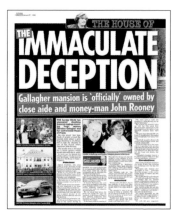

The *Sunday World* broke story after
story about Christina Gallagher and
her controversial prayer centre on
Achill Island.
© *Sunday World*

In one last ditch attempt to get an interview, I asked how could Christina Gallagher afford to lead such a wealthy lifestyle, and why her followers were asked to make cheques out to him. Furious at being questioned further, he once again pointed at my car and ordered: 'Get in and get off my property. If you come back I will have you arrested.'

It was obviously time to go. Clearly this fanatical supporter of Christina Gallagher was not going to be inviting me in for a cup of coffee. Just like Gallagher and Fr McGinnity before him, John Rooney had refused to give one iota of explanation to the Irish people about what happened to the vast amounts of money they had donated. Many people would argue that his behaviour was the classic response of someone in a cult. He had shown complete incomprehension that anyone would dare to question the person he revered more than any other in this world. Indignation is often the only response that cult members can muster when faced with criticism. They are so certain in the knowledge that they are right, and that they are part of the chosen few who could see the truth, that outrage is their only reaction, when faced with a barrage of questions. Gallagher's closest supporters have become so obsessed that they lose all reason when faced with a sceptic. They simply cannot tolerate the notion that they could be wrong. Former supporters said that Fr McGinnity was in the exact same boat. It has frustrated so many of their former followers. Why could none of them explain their position if they had nothing to hide?

The local diocesan office of the Catholic Church in Ohio told me later that day that they were aware of the controversy surrounding the House of Prayer in Ireland, and gave no support to the House in Steubenville. Just as the Archbishop of Tuam, Dr Micheal Neary, had

ruled that the Achill House had no Church approval, the
Bishop of Steubenville, Daniel Conlon, said the house
in their area was also a private concern. A spokesman
said: 'The bishop does not sanction it. It is located in
his diocese but that's it. They are not allowed to have
Mass or confessions or any sacraments, and no priest is
assigned to it. The bishop spoke to the Archbishop of
Tuam before it even opened. It is just a house that has
opened for people who want to pray. If someone wants
to put something in our diocese, there is nothing the
bishop can do except say it is not sanctioned. Just like a
shop opening here, there is nothing we can do.'

After Ohio, it was time to visit the rest of Christina's
Gallagher's sprawling House of Prayer empire across
the United States. The properties, all bought in the last
few years, are many thousands of kilometres away
from Ireland, but they were all partly paid for by
money donated by devout Irish Catholics, particularly
elderly ones. Many people were put under intense
pressure and made huge sacrifices to donate to the
Houses in Minnesota, Kansas, Texas and Florida, not
to mention one in Mexico City, while Gallagher herself
lived in splendour.

The House of Prayer in Minnesota is 20 kilometres
outside an attractive little town called Sauk Centre,
which itself is just over 200 kilometres away from the
main airport of Minneapolis. The House is in a rural
setting in a tiny hamlet called Padua, which is a 15-
minute drive from Sauk, along the Old County 18 road,
and is surrounded by nothing but fields. There are no
signs to the prayer centre and nothing to tell you what
it is once you get there. The building is a former church,
St Anthony of Padua, and the only other building there,
was a bar directly opposite. Quite who would flock
here is a mystery, as it is a long way from anywhere.

A nun in the local Catholic Church of Our Lady of the Angels in Sauk told me that Gallagher had been there the previous year to officially open the centre, which had a dormitory built into the back for staff or visitors. She said the diocese of St Cloud did not promote the House of Prayer but neither did it try to stop it.

Gallagher often speaks of saving millions of souls, but where were they? Most of the US Houses appeared to be open just three hours a day, from 12 noon to 3pm, with just one or two people in attendance. Why people in Ireland should be expected to contribute to the building of such isolated centres was a mystery. Far from saving 'millions' of souls, they would be lucky to get their message across to more than a few dozen.

The House of Prayer in Kansas, however, was a different story. Slap bang in the middle of a town, Humboldt, the house was the base for a property-buying spree. Locals joked that those running it had snapped up half the town. Not only did the organisation buy a disused Presbyterian Church to use as a House of Prayer, which opened in November 2006 after extensive renovations, but it also bought a disused hotel, the Baily, right in the centre of town on the main square. David Haba, the man running the Kansas operation, raised eyebrows further by buying another large historic building on the opposite side of the street from the hotel, which until recently was used as a flea market. He had also bought a number of houses, which locals said he planned to rent out.

'We don't know what they need all this property for if they are just a prayer group,' one local said. 'But they seem to have money to burn. They have turned the hotel into a souvenir shop and rooms for visitors or staff. But at the back they have built a sun room, which is pretty unusual for a church organisation. They were putting in a fireplace and got a deal for two, so they took the other one too, just in case they needed it in the future. People have been wondering where all the money is coming from. Now they have bought this other large place and we don't know what they are going to do with it.'

It is a remarkable spending spree in a rural town of less than 2,000 people in the middle of nowhere. Humboldt, which boasts just one set of traffic lights and no hotels, is deep in farm country and is over 200 kilometres away from the nearest big cities of Kansas and Wichita. The town and surrounding countryside is already served by an incredible 70 churches, including Catholic, Baptist, Mormon, Lutheran, Jehovah's Witnesses, Episcopalian, Evangelical, Methodist, Pentecostal, Presbyterian and Seventh Day Adventists, to name but a few. But locals claim that unlike the others, the House of Prayer people do not mix in the local community.

'They keep themselves to themselves and are not very friendly,' said one local woman who used to attend services in the Presbyterian Church before it was turned into the House of Prayer. 'I see their organiser, David, nearly every day, but he would walk past you and never say hello. He is a very intense man. There seems to be no joy in that place. When Christina Gallagher came for the opening, her followers told everyone not to worry, that she was bringing her own security. We were amazed. Why would she need security for a prayer centre?'

People in the town had been worried about all these properties being taken off the local tax register, but one man made inquiries and found out that the House of Prayer was not being classified as a church because it had no regular services and would therefore have to pay property tax. 'But you do see three or four coaches turning up every couple of months,' he said.

When the *Sunday World* called to the prayer centre, the same David Haba snapped that we could either sit quietly at the back or join him in prayers. He was the only person there. Posters everywhere said: 'No photos, no audio, no video.' The souvenir shop, around the corner, remained shut the whole day. One local said: 'We can't understand why they are here. If they want to pray why don't they just go to the Catholic Church?'

At the same time as the House of Prayer was buying up Humboldt, Christina Gallagher's website still claimed her American houses of prayer were desperately in need of funds. As recently as February 2008, American fundraiser Jim Seelinger, who helped organise the Florida house, claimed only $386,000 of the required $600,000 to complete the prayer centre in Lake Placid had been raised. When we visited one Sunday – a day you would expect to be the busiest of the week – there were just two people saying the rosary. And we were told that all the work was in fact complete.

Richard, who was leading the prayers, told me that this most recent House of Prayer was fortunate to have a genuine relic on the altar – a tiny part of the cross on which Christ was crucified. This indeed seemed a remarkable possession for a small prayer group to have in the middle of Florida, several thousand kilometres away from the Holy Land. Richard wasn't too sure how they got it – nor even how long the House of Prayer had actually been open. 'I am only filling in. The people who run the place are away,' he said. Information was never forthcoming at any of the Houses of Prayer.

The sole woman at the back of the House of Prayer in Leander, Texas, a sprawling place set in the hills outside the state capital of Austin, was the bluntest of all. 'We don't answer questions,' she snapped at me, after I innocently enquired how long the centre had been open. Outside, the enormous car park sat completely empty in the baking desert sun. It was easy to see why.

The Catholic Church in the US has warned its congregations that the Houses of Prayer do not have its support. Bishop Gregory Aymond, of the Diocese of Austin, Texas, issued a statement against the Leander House three years ago, before it even opened. He said it 'should not be considered as sanctioned' by the Church, and he refused to give permission to Fr McGinnity to say Mass there when he arrived with Christina Gallagher for the official opening in June 2006. A spokesman for Bishop Aymond told the *Sunday World*: 'He has not changed his opinion. The House of Prayer is not sanctioned by the bishop or the diocese.'

A Church spokesman in Minnesota said the House of Prayer in Padua, outside Sauk Centre, was allowed to say just two Masses a year, on the feast day of patron saint St Anthony and at Christmas. The spokesman said he was not aware of the controversy going on in Ireland.

While the House of Prayer lost its charitable status in Ireland in 2006, the company which runs the American chain of houses, the Confraternity of Our Lady Queen of Peace, which was set up by John Rooney in 2004 and is based in his own home, still operates as a 'not-for-profit' organisation. Its latest tax return, filed in December 2007, showed it had assets of $6.7 million, a massive rise on the $814,000 from two years previously. Its income was listed as $2.8 million, again a huge increase on the $593,000 it recorded in 2005.

And a large part of that money came directly from Ireland!

CHAPTER TWELVE

The Rebels Revolt

'Christina just had another vision in the chapel! She saw blood over the whole of Ireland. We are all going to be wiped out!'

Another appalling story to come out of the House of Prayer was the way Christina Gallagher and Fr Gerard McGinnity treated one of their most loyal staff, 'Margaret' (not her real name).

For 13 years Margaret was devoted to the House of Prayer, but was sacked in 2006. This occurred after Gallagher and McGinnity discovered that Margaret had her own house which she had kept secret and that she had not handed over to their cause. There were other reasons, too, why Gallagher and McGinnity mistrusted her, one of them being that she refused to give herself body and soul to the House of Prayer. She worked there voluntarily for years, with no financial reward, but always remained her own woman. She did not follow blindly, as others did, everything that Gallagher said.

A deeply religious woman, she was a devout Catholic, rather than a devout House of Prayer follower. Those closest to Gallagher were always taught to be suspicious of the official Church, because it did not support her. But Margaret had no such suspicions, and always remained on good terms with local priests on Achill Island.

Gallagher, on the other hand, had nothing to do with them, and resented anyone who did have contact with them. In fact, one priest later confessed that she and her associates made his life a misery. Her then loyal servant

Mike McCrory was often on their backs, criticising them for not doing enough to support this amazing visionary in their midst.

Relations between Gallagher and the local Archdiocese of Tuam had gone downhill rapidly, within weeks of the official opening of the House of Prayer in 1993. Later, the Archbishop of Tuam, Dr Michael Neary, tried to incorporate the House of Prayer into the diocese. If this happened, the diocese would effectively have wrested control of the prayer centre from Christina Gallagher, but she was having none of it.

The Church, therefore, was always kept at arm's length. But Margaret made the fatal mistake of trying to get them all to get along. One day she made an innocent remark that it would be nice to invite two local Mayo priests round for a meal, as they had both studied under Fr McGinnity when he was teaching at Maynooth College. Margaret, in her innocence, thought that Fr McGinnity might be pleased with such an idea, and would welcome the opportunity to catch up with his former protogés.

But rather than being touched by such a kind gesture, Fr McGinnity was furious. He forbade Margaret outright from inviting them and stormed: 'They are spies for the bishop!' She was told in no uncertain terms that she should not even be talking to them on her regular trips to Mass.

Matters came to a head soon afterwards, when Fr McGinnity discovered Margaret had helped to put away the Eucharist after a service in the local church, the Exposition of the Blessed Sacrament. Rather than being impressed that their loyal member of staff was taking such an important role in local church matters, Fr McGinnity and Gallagher saw this as some kind of disloyalty or treachery and they let Margaret know it.

They also had another, possibly bigger, reason to be upset with her. As they were reprimanding her and telling her that she had to leave the House of Prayer, McGinnity suddenly said: 'There is a rumour you have a house on the island?' The priest asked her the same question three times, after telling her to pack her bags. 'But I wouldn't give them the satisfaction of replying,' Margaret said. House of Prayer manager, Noel Guinan, among others, had said to her on several occasions: 'You are living here now. If you have a house you should sell it and give the money to the House of Prayer.'

Margaret did, in fact, have a house on the island and, ironically, she had been on the verge of giving it to Gallagher and Fr McGinnity, because she wanted to move from Achill. Margaret did a lot of charity work in Dublin, and she was getting tired of the long commute, which was over 300 kilometres. She planned to move nearer to the capital.

She told me how she had actually bought her seven-room home with the House of Prayer in mind. She was doing it up and was going to present it to them. She had built an extension and also prepared the garage, so it could quickly be converted to more rooms. She had already had the garage connected to the electricity and water supplies.

She was going to tell Gallagher and Fr McGinnity that it was for the use of people in the House of Prayer. There was one stipulation: that she would keep one room in the house for the rest of her life, for when she was visiting the area. She was sacked just one week before she had intended to hand it over. The reason that Gallagher and Fr McGinnity didn't know about it, was that Margaret lived in the House of Prayer when she was working there. She had rented out her house, but had asked the tenants to leave for the building work to go ahead. Now it was almost ready.

'They were always saying that if people had homes, they should sell them and give the money to Christina Gallagher,' said Margaret. She left the House of Prayer on 4 July 2006 – never to return. Before she walked out the door, she was asked to sign a form saying that she would never disclose anything that happened at the House of Prayer while she was there. She refused.

As a loyal worker she had been privy to many of the House's secrets, although she claims that she was never one of the inner sanctum. She was too independent-minded and had too many outside interests for that. But Gallagher did trust her enough to tell her, several years previously, that she had bought a house for her daughter. This was before she paid for the €1 million mansion for Mary outside Ballina in 2007. Margaret was surprised to hear Gallagher boast that she had paid for all her family's homes.

Margaret had a fascinating story that she told several other former House of Prayer devotees. She was in the centre one day, when she heard a debate about Christina Gallagher on Joe Duffy's RTÉ radio programme *Liveline*. An engineer had rung the programme to say he had installed hidden cameras and audio equipment in the house. He couldn't understand why a place of worship would need such high-tech eavesdropping equipment.

A House of Prayer spokesperson had gone on the show to deny the story, and said there were no bugging devices. But Margaret said they were actually sitting around the table looking at the electronic equipment while the show was on. A friend of Gallagher's husband, a builder, came in that night and dismantled the whole system. This happened because Christina had invited *Liveline* to see for themselves that there were no cameras. 'Let them try and find any cameras now,' Gallagher said to her followers.

Former devotees believe Gallagher uses whatever information she picks up on cameras and tapes – and the grounds of the House of Prayer are now covered in security cameras – to fool people into thinking she has been given personal information about them from the Virgin Mary.

After so many years working in Achill, Margaret also had plenty of insights into her colleagues at the House of Prayer. Of Majella Meade, one of the main fundraisers, she said: 'Majella has been there four or five years now, but at the beginning they had no time for her. Then suddenly she was being brought up in front of the crowd on a Saturday and praised for her good work. "This great little girl," they said. They must have discovered she had money or something.'

Another boss at the House who is now gone, was a nasty piece of work, says Margaret. 'She used to talk down to everyone and would not eat with us.' She was in charge when Noel Guinan was away, she said. Margaret would be cleaning the chapel or doing other chores, but 'if you put a foot wrong you were told about it'.

Margaret said staff used to take it in turns at night to answer the phones. One evening when it was her turn, a woman rang to complain that her mother was being pestered by the House of Prayer to donate money, and that she wanted to complain to someone about it. Margaret said she didn't know anything about it and was surprised. 'I organised affairs in the chapel and did cleaning and laundry, and had nothing to do with fundraising. The woman said that in that case she would ring the guards.'

Sure enough, a little while later a garda officer came on the phone and asked Margaret: 'Do you know a

John Rooney or know anything about money being collected?' Margaret said she didn't, that it didn't sound right to her, but she was not in charge and would get someone who was.

'I told one of the managers that a woman had complained about Fr McGinnity and Majella collecting money, and that the guards were on the phone. She went scarlet, all flustered. I said, "You have to put the guards straight, that can't be right. Fr McGinnity wouldn't pester people for money."'

Margaret said the phone conversation lasted for ten minutes. She later asked her if everything was okay. The manager replied that she thought the gardaí understood her explanation.

Other former Gallagher followers have revealed that Margaret was treated appallingly by the House of Prayer, after so many years of loyal service. Mike McCrory knew her well, and said her treatment at the hands of Gallagher and McGinnity was typical of what happened at the House of Prayer. The supposedly holy duo had no loyalty to any of their staff, and if you crossed them, you were gone. 'My wife used to say that they chew you up and spit you out,' he said.

Betty Morrissey, also a close friend of Margaret's, said she was one of the most devout people she had ever met. 'She is so holy. She admits freely that she was like a robot up there, and that she was so involved in the spiritual side of it, her mind was only working that way and she was not querying anything. But if she ever went public, Gallagher and McGinnity would deny everything.'

Betty said that it was Margaret who sent her the first *Sunday World* article about Christina Gallagher buying a €1 million home for her daughter. But that was no surprise to Betty, as Margaret had already told her about the house. And Mike McCrory had first told Margaret about it. He had driven out to the Co. Mayo countryside to find the mansion.

Betty said: 'She is such a lovely, gentle, prayerful person, but when Mike McCrory told her about the big house outside Ballina, she set off down there under her own steam to find it. It's not like her to be doing that sort of thing.' Margaret found the house, and was so transfixed by the size of it that she pulled over by the side of the road to take it all in. As she sat there, a car with darkened windows came out of the house and drove past her. The driver, who she could not see, might have recognised her, because whoever was in the car reversed back and stopped. 'She was shivering in her shoes anyway when she saw this big limo reversing back,' said Betty.

Margaret claims that Gallagher took an interest in her the very first time she visited the House of Prayer, back in the 1990s. Margaret was driving a BMW at the time, and the visionary seemed quite taken with it. Margaret says she was always well dressed going down to Achill, and Gallagher probably thought she was wealthy. 'I would say she targeted me at that time,' Margaret said.

Margaret was also one of the few Gallagher followers to be allowed inside her luxury house outside Newport. She was actually driven there from Achill, to help look after Gallagher's ailing father, when he was dying. One friend asked her what went though her mind when she saw all the fabulous furnishings. She replied: 'If it was my house I wouldn't let anyone inside the door.'

When the *Sunday World* revealed that the Newport house had a four-poster bed from Harrods and was filled with expensive crystal and jewellery, Gallagher bad-mouthed Margaret, wrongly assuming that she was the mole. In reality Margaret did not know about the Harrods bed, although she was aware everything in the house was expensive. Margaret was one of the most high-profile victims of the House of Prayer, but there were many, many others, some of whom only visited the place occasionally.

One woman rang me to say her cousin had been completely taken in. Now there was simply no persuading him that Gallagher was in it for the money. 'He is brainwashed and believes implicitly. Christina Gallagher can do no wrong as far as he is concerned and your paper is "satanic". He believes whatever they tell him. I know he gives money, but I have no idea how much. He is a religious person, and his wife can't get through to him.'

The woman said that previously she and a friend went to see Gallagher, when she had a big prayer meeting in Ashbourne, Co. Meath. 'There were between 300 and 500 people there and the place was packed. This priest was with her and two young blonde women. They just prayed, and the question of money was not raised, but these people went round with containers. They were big baskets and then the cash was all poured into one basket. Nobody seemed to put anything less than €10 in. We could not believe it. They must have raised thousands, just from this one meeting. This lady left with a laundry basket full of cash. And it was all paper money.'

The woman said she and her friend thought it was a pure money-making racket. Gallagher played a video at the prayer meeting, in which she talked of all the miracles she had performed and showed pictures of people she had helped. 'But we didn't know who they were.' At the end of the evening Gallagher just disappeared, without saying a word. 'I can't remember if she said anything all night. But there was no thank you or big farewell.'

She said her cousin's wife had tried talking to him, but he wouldn't listen and had an answer for everything. 'This woman can do no wrong, as far as he is concerned. There is a hard core who will believe in her to the death, to the bitter end. You can't tell him anything, and he says the cheques in the paper were forgeries. He says people only handed over money they wanted to give, nobody was forced.'

Another woman, called Noreen, had a remarkable story to tell about a pilgrimage to a shrine at Mount Melleray, Co. Waterford. In 1985 the Virgin Mary was said to have appeared before three young children, over a nine-day period. Nearly two decades ago, Noreen was on a bus going to visit the shrine. She met Gallagher, whom she had been introduced to once before. The visionary was there with Fr McGinnity. Noreen and a friend did an all-night vigil at the grotto. 'The whole idea is that you did not get any sleep and then had breakfast and Mass. I was in the chapel and Mass was being said, and I was feeling light-headed with the lack of sleep. We then piled onto the bus, and Fr McGinnity came on board with his beads. He said, "Christina just had another vision in the chapel! She saw blood over the whole of Ireland. We are all going to be wiped out!" And McGinnity started talking frantically. He was getting the people on the bus into a frenzy, by saying everyone was in danger. It was just not a rational way of thinking, and I was thinking, "This is a load of rubbish." Visions have to be confirmed by the Church, but here was McGinnity repeating everything she had said just a few minutes before – as if it was gospel.

'At that stage, I began to realise we were suffering from sleep deprivation, and that she probably saw something that was not really there. And here was Fr McGinnity telling us she had had a vision. I just thought it was ridiculous. From that point on I distanced myself from her. I thought there was something not right about her. People would often talk to me about her, and I would ask them how she could claim that the whole of Ireland was going to be wiped out, but you would be safe in Achill? I would tell people it was not right. Any time I got a chance I would push this message. I never saw Christina Gallagher again.'

Noreen had first met Gallagher when the visionary was just starting out. Gallagher visited Noreen's prayer group in Northern Ireland. She had heard about this 'wonderful woman' who had been getting astonishing insights and visions, but she did not give a lot of credence to it. When Noreen met her, she was less than impressed. 'She came in, and at one point I was talking to her on my own. I noticed that when she was talking to you she was trying to get an insight into you, and then she started repeating back what you said like a fortune teller. That was my first impression, that she was trying to tell my fortune and I did not like it. She did not ask too many questions, but she wanted me to know she could read me, and that it came from God. I told her a bit about my life and she recited it back to me. I was not too impressed.'

Today, after reading about Gallagher's wealth, Noreen says she feels outrage at the way Gallagher has taken advantage of the old and vulnerable. She was also angry that Gallagher had used her prayer group, and many others up and down the country, to establish herself as a visionary.

'It was a different time and a different Ireland back in those days, and people were more gullible. There was a lot of brainwashing going on in a sense, and she was a charming woman. The people who make money off the vulnerable are like that. Back then Gallagher was involved in many, many prayer groups. It was her way of getting her foot in the door, to get herself known. A year later she had an audience, and suddenly the thing was to set up a house of prayer on Achill and have people come to her. If you were genuine, surely you would not isolate yourself from the very prayer groups you were initiating at the start? How devious she was to get involved in our prayer groups. She used genuine people, sometimes people who were sick. To think she came in and took advantage of them. It makes me so cross. People are so good and they handed over all this money.'

Noreen said a friend of hers was married on Achill, and she told her that the locals there just laughed at Gallagher. 'They think she is pathetic and they know she is not genuine. That big house of hers in Malahide is a disgrace.' As for Fr McGinnity, Noreen thinks that he was totally over the top. 'His sermons can go on for three hours,' she said. 'And these predictions are like the Jehovah's Witnesses predicting the end of the world. The date keeps passing and they come up with a new one.'

Gallagher has in fact been making apocalyptic predictions from the beginning of her career as a self-proclaimed visionary. Every time there is an earthquake or a natural disaster, she claims she foretold it. And yet when she makes her 'predictions', she never says which country the natural disaster is going to hit. She will make vague references to seeing men with cloths on their heads and collapsed buildings, which could be anywhere in the world.

Her supporters claim she predicted the destruction of the Twin Towers on 11 September 2001. An American judge, Dan Lynch, revealed after the disaster that he had stood with Gallagher exactly two years before – 11 September 1999 – in Battery Park, New York, at the tip of Manhattan, in the shadow of the World Trade Centre. The two of them were to speak at a Rosary Rally for Peace. Lynch said he remarked on the Twin Towers as a symbol of America's economic might and its reliance on the priority of power over prayer. 'As I said this Christina waved her arm toward the Twin Towers and prophesised, "Dan, if Americans don't turn back to God, all of this will be destroyed!"'

After 9/11 the judge wrote an article about the incident, claiming it was a direct prediction by Christina Gallagher of what was to come. But opponents of the Mayo visionary argue that it was no such thing. They point out that Gallagher has predicted the destruction of practically everything over the years, and that this was just one more sweeping statement. She certainly never announced the destruction of the Twin Towers in advance. After they did collapse, she was confronted by people in the US, who demanded to know why she hadn't said something, if she knew they were going to be destroyed, thereby possibly helping to save some of the nearly three thousand lives that were lost on that dreadful day.

According to her lawyer, Donal Corrigan, writing on the House of Prayer website: 'She stressed that she tries not to give any message of a serious nature concerning public events, except through her Spiritual Director [Fr McGinnity], as people who do not want to hear may say it is "scare mongering".'

If that was the case, then why didn't Fr McGinnity issue the warning? And isn't an accusation of scare mongering a small price to pay for saving thousands of lives?

On 16 July 2001, just two months before the World Trade Centre attacks, Gallagher gave a typically doom-laden warning in the House of Prayer without once mentioning the Twin Towers. The message supposedly came from the Virgin Mary that morning and was read out three times to those present, who were told it should not be written down.

In it, Our Lady said she was pleased to see everyone in attendance at the House of Prayer, but criticised them for taking so long to respond to her call. 'Even today many of you are here only for sensation,' said the alleged message. Then, presumably referring to a time when the House of Prayer shut down temporarily, it went on: 'You have deserted My House once; do not desert it again. I invite you to come to My House and pray with me while you still have time. Short is your time before the world is drawn into conflict of war. How many will experience the sting of the Locust – that which looks like locusts but is not of the world. Oh, the calamity that is to befall the world and all its people! My House will be the safe refuge for all those I have called. The Third World War is in its permittance. How blood will flow and run red upon the earth! Hunger cries will be heard in the heavens.'

The message said people would turn from God but 'then my triumph will be, as God will purify the earth in his Justice. Fire will fall from the sky; many will lie upon the earth, their corpses will be eaten by wild birds – that which is not burnt in the fire. God's church has entered its purification.'

According to the message, only those who attended the House of Prayer would be saved. 'In all tribulation, disaster and war nothing will touch my House or this little island [Achill] because the Hand of God is upon it.'

The message claimed that those who came to the House of Prayer would be saved on the day of reckoning: 'I desire that my children of the world – especially the youth – come to my House. Those who come in the right disposition will receive not only the gift of the grace of Solace but Eternal Life at this fountain of grace.'

It was these apocalyptic messages that drove away many of Christina Gallagher's former supporters. Some claimed they were pure heresy. Others were horrified to see the traditional Catholic image of Our Lady, as the peace-loving mother of Christ, replaced by one of a vengeful woman, threatening death and destruction on a world scale.

Gallagher has made other vague predictions about the destruction of different parts of the US without specifying where and when. The one time she did name a time and place, Texas in 2006, it did not happen.

While others walked away from the House of Prayer because of these apocalyptic predictions, Fr McGinnity appeared to believe every word. He had no doubt that her predictions were heaven-sent. He claimed his mentor had been shown the destruction of the Twin Towers 'some years before'. Not only that, but she had also been shown widespread destruction 'in many parts of the United States'. He told the House of Prayer website: 'What she has been shown and the knowledge given concerning future happenings is a heavy cross for Christina to bear.'

Why she should choose not to share with the general public where these disasters are going to happen is anyone's guess. Perhaps it's because Gallagher has not got a clue? But once something does happen, like the recent stock market crash, Gallagher claims she 'predicted' it. The rest of the world knows that these things happen in cycles. So anyone can say there will be a stock market crash some time in the future; the same is true of the effects of global warming. Scientists have been warning us for two decades about the effects of ozone depletion, melting ice caps, rising sea levels and changing weather patterns.

Gallagher has been making terrifying predictions about the world's fate for 20 years, and yet we are still very much here. One such message came on 1 January 1995, when Our Lady appeared to be preparing the world for its destruction, at least in the eyes of Christina Gallagher: 'My daughter, the world is in its decline! World purification has begun. Soon the water will be undrinkable. The weather will be so changeable: heat to cold to ice; rainstorms like the world has not witnessed; hurricanes, floods, earthquakes even in unexpected countries; mud slides, disasters throughout the world will increase when the Hand of My Son covers the world. North America – it will be in shambles.'

The message then made a gloomy prediction for Ireland: 'When God's hand comes over Ireland, it will be reduced to nothing. You have told some of my children about the Isle of Achill. They think you are crazy. They are led by the blindness of the deceiver. My Maternal Heart weeps for Ireland and the world. It is steeping in a mud of sin. Be at peace.'

In the following years there were numerous other dire warnings for the people of Ireland and the world. Gallagher also got in digs at the Catholic Church hierarchy for their lack of support for her, and for not allowing the Mass or sacraments to be said at the House of Prayer. While she pretends to be a loyal servant of the Church, she continually attacks its bishops. She and Fr McGinnity even went so far as to say that if the sacraments had been allowed at the House of Prayer, the sexual scandals that swept though the Church from the late 1990s to the present day could have been avoided. She has claimed she was given a vision of the scandals years before they broke, before even the House of Prayer opened. Gallagher and Fr McGinnity said God never wanted the scandals publicised.

In a book of published messages, one dated 23 October 2002, said that if only the Church had responded to Our Blessed Lady and allowed the Adoration of the Blessed Sacrament in her House of Prayer in Ireland, the Church's scandals would have been dealt with 'in God's way and not through the method of exposure which inevitably harms the belief of the faithful'. The message said God's desire to withhold the knowledge of the scandals in the Church was not to leave innocent victims unprotected but rather 'to shield the fragile faith of others. What has already become public is only a small portion of what will yet be disclosed. The human failure to permit Our Lady's House of Prayer on Achill Island to continue as God had desired it to be, renders the Church vulnerable to the enormity of attacks which will bring further damage to the faithful.'

In the same message, Gallagher claimed Our Lady told her to transmit a message to the then President of the US, George W. Bush, warning him of the danger of a third world war. And Fr McGinnity asked: 'By failing to provide the Sacraments and prayers as Heaven's remedy to this immediate danger of a third world war are we going to expose our little country to the fate that will otherwise certainly befall the rest of the world?'

Gallagher has claimed that Our Lady has been warning of a third world war since 1993, if people did not respond to 'her message'. She said God did not desire it, but man was bringing it about. In a message to Gallagher on 25 July 2002, Our Lady supposedly said that Jesus's heart 'weeps with sorrow at the enormity of what is still to befall the world'.

And once again, there was criticism of the clerical scandals and the lack of sacraments at the House of Prayer: 'My Son Jesus was disowned, forsaken and shamed by those who serve Him. I have drawn many to my House to be set free of sin only to be denied God's gifts of his sacraments. Coming to the world are many calamities to purify the stench of sin and evil.' In the same message, Our Lady supposedly told the world to look after her 'servant Christina', and warned that those who deserted her would experience the 'justice of God.' So too would those who had heard her message but had ignored it.

In a message the following year, 21 February 2003, Our Lady allegedly said to Gallagher: 'I want people to take care of you and your every need.' She said that if her servant was to walk away from spreading her message, it would be 'disastrous for the world'. Again there were warnings of the coming Third World War, because 'President Bush has opened the doors and they cannot be closed.'

Then came a call for a series of Houses of Prayer to be set up all over the world: 'I will be present in those houses as I am present in my House of Prayer on Achill Island. These houses will be protected from all calamities, and the people in them also. The people in my Houses are to be the latter day apostles and they will also be a power against the Antichrist. All those who are in my Houses at the appointed time of God will be healed and set free.'

To many, this claim was pure heresy, and was at complete odds with Catholic doctrine. So too was another controversial message the following year. Gallagher said she received it on 4 July 2004 to be read out on the 25th of that month, the annual 'Fraternity Day'. Our Lady allegedly told Gallagher that everyone should wear her 'Matrix medal', which was on sale in the House of Prayer shop. 'Let it always be on your person. Those who die with this medal on their body,

I will save through the merciful Heart of My Son. Jesus will not refuse Me His mercy for the souls who will be wearing this medal,' said the message.

This again was a hugely controversial claim: that anyone wearing the medal would be automatically saved, no matter what sins they may have committed in the past. Many Catholics were outraged. They were no happier at what they then saw as Gallagher's own self promotion in this so-called message. Our Lady allegedly went on: 'Pray for My messenger [Gallagher] that God has placed among you. Those who respond to My call... to help her will receive life in My Son, Jesus. Those who will not respond will not receive from the water of eternal life.' She added: 'She has suffered much through your rejection and the way you scoff at her. She has offered everything to God in generosity.'

By 2008 Gallagher's self-importance had reached new peaks in the Virgin's so called messages. One given on 10 October that year, said that the visionary's efforts to save 'billions' of souls was being jeopardised. The 'millions' of souls that Betty Morrissey had heard about in the secret fundraising meeting in Multyfarnham had now become 'billions'.

'God has put that house there to save billions of souls,' the message said. How a house on the small island of Achill was supposed to achieve such a colossal feat was never made clear. The population of the whole planet is just six billion. Were they all supposed to fit on Achill? Gallagher had claimed on numerous occasions that only those who attended the House of Prayer or contributed to its upkeep could be saved.

Gallagher-watchers had noted that the message of 10 October was also different in other respects. There were far more grammatical errors than usual and, as one man said, it had clearly not been 'polished up' by Fr McGinnity. 'Some of the sentences were almost incoherent and much of the letter was like fan mail to herself saying how great she is. It was pure gobbledegook.'

Gallagher's message, complete with errors, read:

Our Blessed Mother started to speak to me. I was listening to her and forgetting to write. Then there was a silence. Then our Holy Mother said My Child, I desire you to write. My Children, I am your Mother of Truth and Love. I plead with you to read the signs of your times. The world is on the brink of its destruction. The evil one is on every door stop. Your hearts are full aggravation concerning the things of the world and who is right or wrong. Are you unable to recognise all the signs that are before your eyes?

My House of Prayer, My message and My Messenger [Christina Gallagher] are under attack. My messenger endures beyond human endurance. She will be upheld in the Light of God in Truth. You, My Children, who desire to continue to pull My House of Prayer apart through lies will endure the justice of God for the loss of billions of souls. God has put that house there to save many billions of souls especially the souls of the youth. My children, by responding now the multitude of souls may still be saved.

The third world war is imminent. Its destruction is unthinkable. So many of you occupy your hearts in condemnation of My children who have to uphold My message in the most horrible circumstances. I invite you to my call of love and truth and enter My Confraternity in Love and Peace surrendering to do all that is possible to protect My messenger. Otherwise all will be lost in My plan in Ireland and the World, because God has chosen Christina to guide you through His

*guidance in the times that are at hand: you will need
her. Many of the youth of the world maybe lost through
your disbelief in responding to My call. God will not
fulfil My call for souls without My messenger's safety
and that too is becoming unsure. I plead with you to
respond before it has gone past the hour.*

*The anti-christ is drawing his plan together and
drawing with him a multitude of souls all the dangers
I have warned you about are with you. How can you
remain deaf and blind to all I have called you to do in the
past twenty years? How can you run from your Lord
who is Truth and from your Mother who Loves you and
desires to protect you in soul and body.*

I bless you, Father Son and Holy Spirit.

Gallagher then gave her own explanation of the
message: 'My understanding at the time of the message
given was that if people respond now by entering Our
Holy Mother's Confraternity in Love and Peace in all that
she has requested, the billions of souls can still be saved.'

This message was released in the US, where Gallagher
had spent time fundraising that summer.

CHAPTER THIRTEEN

The Church Responds

'Pseudo-visionaries would also be visited by psychiatrists and psychologists, to certify their mental health and to verify if they were suffering from hysterical or hallucinatory diseases or from delusions of leadership.'

The role of the Catholic Church in the whole House of Prayer affair was certainly less than inspirational. It was the subject of much heated debate up and down the country. At best, it could be claimed that the Church authorities sat on the fence, at worst, that they helped the House of Prayer to flourish, by refusing to take action against it. Loyal Catholics around the country pleaded with the Church hierarchy to ban Christina Gallagher's spiritual director, Fr Gerard McGinnity, from the prayer centre, but no such ban was ever put in place.

Countless former devotees of Christina Gallagher have claimed that Fr McGinnity's presence and support of the supposed visionary dispelled any niggling doubts that they had about the false prophet. He once had the reputation of being a devout and revered spiritual leader who gave wonderful sermons about his faith. His presence on Achill Island convinced many people that the House of Prayer must be a genuine holy centre, and that Gallagher was a prophet of our time. How could such a learned and religious man be wrong? Even those who realised early on that Gallagher was not all that she seemed, continued to travel to Achill Island because of his involvement.

The Church was aware within weeks of its opening that the House of Prayer was going to be trouble, and that it had in fact been launched on false pretences. Although the then Archbishop of Tuam, Dr Joseph Cassidy, officially opened the centre in 1993, he did so thinking it was going to be a retreat centre for priests and the laity. He soon realised his error when he saw it rapidly becoming something completely different, a shrine to Gallagher herself, and was forced to write to Christina Gallagher telling her to honour their original agreement. But she was having none of it.

Dr Cassidy's successor as archbishop, Dr Michael Neary, continued the fight and decided to try and incorporate the House of Prayer into the diocese. But he soon discovered that Christina Gallagher was extremely reluctant to hand over control of her baby. In June 1996 he launched a special committee of enquiry to investigate the work of Christina Gallagher, and the claims of miracle cures coming out of the House of Prayer. The committee was made up of two priests and a religious sister. Their report was completed the following year, and was presented to Archbishop Neary who, on 16 December 1997, issued a public statement about the findings. The statement was to set the tone for all further utterances about the House of Prayer over the next few years. The Archbishop said that on the one hand there was no evidence to question the integrity or sincerity of Christina Gallagher, but on the other hand there was no proof of supernatural phenomena at the House of Prayer.

He said that there was a great deal in the work of the House of Prayer that was 'wholesome and good' and was a force for good in the faith and in the lives of people who went there. He wrote: 'My chief concern at this point is that the House of Prayer be integrated into the life of Achill Parish, of this Archdiocese and of the Church in general, in a more stable and ordered manner than has heretofore been the case.'

He said he also wanted it to adhere more closely to the original plan, that of it being a centre of retreat. To achieve these aims he wanted, with Christina Gallagher's agreement, the House of Prayer to become a private association of the Christian faithful to operate in conformity with canon law. It would provide a 'clear and unambiguous' statement of its aims, including the adoration of the Blessed Sacrament, the recitation of the rosary and the provision of a place of spiritual retreat for priests. 'These ends are those originally agreed upon by my predecessor, Archbishop Cassidy, and Mrs Gallagher and I observe that the clarity of this agreement may have become somewhat obscured during the intervening years,' wrote the Archbishop.

Then in the next clause, possibly the most crucial – certainly in the eyes of Christina Gallagher – he said he would be in charge of the House of Prayer donations. 'As is required by canon law, the new Association will be subject to my authority as diocesan bishop in all matters concerning the administration and disposition of funds either donated or left in bequests to it for pious causes.'

He also said it was his duty to ensure that all the House of Prayer's 'goods and property' were used for the proper aims and that it would have to submit accounts. Under this new scheme the Parish Priest of Achill would be the chaplain of the House of Prayer, and the curate of Achill Sound would be the assistant chaplain. 'These two priests alone will have faculties to preach and hear confessions in the chapel. Furthermore, no priest, other than these two, may celebrate the Mass in the Chapel without permission from me.'

Christina Gallagher must have been spitting blood when she read the Archbishop's statement, because it basically took control of the House of Prayer away from her. Not only would she be losing control of its finances, but she would also be losing the services of her beloved Fr McGinnity, the priest who gave her credibility. Only the chaplain and assistant chaplain would be allowed to preach and say Mass under the new order.

Needless to say, Gallagher was never going to accept these terms. As a result, relations between her and the Archbishop went from cool to frosty. In fact, Gallagher's anger seethed away for months. She was so furious at the Archbishop's response that the following summer she announced the closure of the House of Prayer, claiming the decision had been forced upon her by Archbishop Neary. She claimed in a radio interview that she had been badly treated by the diocese. The Archbishop replied with his own statement, on 3 July 1998, saying that he heard the news of the closure with 'considerable surprise', and denied any role in it.

'I wish to state clearly and emphatically that at no time have I ever instructed Mrs Gallagher, either verbally or in writing, to take this step,' he said. 'On the contrary, I have repeatedly stated, both verbally and in writing, that it was not my intention to close the House of Prayer. This decision was made by Mrs Gallagher.'

He said that he had major reservations about the advice she had been given throughout the time that the House of Prayer was open. He pointed out that Gallagher had gone her own way, as soon as the Achill prayer centre was opened by Dr Cassidy in 1993. 'Dr Cassidy explicitly and repeatedly stated at that time and afterwards that the House of Prayer was intended to be a place of quiet where the adoration of the Blessed Sacrament, the recitation of the Rosary and the provision of a place of retreat for some priests would be the only activities,' said Archbishop Neary.

'Within a fortnight after the opening he found himself obliged to write to Mrs Gallagher in protest against persistent deviation on the part of the House of Prayer from the original simple vision. This tendency to stray from the terms of which the Archbishop had permitted the House of Prayer to function was to continue. Instead of a quiet place of retreat a de facto shrine was coming into being, attracting large crowds of visitors weekly. In a letter to Mrs Gallagher of 15 September 1994, Dr Cassidy criticised these developments again and refused permission, as requested by Mrs Gallagher, for an extension of the actual premises.'

Archbishop Neary revealed that he, too, had had run-ins with the single-minded head of the House of Prayer. 'In my most recent letter to Mrs Gallagher I was obliged to ask for clarification in the matter of Sunday Masses being allegedly celebrated in the House of Prayer in direct contravention of my express instructions in the matter. I found myself furthermore obliged to note in the same letter her tendency, persistent throughout my dealings with her, to misunderstand and misinterpret legitimate directives and to consequently misinform her associates and supporters.'

The Archbishop said he had also asked Gallagher for detailed accounts of any money that might have been donated or willed to the House of Prayer since it opened, but he had not received them. He said he would continue to push for them, even though the House of Prayer was now closed.

But, of course, it was not long before Christina Gallagher reopened her house. She was back in business, albeit with no authorisation from the Church, which she never bothered officially informing. The Church now regarded her venture as a completely private affair and, as such, it had no right to hold Mass, Confession or any of the sacraments within its walls.

Relations with the archdiocese were simply non-existent for the next ten years. If newspapers rang with queries about the House of Prayer they were simply told to see Archbishop Neary's previous statements on the matter. The Archbishop's secretary, Fr Fintan Monahan, told me in December 2007: 'The only thing the Archbishop has to say is that the situation is the same. As far as we are concerned the House of Prayer is officially closed. We did try to integrate it but it didn't happen. It is a private concern and does not have our support.'

But all that was to change in 2008 when the first stories about Gallagher's wealth hit the *Sunday World*. The Archbishop's office was flooded with phone calls and letters from worried Catholics, who regularly visited the centre. And it faced a barrage of media questions from newspapers and radio and TV stations, which were keen to follow up the story.

His office received so many requests for information that Archbishop Neary decided to publish a press statement on Friday 29 February 2008, for the attention of 'Newsdesks and Religious Affairs Correspondents'. The statement said:

> The Tuam Diocesan Office has recently received a considerable number of media enquiries regarding this matter. In 1996 I established a diocesan commission of enquiry to investigate certain claims regarding and emanating from this work. In 1997, acting on foot of a report from the commission, I issued a lengthy public statement to the effect, in essence, that no evidence of supernatural phenomena had been observed but that the persons involved gave every evidence of good faith.
>
> Arising from that, I proposed a basic canonical structure that would gradually integrate the work of the House into the life of Achill Parish and the Archdiocese. While this was

then attempted by the Archdiocese, I became increasingly perturbed by an apparent absence of enthusiasm on the parts of Mrs. Gallagher and her associates.

The relationship deteriorated to the extent that Mrs. Gallagher, in July 1998, closed the 'House of Prayer' at Achill, expressing to the media at the time a sense of having been harshly treated by the Archdiocese. In order to clarify the issue for the faithful I issued another statement, regretting the development and expressing grave misgivings as to the wisdom with which Mrs. Gallagher had been advised and had acted in the matter.

Diocesan efforts to integrate this work ended in July, 1998 when it was closed by Mrs. Gallagher. Celebration of the Sacraments and reservation of the Blessed Sacrament at the "House of Prayer" are not permitted. Any work carried on since then has been entirely of a private nature and has no Church approval whatever. Neither, for reasons given above, does such work enjoy the confidence of the Diocesan authorities. Nothing has been brought to my attention to indicate that I should change from this position in the future. Over the years since then, the Tuam Diocesan Office has clearly and consistently replied to enquiries in respect of this work, which Mrs. Gallagher recommenced.

I respect the faith and devotion of many people who have been impressed by this work in the past, some of whom have expressed their sadness at my stance. Finally, I wish to remind all Church members that they should not hesitate to enquire, as a matter of course, at local diocesan offices regarding the standing of any work describing itself as Catholic, should they be in doubt.

In summary the 'House of Prayer' has no Church approval and the work does not enjoy the confidence of the diocesan authorities.

This was the last public statement made by the Church about the House of Prayer. Despite repeated calls to be more pro-active, the Church seemed to have washed its hands of the problem, regarding it as a thorn in its side. Many people were disappointed by its stance, believing it had not done enough to discourage people from travelling to the Achill centre.

Many devout Catholics were also hugely frustrated that Cardinal Seán Brady did not do more to prevent Fr McGinnity's involvement. Cardinal Brady was Fr McGinnity's superior, as head of the Armagh Diocese since 1996, and was also the head of the country's Catholics, as Primate of All Ireland. Cardinal Brady never banned his priest from leaving his own parish in Knockbride, Co. Louth, and attending the House of Prayer most Saturdays. What was worse, he seemed to believe everything that Fr McGinnity told him. At one point, he called in the priest to question him about his role in the House of Prayer, but appeared to swallow everything he was told at the time.

Cardinal Brady declared in a private letter, seen by the author, that Fr McGinnity had assured him he was not involved in fundraising. Furthermore, if someone was unhappy that a family member had donated money to the House of Prayer, that money would be returned.

Fr McGinnity's claims to the cardinal were obviously blatant nonsense. He was at the heart of House of Prayer fundraising, and had been for many years. And if the organisation was happy to give back cash to disgruntled donors, why did three of them have to take legal action in 2008 to get back their €250,000?

Cardinal Brady met with a group of eight concerned Catholics in May 2008. The group left the meeting believing the cardinal was going to act. The result they hoped for was that the cardinal would stop Fr McGinnity from preaching at the House of Prayer. If this occurred it would deprive Christina Gallagher of the one man who could pull in the crowds for her. But once again, weeks went by and nothing was done. Betty Morrissey became so frustrated that she wrote to the cardinal, asking why Fr McGinnity was still being allowed to preach in Achill. She urged the cardinal, once again, to take some kind of action. Cardinal Brady sent her a reply in October, but it was not the one she was hoping for, as he failed to address the issues she had raised.

'He told me that he had spoken to Fr McGinnity, and that McGinnity had asked for more time,' said Betty. 'The cardinal said this was the second time he had spoken to him and that "progress was being made".' The cardinal then asked Betty to confirm that matters had been resolved to 'my satisfaction'. This was a reference to her lawsuit against the House of Prayer to get her money back. 'But of course I will never get satisfaction until that place is closed and McGinnity is stopped from preaching his heresy there. How can these talks the cardinal is having with McGinnity still be going on after all this time? We went up to the North to meet him in May and told him about our concerns. That was five months ago.'

She felt compelled to write again on 10 October 2008. She sent copies of her letter to Dr Michael Neary, and the Papal Nuncio in Dublin, Archbishop Giuseppe Leanza. In it she said that the cardinal had failed to address the issues that had driven her up to Armagh to meet him in May of that year. 'I went to you not just to represent myself but so many other people whose faith has been seriously damaged by the activities of Fr. McGinnity and Christina Gallagher and indeed the great damage done to the Catholic Church in general here in Ireland,' she wrote.

She enclosed a booklet of Gallagher's apocalyptic

messages, which the so-called visionary claimed she received direct from heaven. She begged the cardinal to read them, because these 'were used by Fr. McGinnity and Christina Gallagher to extort money from me and hundreds of others over the past 15 years'. She said: 'I can look back at everything now, in the cold light of day, and see we were part of a cult, brainwashed and frightened by the extraordinary apocalyptic messages of gloom and doom, as perpetrated by the prophecies of Christina Gallagher.

'I recently spoke to people confidentially, who worked within the inner sanctum of the House of Prayer. They describe a similar place shrouded in secrecy, cameras everywhere and where Christina rules with an iron hand. I have been told also by a witness that her reported stigmata is self inflicted. All this has been told to Bishop Neary, who insists that it is your job, Your Eminence, to deal with this.'

Betty Morrissey told Cardinal Brady that Fr McGinnity had even made veiled references to Bishop Neary and the hierarchy of the Catholic Church 'being under the influence of "Satan or the Beast" for not supporting Christina Gallagher.'

'I am pointing out these messages to you to explain how simple, elderly people like Michael [her husband] and myself were coerced through fear, and trusting Fr. McGinnity as a man of integrity and "Holiness", in to handing over large sums of money for their cause. All the newspaper articles since January 2008, which have exposed Gallagher's vast accumulation of wealth and lavish lifestyle, paid for by gullible, vulnerable people such as ourselves and so many others, I can verify to be absolutely true.'

Betty said the 'devastation' to her and to many others was difficult to express. She said she had trusted Fr McGinnity, but now she believed he was 'a fraudster', both controlled and manipulated by Christina Gallagher. 'The more I study everything, now I see that she controlled him absolutely and totally. She expanded his pride with her many messages from "Our Lady" to "My son Gerard".'

Betty said that Gallagher, in June of that year, had boasted openly to the crowds that Fr McGinnity was 'Cardinal Brady's best friend', and therefore untouchable. 'Could this be true?' asked Betty. 'I beg you to stop this priest who has done so much harm to my faith, to so many others and indeed the Church in general. Please intervene as head of the Church here in Ireland, as I feel it is your responsibility as his bishop and stop him going to Achill every Saturday and preaching his heresies which must be an affront to you and the whole Catholic Church here in Ireland.'

The battling pensioner then said that she expected a reply to her letter which was written 'with a broken heart'. She warned that if the cardinal felt he could do nothing about the situation, then she and others, who felt just as strongly about the situation, would have no choice but to approach higher authorities in Rome.

What was Cardinal Brady's reply to this heartfelt letter? Betty Morrissey never got one.

Fortunately, not all the Irish clergy were as trusting of Fr McGinnity, as Cardinal Brady. One Co. Mayo cleric wrote to me in February 2008, praising the *Sunday World* investigation. The cleric said: 'As a priest of the Archdiocese of Tuam, I wish to compliment you and your paper for your courage in blowing the cover on something that has been a source of major concern to many right thinking priests and laity for many years – i.e. The House of Prayer on Achill and the activities of its leadership.

'Anybody who dared question what happened there down through the years was accused, as you have been, as working for Satan or was threatened with legal action. I listened to the pathetic explanations, given by Gerry McGinnity on Joe Duffy's *Liveline* and on our local radio station here MWR, for all that your newspaper has uncovered. Their reaction to your revelations is the classic reaction of a cult when its cover is blown.'

The priest, who asked not to be named because of the abuse critics of the House of Prayer receive from Gallagher's followers, said: 'You have done everyone a favour. People dare not criticise her because they are then lashed for being agents of the Devil. These kinds of threats are classic cult behaviour. The House of Prayer has a lot of the hallmarks of a cult, the secrecy, the threats and the focus on one person.'

Another Co. Mayo cleric said: 'A lot of priests who used to work in that area are glad all this has been exposed. They used to get a lot of hassle from the House of Prayer. Most of the people who go there are good people, but a small number are fanatics. They are like "the faith police" telling priests what they should be doing and how to run their parishes.

'What I want to know myself is where Christina Gallagher goes to Mass herself? They can't say Mass at the House of Prayer, and she doesn't go to the church on Achill, and I know she didn't go to the parishes where she used to live around Newport and Castlebar. Does she even go? And she is supposed to be this holy woman? I have been questioning for years this whole financial side of things. The priests would talk about it among themselves.'

Another cleric said: 'I have not met a single priest who is not happy with what you are doing. Everyone has been really worried about that place for a long time.' He said he was more than disappointed in Fr McGinnity for getting so involved. He hadn't spoken to him for a couple of years, because all he talked about now was Christina Gallagher. He said he didn't know of another priest who in any way supported the House of Prayer, because Gallagher played on the vulnerable and took their money.

'People always wondered about her wealth,' he said. 'Christina Gallagher has her fans, of course, and they will not be happy. She appeals to a certain type of traditionalist who likes to deal in signs and wonders. They are on the right of the church, and would be addicted to religion rather than faith. You get that in every religion, people who say "if you are against me, you are the work of the Devil". That has little to do with faith and more to do with psychological factors.'

In October 2008 rumours began to circulate among former believers that Cardinal Brady had finally banned Fr McGinnity from preaching at the House of Prayer. He was allowed to attend, as a person of free will, but could no longer preach to the faithful there, so the story went. The rumour caused quite a stir, as people thought the official Church was finally taking action.

But their excitement was premature. Calls to the Archbishop's office on 10 October, poured cold water on this hot news. Although the cardinal was said to be in Rome until the end of the month, and was not available for comment, press inquiries were directed to Martin Long, the director of communications for the Catholic Church based at Maynooth. He made inquiries and came back with the official line that nothing had changed. 'Discussions are on-going between the cardinal and Fr McGinnity. There are no restrictions on Fr McGinnity,' said the spokesman.

Nine months into the scandal and the Church was

still refusing to take any action that might resolve the situation. Heads were still stuck firmly in the sand. It was also clear by this stage that the whole House of Prayer issue had driven a wedge between Archbishop Neary and Cardinal Brady. It appeared that both men were claiming, confidentially, that it was up to the other to deal with the matter. The result was that nothing was done.

There could have been several reasons for this inaction. One was that the Church was reluctant to alienate formerly disenchanted Catholics who had returned to the fold because of the House of Payer. The hierarchy accepted that many genuine people travelled to the Achill prayer centre, and it did not want to set them against the Church. Some lapsed Catholics who had fallen by the wayside, perhaps bored by the routine of the everyday Church, were revitalised by their trips to the West. Conservative people, who disapproved of the way Irish society was going, were also inspired by the fire and brimstone messages coming out of the House of Prayer.

Some worshippers spoke about the personal fulfilment they received from their weekends in Achill. There were also reports of non-Catholics being converted there. As Archbishop Neary's earlier statement said, the Church accepted that there were elements that were 'wholesome and good' about the House of Prayer. Nobody was keen to smash those elements. The Church was happy that people were praying, and it didn't seem to matter too much where it took place.

Archbishop Neary's spokesman, Fr Fintan Monahan, also told me in January 2008 that the diocese could not act, because the House of Prayer was a completely private affair, adding: 'A lot of good people go there. A lot of good things were going on there.' He said:

'The Church has to be very circumspect in dealing with extraordinary claims. A lot of observations and testing have to be carried out. But it will become clear in good time. Knock only got Church backing in the 1960s.'

But if Archbishop Neary was reluctant to make any tough pronouncements in Ireland, he was not so reticent in advising foreign Church bodies about the House of Prayer. He wrote to the Catholic Bishops' Conference, in the Philippines, in early March 2008. He said that the House of Prayer had neither the approval nor the confidence of Irish diocesan authorities. 'A large number of people from the Philippines visit the place on a regular basis. I would like to make people aware that it has no ecclesial authority whatsoever, and urge the greatest circumspection in consideration of a visit there,' Dr Neary said in his letter.

The Irish Bishops' Conference had also been informing other Catholic bishops' conferences worldwide that Gallagher's activities did not have the consent of the Catholic Church. It called on other prelates to caution their flocks about Gallagher and her organisation.

There could have been another reason for official inaction, too. The Church had been plagued with a whole series of scandals over the previous years, from Bishop Eamonn Casey and his love child to a horrendous catalogue of horrors suffered by children at the hands of paedophile priests. The Church may not have wanted to add one more scandal to the list by announcing publicly that this supposed holy place, attended most Saturdays by one of its own priests, was in fact a money-making operation.

A third reason might also have been that they did not want to turn Fr Gerard McGinnity into a martyr. The Church hierarchy had already been forced to make an apology to the priest in 2005, over the way he had been treated in the Micheál Ledwith affair. Cardinal Brady, it was claimed in some quarters, was now reluctant to be seen to be coming down hard on a man, who had already been so badly treated by the Church.

Whatever the reason, absolutely nothing was done about Fr McGinnity's weekly departure from his own parish, and his appearance at the controversial centre. Devout Catholics, who had quit the House of Prayer after waking up to its true nature, grew ever more frustrated.

But there were individual priests who did their best to stop people going to the House of Prayer. In October 2001, a Redemptorist priest giving a sermon at a parish retreat in Castlebar, Co. Mayo, spoke out against Christina Gallagher and accused her of 'heresy'. He also criticised her alleged prediction of 9/11. This is now a matter of public record, because the House of Prayer lawyer, Donal Corrigan, criticised him in a letter, weeks later, in *The Irish Family*. This was a newspaper, now closed, which was run by Dick Hogan, a former director of the House of Prayer, and one of Gallagher's biggest supporters.

In the letter Corrigan expressed his 'sheer disgust at the grave injustice done to Christina Gallagher' by the preacher on the final talk of the retreat, on the 9 October 2001. He said the priest took a 'cowardly swipe' at the local visionary, and 'tried to undermine her reputation'. Corrigan said: 'She cannot understand how a priest could be permitted to destroy her good name in this way… Mrs Gallagher cannot but think that the way she is treated is quite the opposite of what Christ urges His followers to practice towards each other.'

It would appear that Christina Gallagher was developing something of a martyr complex. Corrigan, who failed to mention in the letter to the newspaper that he was a director of the House of Prayer and its solicitor, went on to say that the stress from such attacks had caused Mrs Gallagher 'to suffer a heart-attack some years ago', and the 'maliciousness' was once again affecting her health. In reality there is no evidence Gallagher ever suffered a heart attack.

The Redemptorist priest was not the only one to attack Gallagher. A priest in Knock used to advise visiting American pilgrims in the confession box not to go to the House of Prayer. Lawyer Corrigan attacked him, too, in the same letter. He said protests were made to the priest's superiors, but he kept up his campaign. Corrigan finished by saying he was shocked at the misinformation spread about Christina Gallagher. Especially, when there was 'clear evidence available from the top medical experts' of miraculous healings at the House of Prayer, and through the use of the Matrix Medal 'thereby indicating the power of God in the work Christina carries out'.

The only problem here was that one of 'the top medical experts' who authenticated some of these 'miracles', Dr Michael Anketell, later became one of Christina Gallagher's most outspoken critics. He withdrew his support for the House of Prayer. He wanted it closed down, accepting that he had been duped.

If the Church authorities were reluctant to move against Gallagher in Ireland, Pope Benedict XVI's promised crack-down on false Marian prophets gave them some comfort. It was revealed in January 2009 that the pontiff was planning such a move, and had drawn up a 'directory' of action, which he planned to send to his bishops all over the world.

His first directive was that 'so-called visionaries' remain silent, while their claims were being investigated. Genuine visionaries, it was argued, would be able to follow the orders of their local bishops. But those who continued to publicise their alleged contact with the Madonna would have already given a sign that showed the falseness of their mysticism.

Pseudo-visionaries would also be visited by psychiatrists and psychologists, to certify their mental health and to verify if they were suffering from hysterical or hallucinatory diseases or from delusions of leadership.

A third step would be to check if the proclaimed mystic was studying theology or Mariology on the internet, a great source of information for any would-be prophet. Crucially, in the Pope's directory, bishops would also be asked to determine if the person being investigated received any economic benefits from the pilgrimages to where they claimed to see the Virgin Mary, or from the sale of religious souvenirs. Messages from the Madonna would also have to be in line with the Gospels or Catholic doctrine. If they passed all the above tests, then they would have to be visited by a demonologist or exorcist to exclude the possibility that Satan was hiding behind the apparitions to deceive the faithful.

It is clear that Christina Gallagher would fail the Pope's test on several fronts. There would be little chance of her remaining silent, while the Church spent years investigating her claims. Many of her pronouncements are already thought to be heretical. As for having 'economic interests' in pilgrimages, and the sale of souvenirs – people only have to look at her lifestyle and where she lives.

CHAPTER FOURTEEN

The House of Prayer Fights Back

*'In light of the above, the Sunday World
strenuously denies any breach of the code.'*

Christina Gallagher had been blasted in the media as a fraud and a liar, who had grown rich at the expense of elderly people all over the country. What did she do to defend herself against such shocking allegations in the immediate aftermath? Nothing. If these accusations had been untrue, they would, of course, have been libellous, and therefore, subject to possible litigation from the offended party. Lawyers across the country would have been queuing up to represent Christina Gallagher for a big payday in court. But the stories were true. Gallagher was always going to be reluctant to take legal action, because that would have meant standing in a witness box, under oath, and being questioned about all manner of things that she would much rather keep hidden.

But after more than a year of exposés about her wealthy lifestyle, Gallagher must have felt that she had to do something to stop the avalanche of stories. She had told her devoted Saturday afternoon supporters that she was taking legal action, and was going to get a huge payout, but this was a blatant lie.

The number of people turning up at the House of Prayer had dropped radically, and so had Gallagher's income from donations and from sales in the shop. Even those who remained loyal to her might have thought twice about handing over large sums of money.

In February 2009, the House of Prayer began to fight back starting with an article in *Ireland's Eye* magazine. In each issue of the monthly magazine there's a fawning two-page article about Christina Gallagher. In this particular issue, the organisation's self-proclaimed fundraiser, Majella Meade, went on the offensive and lashed out at 'fabricated' media stories. Meade said that no press outlet had tried to get any information from her at any time in 2008. A subsequent article in March and another in April continued on the same theme. The *Sunday World* was singled out for particular criticism for not interviewing Majella Meade to check facts. A 'reader' called Josie Butler, said it was 'highly revealing' that nobody had tried to interview Meade, when she was the main organiser of fundraising meetings.

What the articles failed to say, however, was that the *Sunday World* had tried to get interviews with all the main House of Prayer players, including Christina Gallagher herself, Fr McGinnity and John Rooney in America. The paper was not interested in interviewing Meade; it wanted to talk to people higher up in the centre. It was clear that Gallagher and McGinnity were the main fundraising powers at the House of Prayer. We will never know for sure just how many people gave money as a direct result of Gallagher urging people to support the House of Prayer in order to earn salvation. Gallagher claimed, in her repeated messages over the last 15 years, that only followers of the House of Prayer would be guaranteed eternal life. Fr McGinnity's role in fundraising was much more hands-on, as he attended meetings all over the country. It was McGinnity who urged people to give as much as they possibly could.

When the *Sunday World* investigation began, Majella Meade was not known. And she certainly was not known as being a key player in the centre. When the

Sunday World did get in touch with her, as a result of the *Ireland's Eye* articles, she refused to talk. She put the phone down, which was the typical response from anyone in authority at the House of Prayer.

It is interesting to note that Josie Butler was part of the House of Prayer set-up. She was not just a keen reader writing in to the magazine. She was one of the two people who turned up on Betty and Michael Morrissey's doorstep in a desperate bid to woo them back into the cult. This was after the couple first went public about their experiences, and told how they had been brainwashed into handing over vast amounts of money. We can only assume that this intimidating move was made on the orders of Christina Gallagher.

The *Ireland's Eye* articles failed to answer any of the serious questions the *Sunday World* had raised about the finances of the House of Prayer. In fact, these questions were dismissed by Majella Meade in an almost infantile response: 'All that stuff about personal wealth and houses and so on is just rubbish.' This was hardly a professional response from an organisation under public scrutiny.

By this stage it would have been wise for the House of Prayer to come up with a better response than Meade provided. It was clear that Meade was not familiar with PR or communications. Meade said that Christina Gallagher lived in 'a private and secure place of refuge' to get away from the media. She said: 'The media people attacking Christina over houses and alleged wealth are the very ones from whom she needs protection.'

Unfortunately, it was a very weak and vague response to explain why a supposedly holy woman with 'no interest' in material things was living in a €4 million mansion on a millionaire's row. This was not a 'refuge' but one of Dublin's most magnificent homes.

What's more, Gallagher had moved into the house two years before the media stories even began. Her previous home in Newport, which she still owns, was actually far more secure in the first place, with its high walls, making it impossible to see into the house from the road.

Mullingar journalist, Dick Hogan, also defended Gallagher in the same magazine article. He claimed that the media attacks on the Mayo woman constituted the worst case of distortion and suppression of truth he had seen in 50 years of journalism. A fact he managed to suppress himself, was that he is actually the owner of the magazine he was being quoted in. He also forgot to say that he had been a director of the House of Prayer for a decade, up until the previous year. This was something that readers might have thought was relevant to any article on the House of Prayer. Instead, as publisher, he hid these facts and was quoted as if he were just another interested reader.

Not content with these broadsides in *Ireland's Eye*, the House of Prayer stepped up its campaign to stop the *Sunday World* investigating Christina Gallagher, by launching a series of complaints over the newspaper's articles to the Press Ombudsman. Gallagher did not write the complaints, but got Majella Meade and Dick Hogan to do her dirty work for her. The first one came in a rambling six-page letter dated 23 February 2009. Meade said that she had been affected personally by the 'on-going media-based campaign' against the House of Prayer, Christina Gallagher, Fr Gerard McGinnity and 'all the members of the public' who supported the prayer centre. She called the *Sunday World* articles 'an unjust and unbalanced vendetta', which contained 'untruths, lies, distortion and deception'. She said the stories amounted to an incitement to hatred. Again, Meade claimed that she was the person responsible for organising and conducting 'all meetings that have taken place around the country'. Yet the paper had chosen to target 'innocent people' with 'unfounded and untrue allegations.' Meade then claimed that the series of articles was endangering people's lives.

She argued that eight principles of the Journalistic Code of Practice had been repeatedly broken. She then listed seven of them: truth and accuracy, distinguishing fact from fiction, fairness and honesty, respect for rights, respect for privacy, protection of sources, and incitement to hatred.

The Press Ombudsman forwarded Majella Meade's complaint to the *Sunday World* on 20 April. The newspaper gave a detailed reply dismissing the complaint and said it had begun its investigation into the House of Prayer at the behest of some of its own former members. These members were concerned about the possible misuse of funds, and that its investigation was not, and had never been, a private 'vendetta'.

The prayer centre's accounts for 2006 showed profits carried forward of over €2 million. This was money that had been donated by the Irish public, and therefore, was a matter of serious public interest, said the newspaper. It highlighted the properties which it had discovered that Gallagher owned. It also explained how former followers had revealed the enormous pressure they had been put under to make donations to the House of Prayer. These people were now asking what happened to their money.

'We revealed how donors were asked to sign cheques in the names of Christina Gallagher's key aides, Fr Gerard McGinnity and John Rooney, instead of to the House of Prayer, with no explanation,' the newspaper continued. 'We then uncovered documentary proof that Mr Rooney, in whose name donations were made, purchased the €4

million house in Malahide where Christina Gallagher
was living and where she was photographed by *Sunday
World* staff. We have still received no satisfactory answers
to questions this obviously raises in the public interest
over the purchase of this house.'

It was pointed out that the complainant, Majella
Meade, had told *Ireland's Eye* that she was involved in
the purchase of this house. Her explanation for this was
that the Virgin Mary, in messages to Christina Gallagher,
informed her followers that she needed a shelter from
the storm of media criticism she was subjected to. But
the mansion was bought two years before the storm
broke – and was in fact the cause of that very storm.

The newspaper reminded the Press Ombudsman
that the House of Prayer had been forced to hand back
€250,000 to three donors in August the previous year.
This was after they took legal action following revelations
about Christina Gallagher's properties. The gardaí and
the Revenue Commissioners had also launched their
own investigations.

'Our investigations were of high public interest
and were followed up by numerous national and local
media outlets,' said the paper. 'We endeavoured at all
times to get answers from the two central figures who
run the House of Prayer, Christina Gallagher and her
spiritual director Fr Gerard McGinnity, about how the
huge amount of donations were being spent. But they
have consistently refused to speak. We even travelled
to Ohio in the United States to talk to the House of
Prayer's main American fundraiser, John Rooney.
But he, too, refused to explain why donors were asked
to sign cheques of up to €50,000 to his name and why
he owned Gallagher's mansion. We revealed how the
Church in the US and other countries had issued public
warnings about the House of Prayer.'

The newspaper's reply to the Ombudsman said that, significantly, Majella Meade made no complaints about any of the financial revelations above, and they had never been challenged by the House of Prayer. It was the organisation's own volunteers who first raised doubts about the religious centre's accounts early in 2007. This was because Gallagher owned an extensive house in Newport, and had bought properties for her family, despite having no income. These supporters felt a luxury home was an unusual possession for a visionary devoted to spiritual matters, or of a woman who had consistently claimed, for two decades, that she had no interest in material things.

The newspaper pointed out that one of these sources was Mike McCrory, who had devoted four years of his life to the House of Prayer. He and his wife had even left their home in the US to live next to it. The basic question that McCrory and other former devotees had raised had never been addressed by the House of Prayer: Just how did Christina Gallagher pay for her extraordinary lifestyle?

Instead supporters of the House of Prayer threw up numerous smokescreens and unsubstantiated allegations against the *Sunday World* and its reporters, including allegations of 'gutter journalism,' 'invasion of privacy,' 'untruths and lies'. To date there has not been a satisfactory explanation as to why money donated to the House of Prayer had been used to pay for fabulous homes for use by Christina Gallagher or why the House felt obliged to pay back €250,000 to former donors following our investigations.

'This crucial question has been at the centre of all our stories and is of enormous public interest, particularly as people from all over the country have donated to the House of Prayer,' the newspaper told the Ombudsman.

It had taken almost a full year for the first story to appear, after that initial meeting with disaffected former members. 'Nothing was ever printed until it could be proven and the newspaper carried out extensive inquiries into each and every allegation. Even today we are aware of several further serious claims, but they will not be printed until they can be independently and fairly confirmed.'

The newspaper explained that it decided to publish the first story, after discovering that Gallagher had bought a €1 million home for her daughter. It had also received a copy of an extraordinary letter written in 2003 by a House of Prayer fundraising priest in America, Fr Robert Burns of Omaha, saying that Christina Gallagher wanted cash only from now on and 'no checks'. The money was to be sent to her home address, so she could thank donors personally. This was a highly suspect method of fundraising, to say the least, but 'did not warrant a mention in Ms Meade's complaint'.

The *Sunday World* told the Ombudsman that attempts to get an interview with Gallagher at that time had been turned down. Days later, the newspaper was just as unsuccessful when it sent a reporter and photographer to the secret mansion in Malahide, which the newspaper had uncovered, and where Gallagher had lived for two years. An assistant claimed she had never heard of Gallagher, even though we had photographed them together days before. The point was that the House of Prayer had been given ample opportunity to give their side of the story, but always turned them down.

The Ombudsman was also told how the House of Prayer had lost its charitable status, two years earlier. Despite this, the House still illegally claimed on its website that it was a charity, and that funds were 'urgently needed'. The newspaper revealed that the

Archbishop of Tuam, Dr Michael Neary, had declared that the House of Prayer had no Church backing 'whatever'. Church authorities had banned Mass from being said there for the previous decade. 'These were all hard facts, not conjecture.'

In its written reply to Majella Meade's complaint, the newspaper also retold the story of Betty and Michael Morrissey. It mentioned how the couple had handed over a fortune to the House of Prayer, and ultimately believed they were just funding her opulent lifestyle. The couple claimed the centre was 'a cult' and that they were 'brainwashed'. These were words which Meade took offence to in her complaint. The Morrisseys subsequently sued the House of Prayer and got their €150,000 back. Another man, Paddy Woods, had the €100,000 that he donated returned to him. Majella Meade claimed supporters were never pressured into donating money. Why then did they have to hand back €250,000 last August?

'All of our stories have been substantiated by documents and by former supporters of the House of Prayer, some of whom had worked there for up to 13 years, or from their close relatives,' the Ombudsman was told. 'We carried Land Registry documents showing Gallagher's extensive property portfolio, even though her spiritual director Fr McGinnity claimed on live radio that she did not own any property. We published copies of the cheques which donors were asked to sign to Fr McGinnity and Mr Rooney after the priest claimed that they were 'fake'. And we carried copies of High Court papers relating to the Morrisseys' legal action against the House of Prayer after supporters were told one Saturday afternoon at the house that the writs were a "*Sunday World* hoax."'

At the heart of Majella Meade's complaint was the

fact that reporter Jim Gallagher did not ring her until March 2009, said the newspaper's response. But he was not writing about her. He was writing about Christina Gallagher, Fr Gerard McGinnity and John Rooney, and so it was they who he approached for comment, even travelling to Ohio to try to talk to Rooney. But none of the three would speak. The fact is that no matter how many times they are contacted, the House of Prayer leaders refuse to answer any questions.

'In light of the above the *Sunday World* strenuously denies any breach of the code.'

Replying to specific allegations, the *Sunday World* said that Majella Meade may well organise fundraising meetings, but everything she did was under the auspices of Christina Gallagher and Fr McGinnity. The self-proclaimed visionary had complete control over the House of Prayer. So it was 'fanciful' to suggest that she was not responsible for its fundraising activities. Her name and her pronouncements were regularly invoked when House of Prayer fundraisers were seeking funds, as was evidenced by the American fundraising letter obtained by the *Sunday World*.

Meade had complained of words and phrases like 'elderly', 'gullible', 'touched' and 'simple minded' being used in *Sunday World* articles about the House of Prayer followers. The newspaper said these terms were often used by former followers themselves, or the families of victims, and were often in quotations marks. It was a simple fact that many were elderly.

Meade complained that a report in the *Sunday World* which stated that Gallagher was claiming she was going to be 'assumed' into heaven was 'ridiculous' and 'laughable'. But Gallagher did make the claim, and so did her chief followers, Fr McGinnity and an ex-nun Sister Treasa, and the newspaper had witnesses. The paper asked: 'Is it any more ridiculous than [Meade's] claims to *Ireland's Eye* that she personally organised fundraising for a €4 million mansion in Malahide for Mrs Gallagher on the instructions of the Virgin Mary?'

Meade had told the Ombudsman that Betty and Michael Morrissey's version of the high-pressure meeting in Multyfarnham was 'totally incorrect'. This is where they were ultimately persuaded to write a cheque to John Rooney for €50,000. Meade said that the *Sunday World* version of that story was 'sensational tripe'. If it was inaccurate, then why were they forced to hand back a total of €150,000 to the Morrisseys in August 2008? Majella Meade was not, as she maintains, the 'only person who ever interacted' with the couple. They signed cheques at Fr McGinnity's request to his own name, one for €40,000, as proven by the documentary evidence.

Meade even hinted in her complaint that the Morrisseys might not have complained at all. She wrote: 'The *Sunday World* has published several times a distorted and untrue article, concerning a couple who have allegedly complained about Fr McGinnity and Christina Gallagher having "taken" money from them. Such claims are totally incorrect.' Meade's comment begs the question: what was 'alleged' about the Morrisseys' complaint? The couple went public in the newspaper with their story. Michael was even photographed, and the couple made a formal complaint to gardaí in Co. Mayo about being defrauded. It is intriguing that Majella Meade was questioning whether they had complained at all – six months after her organisation gave the couple their money back.

Meade had also denied in her complaint to the Ombudsman that Christina Gallagher had ever asked people directly for money, a claim that the newspaper now refuted. She had also taken issue with the use of such terms such as 'money-making scam' and 'cash racket'. But the newspaper said nobody at the House of Prayer had ever been prepared to explain their dubious fundraising techniques. Former members themselves called it a racket. A garda investigation into these allegations only ceased when money was repaid to those who had made an official complaint.

Majella Meade had also denied that anyone was ever pressured to sell their homes and give the money to the House of Prayer. In its reply, the *Sunday World* said that several people who had worked in the House of Prayer confirmed that the opposite was true. Michael McCrory heard several volunteers at the House of Prayer being told just that. And one woman told us of how she was sacked after years of service, when Fr McGinnity and Mrs Gallagher discovered she owned a house on the island.

Similarly, Meade had claimed that warnings of eternal damnation were never used 'as a means to solicit donations'. The Morrisseys and many others begged to differ. The threat of apocalyptic messages was also well documented on the House of Prayer's own website. The website included a message that threatened that much of the state of Texas would be devastated, unless money was raised to complete the House of Prayer there.

Meade had taken offence at the newspaper's use of the world 'cult', and said that she and other followers of the House of Prayer had been presented as 'subversives or criminals'. The newspaper denied suggesting any such thing. It defended its use of the word cult, pointing out that well-known Irish cult expert, Mike Garde, had called the House of Prayer a cult for many years. Relatives of people caught up in the House of Prayer used the same term, as did many former members.

With reference to a complaint that the newspaper had

invaded people's privacy, it replied that it had never questioned people's rights to pray. 'Our stories focused on the dubious fundraising tactics of the House of Prayer and Gallagher's millionaire lifestyle.' It also denied claims of incitement to hatred, insisting that it was following a legitimate inquiry of great public importance.

Majella Meade's complaint and the *Sunday World's* response was later referred by the Ombudsman to the Press Council for adjudication. But before they had time to even look at it, another two complaints were made to the Press Ombudsman, first by Dick Hogan and then by Majella Meade again.

These complaints carried the same arguments as before, but with particular reference to separate articles. Dick Hogan took offence to an article on 1 February 2009 in which the *Sunday World* revealed that the complete board of directors at the House of Prayer had resigned and been replaced, a fact proved with records from the CRO.

Much of Hogan's letter of complaint was irrelevant to the principles in the Press Council's Code of Practice. It rambled on about the newspaper breaching Principle 1, Truth and Accuracy, and Principle 2, Distinguishing Fact and Comment, but did not explain why, other than to vaguely refer to the story as 'one-sided'.

He also complained that the story gave the misleading impression that he had resigned 'hurridly' [sic] or 'in haste', and yet these words, which Hogan attributed to the article, were never used. The newspaper said, in its response, that the facts used in the article were taken from official records. These records were 'reported truthfully and accurately', and there was therefore no breach of the Code of Practice. Hogan also took umbrage at being called a 'right wing Catholic' in the article.

Like Majella Meade, he also complained of the newspaper's use of the words 'cult' and 'money-making scam', but once again it was explained that these were the words of former followers who had turned against the House of Prayer and who were expressing their opinion in the article in question.

Hogan's complaint then got more bizarre, as he lashed out at the _Sunday World_ by claiming that the phrase in the article that the directors had 'handed in their resignations' allowed only one interpretation. It did. It meant they had resigned. And they had! The newspaper replied: 'Mr Hogan either does not understand the code, or this is a vexatious complaint aimed to deter the _Sunday World_ from further investigations and to consume considerable time and resources.'

Hogan asked why the paper had called Annette Casey, the new company secretary and director, 'Casey'. It replied: 'It is her name and again is irrelevant to any alleged breach of the code.' Similarly, Hogan asked why the article had carried the ages of the new directors. The newspaper replied that it was common practice to carry people's ages in news stories, which 'one might have expected a newspaper editor like Mr Hogan to know'. It added: 'This also illustrates the bizarre and vexatious nature of this complaint.' Hogan also wanted to know why the newspaper had called the incoming board of directors 'little-known Gallagher supporters?' The answer was: 'Because that is what they are.' They were not high-profile supporters, like Mr Hogan.

The _Sunday World_ also dismissed Hogan's claim that reporting that a board of directors of a company had resigned was in some way an invasion of privacy. The story was based on public records, and was a matter of clear public interest. Likewise, the paper denied that it was an incitement to hatred, as Hogan claimed, or that calling him a millionaire constituted an invitation to rob his home.

The newspaper had a hard-hitting conclusion in its reply to Dick Hogan: 'The *Sunday World* rejects any allegations of a breach of the code of practice in relation to the article of February 1. Furthermore it is our belief that in the course of a rambling eight-page letter there is insufficient evidence of any such breach to have even warranted this complaint being considered by the Ombudsman's office. As we have made clear, the complaint frequently refers to things that never appeared in the article under review, in a bid to prove breaches of the code of practice. It is clear that followers of the House of Prayer are intent on tying up the resources of the *Sunday World* with vexatious complaints in a bid to deter further investigation, and are deliberately misusing the office of the Ombudsman to achieve this in a manner that is likely to call the entire press complaints procedure into disrepute.'

But this was not the end of the matter. The Ombudsman's office soon informed the *Sunday World* that it had received another complaint, again from Majella Meade. This time the complaint was about an article on 15 March 2009. The letter was dated 26 April, but was not received by the Ombudsman until 29 May. The article in question, 'Still Praying on the Elderly', said that Christina Gallagher was still 'conning gullible elderly Catholics out of their cash'. It recounted how she had told followers that the Virgin Mary had guided her to the house in Malahide, and that the House of prayer was still desperately in need of funds. The story also revealed how the House of Prayer was hitting back at the newspaper through the pages of *Ireland's Eye*.

Majella Meade's letter to the Ombudsman contained a whopping 57 complaints about the article.

But the Ombudsman immediately dismissed 51 of them, claiming that they did not provide 'prima facie evidence' of a breach of the Code of Practice. In the circumstances, only six of the complaints warranted a reply from the newspaper.

The *Sunday World* subsequently defended its story, claiming it was true and accurate.

At the same time as bombarding the *Sunday World* with press council complaints and of denouncing the newspaper in *Ireland's Eye*, the House of Prayer also set up a new website in which it blasted all media outlets that had dared to criticise it. As well as haranguing me, it took pot-shots at *The Irish Catholic* newspaper, and ridiculed a variety of other journalists, including one who inadvertently got Fr McGinnity's first name wrong. The House of Prayer was clearly doing its best to put journalists off writing about it.

The first reply to the series of House of Prayer complaints to the Press Ombudsman came in July 2009, when the *Sunday World* was informed that Dick Hogan's complaint had been rejected.

In a letter to the newspaper dated 6 July, the Press Ombudsman, Professor John Horgan, said that he had decided not to uphold a number of complaints about the 1 February article. He said: 'The information contained in the article supports the newspaper's contention that its investigation was in the public interest, and material in the article was appropriately sourced either to documents in the public domain (for instance the Companies Registration Office) or attributed to specified sources.'

Although the complainant objected to some of the statements, Professor Horgan said, 'The freedom of newspapers to publish such matter is protected under the Code of Practice as long as their attribution to a source is clear.' He said the statements under complaint were not, therefore, in breach of Principles 1 or 2 of the Code of Practice.

'There is no evidence to suggest that the newspaper knowingly published matter based on malicious misrepresentation or unfounded accusations. Its attempt to contact the complainant supported its contention that it took reasonable care in checking facts before publication. The complaint under Principle 4 is therefore not upheld.'

The Ombudsman ruled that there was no invasion of privacy, because what the complainant referred to as his private affairs were in fact: 'public affairs as documented in the Companies Registration Office'. A breach of Principle 5 could not, therefore, be upheld.

Similarly, there was no incitement to hatred. 'Although the complainant provides evidence of a feeling of vulnerability because of the publicity that has accrued as a result of the publication of the article concerned, this falls far short of the evidence required to prove that a breach of Principle 8 has occurred.'

Finally, the Ombudsman ruled: 'The complainant's belief that the article generally cast him in a poor light was not supported by sufficient evidence to enable the Ombudsman to conclude that this amounted to a breach of any of the Principles of the Code of Practice cited by him.'

Just two days later, the Press Council announced that it had dismissed Majella Meade's first complaint about four separate *Sunday World* articles, after the matter had been referred to it by the Press Ombudsman. In a letter dated 8 July, the Council said it had discussed the complaint, at its meeting on 3 July, and decided not to uphold it.

'There was no evidence that the newspaper did not strive for truth and accuracy in the articles under complaint. In addition, there was no concrete evidence that the articles contained any significant inaccuracy, misleading statement or distorted report. In the circumstances, the complaint under Principle 1 was not upheld.'

The comments complained of were also always attributed to named or unnamed sources and 'their attribution was clear,' so there was no breach of Principle 2 (Distinguishing Fact and Comment).

The Press Council noted that the *Sunday World* had made 'significant efforts' to contact the people mentioned in the articles for comment. 'The fact that Ms Meade, who had not been mentioned in the articles, was not approached did not, in the Council's views, constitute a breach of Principle 3.' (Fairness and Honesty).

In relation to Principle 4 (Respect for Rights), the Press Council found no breach of the Code, since the published material was not based on 'malicious misrepresentation or unfounded accusations', and that reasonable care had been taken by the newspaper to check facts.

Rules of privacy had not been broken, and the articles were in the public interest, so there was no breach of Principle 5. The complainant had not put forward any legitimate grounds for her complaint under Principle 6, which states that journalists will protect confidential sources, so that was not upheld.

Finally, the Press Council threw out Meade's complaint that the articles were an incitement to hatred, which would have been a breach of Principle 8.

The Press Ombudsman subsequently threw out Meade's second complaint without referring it to the press council.

CHAPTER FIFTEEN

Immaculate Deception

*'The birth-pangs are over. The world is handed over to the
Antichrist. Civil war will break out in the United States,
and many will fight and kill each other. "Nests"
of foreigners have already been placed in the U.S.'*

Christina Gallagher might have thought that her
supporters' complaints to the Press Council had
silenced the *Sunday World*. Indeed, she was so confident
that they had done just that – there were, after all, no
new stories about her for three solid months – that she
began telling her loyal followers that she had stopped
the press once and for all. Our Lady even told her the
campaign of vilification was over, she said.

How wrong Christina was. On 5 July 2009 the
Sunday World revealed that Gallagher's US operation
had brought in nearly $3 million in the last year. This
interesting figure came from an official US charity
website. At the same time the US arm of the House of
Prayer had assets listed at $6.7 million, compared to less
than $1 million, just two years previously. Much of this
cash was believed to have been raised by Irish donors.

The full figures filed by the Confraternity of Our Lady
Queen of Peace in the US were for 2007, and showed
annual income of $2,813,504. This was a rise of nearly
500 per cent on the $593,867 recorded for 2005. When
it came to assets, the Confraternity listed the value for
2007 at $6,704,392, a rise of more than 800 per cent on
the $814,287 it recorded two years earlier.

Despite seeing profits rocket into seven figures, Christina Gallagher's own website still urged people in Ireland and elsewhere to dig deep and give even more money to the House of Prayer's five sister houses across the US. The message said: 'Funds are urgently needed to complete the work on the existing Houses as well as for the upkeep and maintenance of Our Lady's chain of Houses.'

And yet when I visited all five Houses in Ohio, Minnesota, Kansas, Texas and Florida, the previous summer, the building work was all but complete. The newspaper story revealed that Gallagher had finally removed the 'charity status' claim for its Achill house from her website. The houses in the US, however, still retained their tax-exempt, not-for-profit status. It was unlikely that the US authorities were aware of the controversy surrounding the House of Prayer in Ireland and its dubious fundraising techniques.

The 5 July article said the latest findings would increase pressure on Christina Gallagher and her House of Prayer organisation to explain why they were still raising large amounts of money in Ireland, and why they were using terrifying messages to do so. One of Gallagher's most recent and chilling messages was specifically aimed at Americans. Posted on her website, it suggested that only those who attended her Houses of Prayer would be saved on the rapidly approaching judgement day. The message, dated 29 March 2009, said (the grammatical errors have been left in):

The birth-pangs are over. The world is handed over to the anti-Christ. Civil war will break out in the United States and many will fight and kill each other. "Nests" of foreigners have already been placed in the U.S. Christina was shown a scene of what will take place, the weapons being used and the blood flowing. The horror was overpowering for her.

Christina was then allowed to witness the explosion of a bomb which will be dropped on America. Its impact was horrific. She was shown that an earthquake will follow some time later. (She, herself believes that the earthquake will be a direct consequence of the bomb.) The events in the U.S. will also filter throughout Europe and then throughout the world. A great suppression will come about... Many, including Church authorities will go willingly in union with the anti-Christ. She was then shown the global Church descending into a great blackness and exuding misty vapour. This scene was surrounded by a multitude of angry demons wanting to get rid of the Church and Christianity. Christina was then shown Blessed Michael, clad in red and gold and holding his sword upright. Behind him could be seen Our Blessed Lady and a multitude of angels in red, in haste to do battle with the adversary. Pestilence will accompany the civil war and the suppression. Mosquitoes will carry all kinds of new diseases. Locusts such as have never been seen before will form a plague; it will seem as those themselves have an evil intent, almost as if they have an awareness that they are to wreak destruction. Christina understands that if people in the US wish to gain the graces of protection as invited by Our Blessed Lady, they should ...pray frequently in Her Chain Houses and upholding them – now, beforehand – as it will be too late for them when these events have begun to happen.

A week after this report, on 12 July, the *Sunday World* carried another story revealing how it had obtained remarkable video footage of Fr McGinnity directly asking followers to donate an incredible IR£250,000 to the House of Prayer.

It explained how Gallagher's top officials had been claiming all year that Fr McGinnity was not, and had never been, involved in fund-raising activities. The priest had even told his superior, Cardinal Seán Brady, that he was not involved in collecting money for the controversial prayer centre on Achill Island.

But the newspaper revealed it had discovered video footage of Fr McGinnity preaching from the pulpit and begging supporters to come up with IR£250,000 to build an extension to the House of Prayer, back in 1995. The priest falsely claimed that the extension was to allow more priests to come on retreat to the centre, as there was a severe shortage of beds.

'Facilities for the priests are so inadequate that sadly priests are coming to do their retreat, but often have to be directed to B&Bs locally,' Fr McGinnity told a packed church in Whitechurch, Co. Cork, where he was leading a prayer and fund-raising session. 'We have to appeal to you very directly that if we were to extend it the way we would like for the priests, it would take IR£250,000. But everything is possible for God. I place that before you tonight because I know Our Blessed Mother would desire it and I know you would wish to be generous.'

What Fr McGinnity did not tell the audience was why there was a shortage of beds. Maybe he didn't want to inform them that they were demolishing several cubicles, originally built for visiting priests, in order to build a luxury suite for Christina Gallagher and private rooms for Fr McGinnity.

And when the extension did finally go up in the new millennium, after many years of fundraising, it was nothing like devotees might have expected. Rather than building small humble rooms or cubicles for fasting priests, as donors might have expected, the money raised went into the most luxurious furnishings that money could buy. Stunning rooms with deep pile carpets, each with satellite TV and with Jacuzzis in the bathrooms, were then rented out at €120 a night to visiting Americans to raise yet more money.

Gallagher also got her own luxurious suite in the extension, which included expensive furniture and her own Jacuzzi. Few priests were going anywhere near the place by this stage. Two former loyal followers of Gallagher were so shocked when they were given a tour of the extension that they later quit, the *Sunday World* said in its 12 July report. One man said: 'I nearly died when I saw the extension because I knew the people of Ireland had paid for it. Fr McGinnity was always going on about television being the "tabernacle of Satan", a line he took from Padre Pio, and here were these satellite TVs in every room which could get porn channels. I just couldn't believe it. It was like a five-star hotel with the grand staircase and the chandeliers. I was flabbergasted by the amount of money that it must have cost.'

The man said he asked what priest could possibly afford to stay in such luxury and was told it was aimed at American visitors, who were coming in large numbers in tour buses. 'Christina does not want them to go to Knock,' the two men were told as they were given their tour. They were so appalled by the lies told to raise the money that they both began to pull away from the House of Prayer.

John Rooney, Gallagher's US money man, was among those who stayed in the fabulous extension. 'Fr McGinnity would always make a huge fuss over John Rooney whenever he was there. He and Christina would always grovel over people with money,' said one former follower. Rooney joked about himself being 'the moneybags' when he arrived in Achill and always got the best suite.

Gallagher's officials had claimed in their complaints to the Press Council that nobody had ever been put under pressure to hand over money or to sell their homes. But the former follower, who gave me the video of Fr McGinnity asking for IR£250,000, revealed how he had to stop two of his friends selling their home and business to give money to Christina Gallagher.

'She tells people that "Our Lady wants you in Achill" and my friends were going to sell their restaurant and bar and move there,' he said. 'I told them not to be stupid, that they had two children to rear and how could they make a life there. They are very thankful now that they listened to me.'

Another week went by, and then a third story appeared on 19 July, which carried extraordinary photographs of Christina Gallagher going into 'ecstasy'. The pictures were taken from rare video footage filmed inside the Achill chapel. Normally, cameras and video recorders are banned, but on this occasion the event was filmed. Her most influential and generous supporters had been specially invited, and she planned a day they would never forget. (It was the day she bent over backwards at an angle some thought was impossible.) The rare footage gave an insight into Gallagher's routine, which had 'hooked thousands of followers and helped Gallagher amass a fortune in donations,' said the newspaper. 'It is in these moments that she claims to receive messages direct from the Mother of God about the impending destruction of the world. Her states of ecstasy are frequently followed by appeals for more cash to extend her House of Prayer empire.'

The newspaper published the photographs on the same day that it reported on how it had travelled to

Achill in an unsuccessful attempt to get an interview with the press-shy religious leader on the House of Prayer's sixteenth anniversary, 16 July 2009.

Hundreds of people had gathered at the Co. Mayo House to see if Christina would get a message from Our Lady. But neither Christina nor Our Lady were in the mood to speak. Our presence caused a flurry of activity among security staff, who began whispering into their FBI-style headpieces and walkie-talkies, once we revealed ourselves.

I asked Noel Guinan, House of Prayer manager, if I could meet his revered leader, and was told there was 'no chance'. He said: 'You have tried to destroy this place.' I replied that I had simply asked Gallagher to explain her wealth. 'That is none of your business,' I was told. I insisted the public had every right to know what happened to the millions of euro they had donated to the House of Prayer since it opened in 1993. Why did she live in a mansion in Malahide?

'That's none of your business and that's all I'm saying,' said Guinan. I asked why she wouldn't just come out and talk to me, if she had nothing to hide. 'It's up to her who she speaks to. You are not welcome here, and I would like you to stand on the other side of that gate,' he said, pointing to the road at the main entry to the House of Prayer. Then, presumably referring to my chances of reaching the afterlife, he said: 'You will find out in the end who is right!'

Security staff also stopped me going into the House of Prayer, claiming it was full, though other people were allowed in afterwards. A man aged about 30, who refused to give his name, then came over and accused me and the *Sunday World* editors of being 'Freemasons' for attacking Gallagher.

He dismissed our stories about her wealth, and

said that he had been a non-believer until three years
ago. But he had since seen the sun 'spinning' over the
pilgrimage sites of Fatima, Lourdes, Medjugorje and
also Achill, and now he believed.

Gallagher often falsely accused her opponents of
being Freemasons. John Beighton, the English solicitor
who walked out of the House of Prayer never to return
in 1998, had been dubbed one of 'England's biggest
Freemasons, out to destroy the House of Prayer'.

Between 400-500 people turned up in Achill for the
anniversary, one of the biggest days of the year for the
centre. This figure was well down on the thousands
who arrived in previous years. An undercover *Sunday
World* reporter, Lauren Kansley, had gone into the
chapel earlier in the day to see if Gallagher would
deliver her annual message of death and destruction.
The journalist noted that 'Gallagher was treated as
every bit the celebrity she seems to think she is.'

She went on: 'The excitement that she may be there
in person was palpable inside the small prayer house.
When stewards with ear pieces lined the aisle, the
excitement reached fever pitch. But like the pro that she
is, Gallagher knows the value of anticipation, so she left
the crowd hanging on for a further 15 minutes before
she eventually emerged, dressed all in black, from
a door marked "private" at the back of the building.
Pensioners reached out to her but Gallagher swept
straight past to the altar.'

The reporter said that Fr Gerard McGinnity took to
the pulpit first and reminded the adoring crowd just
how honoured they were to be in Gallagher's presence.
'To all the pilgrims who have travelled here from all
over the world, we welcome you,' he said. 'Today we
will be lucky enough to have Christina lead us in the
rosary.'

For the next hour and a half Gallagher painstakingly recited the rosary, pausing at the appropriate moments for emphasis.

She didn't go into 'ecstasy' while our reporter was there. But the congregation, nonetheless, enjoyed the show. One man regularly kissed a picture of the Virgin Mary, and another old woman had her hands lifted up to the ceiling. Afterwards, the congregation poured out to make way for the next wave of pilgrims waiting their turn to come inside. Nobody seemed to mind that Christina hadn't gone into ecstasy. 'Hopefully our Lady will still come through with a special message,' one woman commented hopefully. 'Ah, but Christina was great anyway,' another woman replied.

The same day as Gallagher and her followers celebrated the anniversary, *The Irish Catholic* newspaper published a hard-hitting letter from 'a professional man' who had once been a big follower of the Mayo housewife, but who had now distanced himself completely and was calling for more clarity from Gallagher. The man supplied his name and address to the newspaper, but asked for it not to be published. In the letter, he exposed the lies that Gallagher had told him when he confronted her, the previous year, about her Malahide mansion and the properties she had bought.

He began by saying he had been associated with the House of Prayer since the late 1990s, when he used to bring an elderly relative. 'I was initially impressed at the eloquence and spirituality of Fr G McGinnity, but the final straw for me (as the message, purportedly from heaven, had become increasingly disturbing in recent times) was 16 July 2006, when Fr McGinnity read out a message as per Ms Christina Gallagher in which she stated that Our Lord threatened to destroy the State of Texas if a large sum of money was not paid within nine

months to complete one of her Houses of Prayer. This
to me was an insult to anybody's intelligence.'

The writer then jumped forward to January 2008,
when he said he rang Gallagher after being shown a
story about her in the *Sunday World*. 'I was astonished
when I read the article and saw the pictures of vast
houses and a BMW car. After all, I had often heard
this lady say she had no interest in material goods and
would gladly live in a tent. As I didn't know what to
believe, I spoke to her directly. She reacted angrily
and spoke disparagingly of a former devotee [Mike
McCrory] who she said had spoken to the press, told
lies about her and had libelled her and her family.'

Gallagher told the writer that she had been forced
to sell her Newport house, and that it had been bought
by House of Prayer devotees, as a shrine to herself, and
was to be called the Blue Ivory Trust.

'When I questioned her about her daughter's house
in Ballina, she stated this was purchased from the
proceeds of the sale of her Newport house and it was
her daughter's inheritance.

'On her €4 million Malahide mansion, she denied
any knowledge of this and said it was a fabrication by
the press. She said the only time she went to Dublin was
to visit a hospital for medical treatment and on those
occasions stayed with her sister. I asked, "does that
mean that you are homeless?" and she reacted angrily
again and stated she was happily married and living
with her husband in Knockmore, Co Mayo.'

The letter writer said that at the time he accepted
Gallagher's explanations, and asked what she was
going to do about the press reports. 'She said she was
heading for the High Court to sue for libel and character
assassination. I agreed this would be the correct course
of action.'

But as time went by, and the press reports became more shocking, he waited for Gallagher's legal proceedings to silence the press, but in vain. 'There was nothing,' he said. Then the broadsheet newspapers took up the story, asking questions about the House of Prayer's finances. The Church also spoke out and made its disapproval clear.

'I listened with dismay to Fr McGinnity's weak replies to Joe Duffy, denying any knowledge of Ms Gallagher's wealth. I watched in astonishment his disappearance behind a door on *Primetime*, refusing to be interviewed – he who could have brought clarity and truth in relation to what was now becoming a national scandal.

'I read with further dismay how Ms Gallagher settled vast amounts of money to her disgruntled elderly followers and even silenced them with a legal clause. What does this all speak of? Why the failure to speak out publicly and provide clarity if they have nothing to hide?'

The author of the letter said he was writing with great sadness, because there were many people who were hurt and bewildered by what had been uncovered. He asked where the transparency was in this 'sordid situation'.

'I know I will be relegated to the ranks of the Antichrist or an agent of the Devil for daring to criticise Christina and Fr McGinnity, but I challenge them to come forward now, and speak openly and provide clarity regarding the issues raised in this letter. If not, their silence speaks for itself.'

The letter would have been an unpleasant shock for the House of Prayer hierarchy because they knew *The Irish Catholic* was the one newspaper that most of its supporters would read. Readers might have been surprised to hear Gallagher denying all existence of the Malahide house, as she and her staff had been admitting all through 2009 – which they confirmed again in the press council complaints – that she did in fact live in the Malahide house. But of course they had put a spin on it by claiming the visionary was forced to flee there to take 'refuge' from the press, when in fact she moved into the house two years before the exposés began.

The letter may have been a surprise to the House of Prayer, but it was no surprise to me, as I had already interviewed the author in his home in the south of the country. I spent five hours listening to his astonishing story of how he was sucked into the House of Prayer and, in his own words, 'made an eejit of'. Unfortunately, as a professional man, he did not want his name used, as he thought it would lead to public ridicule.

But he told me how he had had been welcomed into the 'inner sanctum' of the House of Prayer from his very first visit in 1996, once Gallagher was made aware of his professional background. For the next ten years he was a regular visitor and a close confidante of Christina Gallagher, who would occasionally phone him for advice.

The man, whom we shall call Patrick, recalled every detail of that first visit on the House of Prayer's big anniversary day of 16 July 1996. He remembered being taken aback by the huge number of people there and the large queue of buses. He was also surprised by the length of Fr McGinnity's Mass, which at two and a half hours was 'the longest thing I ever went through'. But what really caught his attention was Fr McGinnity's jerking, stuttering and flailing movements during the consecration part of the service.

'I wondered what the hell was happening and got a terrible fright. I thought he had epilepsy. I asked an old lady next to me what was happening and she said, "Oh, he is a saint. He is undergoing the same thing as Padre Pio, the Passion." It was an extraordinary performance, very theatrical.'

Fr McGinnity then launched into one of his favourite topics, said Patrick, the evils of the Maastricht Treaty, which would help bring about a one-world government and a single global currency, leading to 'the mark of the beast and the Antichrist'.

'It was very entertaining – it was better than *The Omen*,' said Patrick, referring to the classic 1976 horror movie about the Antichrist. 'At the same time, it was very frightening and threatening stuff. There were terrible times ahead of us and terrible chastisement, and the people of Ireland were doomed like the rest of the world. It was very conservative stuff, almost critical of Vatican II, although it was done subtly.'

Fr McGinnity told the crowd that the Blessed Mother did not want her followers to receive Holy Communion in the hand, as had now become common practice, but in the mouth, as in the old days. 'He was a very eloquent and powerful speaker,' recalled Patrick. 'But I couldn't understand his convulsing.'

Patrick was later introduced to Christina Gallagher. His first impression of her was that she was a simple kind of woman. Years later he would have a completely different opinion of her: 'She is the greatest actress and would probably win an Academy Award for her ability to communicate. She went through the crowd that day like she was walking the red carpet, while Fr McGinnity was eulogising her. Christina was treated like a prima donna and thoroughly enjoyed that in front of the crowds. I was not discerning enough to see through it back then in 1996.'

Patrick said that he never really warmed to Fr McGinnity, who he found to be distant and very effeminate in his ways. 'You could never talk to him about football or hurling. He was always holier-than-thou, with his eyes nearly always raised to heaven.

It was strange; I had never met a priest like him, and I could not figure out if he was a saint or if it was put on. It was a puzzle at the time.

'People still think of Fr McGinnity as a walking saint, but he is another actor as well. He was very sour over the Ledwith affair, but other priests said his role was grossly exaggerated. People saw him as a very odd character, but he was very brilliant and had published two books before he was 30. He specialised in Marian theology and his doctorate was in it. He was one of the first priests in Ireland to go to Medjugorje and bring groups there.'

Patrick said there was a magnificent dining room in the House of Prayer, which is adorned with antique furniture. Fr McGinnity would sit in there on his own, and be served his dinner. He would hardly say a word to the staff, and they would almost bow to him. Only when he got on the altar did he become eloquent.

Patrick said one unforgettable memory he had from that first visit was of Gallagher's bodyguard, Tony Fitzpatrick, playing the guitar to her, as she sang along 'without a note in her head' in the House of Prayer kitchen. 'She liked country and western and she was smoking non-stop,' he recalled.

Over the following years Patrick kept returning to the House of Prayer, because his elderly relative was completely entranced by Gallagher. Once there, Patrick would wander off on his own and would call into the office to have a chat with the then manager, the late Martin Scally. Martin would tell him all sorts of interesting things that Christina had been up to. He told Patrick one day how Christina claimed she saw Jesus come through the office window and throw his arms around him. 'He was sceptical and he used to tell me these things tongue in cheek,' said Patrick.

Scally also told him how Gallagher used to build up Fr McGinnity by telling him that he was going to become the next Cardinal of Ireland, that he was going to be the head of the Church in Ireland. 'It was "my son Gerard" all the time,' said Patrick . 'This was great for Fr McGinnity's ego. He was a broken man and she was telling him he was destined for high things. As a priest once said, even when he was in Maynooth, if someone told McGinnity that Our Lady was appearing in the toilet, he'd be down there. He was absolutely, totally gullible.'

Patrick said Christina Gallagher saw Fr McGinnity's vulnerability and used it for her own ends. 'She was telling him Our Lady loved him so much and how he had suffered so much for the Church, and how he had been so maligned by his fellow priests and bishops. She was playing him.'

Patrick said he was at the House of Prayer in July 1998, when Gallagher suddenly announced its closure, following her battles with the local archdiocese. People were distraught and one woman, who was about to sell her home and move to the House of Prayer with her husband, was frantic, saying, 'I have to ring the bishop.'

'People were crying and weeping, but Fr McGinnity was chirpy and did not seem put out at all,' said Patrick. 'Then I heard Christina say to Fr McGinnity, "Take away the Blessed Sacrament." She told the crowd that the archbishop had ordered it, but he had not. The minute the Blessed Sacrament leaves the church, the building becomes private property, as God has gone out of the place.'

The House of Prayer was now closing, and Patrick recalls that he said his farewells and wished Gallagher good luck and thought that that was the end of it. He thought the whole House of Prayer experience was now over. But he could not have been more wrong.

Weeks later he was given the shocking news by one of
Gallagher's supporters that the visionary had suffered
a heart attack and was now recuperating. 'I rang her
daughter and asked which hospital she was in, but the
daughter would not tell me and was evasive. She didn't
seem to know anything about it.'

Patrick was horrified to learn years later that
Gallagher never suffered a heart attack. This was
used as a smoke screen, so that she could get away
for a while. This is the time she spent in Devon with
Chalky White and Esther. Instead of lying in a sickbed,
Gallagher was out drinking double Baileys every night,
having the time of her life in the English seaside town
of Paignton.

It was years later, too, that Patrick discovered
what happened between Gallagher and the woman
making the frantic phone calls the night the House of
Prayer closed. The devout Catholic discovered that the
Archbishop had not ordered the Blessed Sacrament to
be removed, nor the House of Prayer to be closed down,
as Gallagher had told the crowd.

'She confronted Christina. They had a big row and
Christina told her to f**k off. The woman and her
husband were her most devoted followers. They were
shocked, because she had thought Christina was God
Almighty. They left and never came back and I did not
understand why. I only contacted them last year and
she told me exactly what happened that day.'

Patrick said it was only later that he realised why
Gallagher and McGinnity were so cheerful that day.
The fact was, the House of Prayer was now going to be
their own private concern, and they would never again
have to answer to the Church or the local archdiocese.
'It was going to be their private club. It was separate
from the Church now.'

Meanwhile, the House of Prayer did not remain closed for long. 'In 1999 we heard it was reopening and on 16 July we were back,' said Patrick. And Christina Gallagher had a very special day lined up for her fans. This was the day she went into ecstasy and a 'host' mysteriously appeared on her tongue.

'There were thousands of people there,' said Patrick. 'There was supposed to be a very special promise from Our Lady.'

Patrick said that Fr McGinnity seemed to have known in advance what was happening to Christina. He told the crowds that when she opened her mouth the Archangel Michael had appeared to her, and given her Holy Communion.

Patrick said that during the ecstasy Gallagher started 'moaning and groaning', and the whole thing went on for about 12 minutes. 'I certainly believe it was a gimmick now. But on that particular day I thought something unusual and extraordinary was happening, because of the backward position she held.' He said that one minute the 'host' did not appear to be there and the next it was. But there was something peculiar about it. He mentioned it to Gallagher later, and she immediately asked: 'Was there a gimp in it?'

'I did not take much notice at the time, but it wasn't a perfectly shaped host. There was a slight twist on it. It was not a perfect circle. It was as if there was a small piece missing off it. And she said it to me afterwards – and it has stayed in my mind ever since. She must have realised what she was pulling off was not totally perfect. I think now it was a bit of something she stuck at the top of her mouth and dropped it down onto her tongue, although that is only my opinion. It certainly was not the angel from heaven. It didn't stay on her tongue for long, as she swallowed it very fast.' He said it could not have been a normal communion host, as it would have melted in her mouth.

The Virgin Mary supposedly gave Gallagher a very special message during this ecstasy, that of the famous seal. 'It came out of the Book of Revelations. The seal is the protection guaranteed in the book of John which will protect everyone from the Antichrist. It will protect people from taking the mark of the beast,' said Patrick.

Patrick said that this was one of Gallagher's greatest ever money-making gimmicks. She claimed that Our Lady had appeared to her in gleaming light and told her she was going to grant the seal to everyone who was present there that day. They would all be protected from this mark of the beast which Fr McGinnity explained as the microchip that was going to be inserted into people's hands, when one world government was imposed on the planet.

'It was extraordinary stuff, great entertainment!' said Patrick. 'Our Lady said, it seems, that there were certain people present there that day who did not deserve the seal, but Christina was supposed to have pleaded with Our Lady, and this is where she went into the moaning and groaning. She was supposed to have suffered greatly over the seal, and Our Lady smiled at her and said, yes, she had given the seal to everyone. Half the men had gone down to the pub, as their wives had dragged them there, and those who were in the pub got the seal that day too. It was the biggest gimmick of all time!'

Our Lady had supposedly claimed that the seal would go on for two years, and the only place to get it was the House of Prayer. She urged people to travel from all over the world to the prayer centre in Achill. 'It became the biggest money-spinner of all time,' said Patrick. 'It ran from 1999 to 2001 and people came in their droves from all over the place.'

One thing that annoyed Patrick about the Saturday afternoon prayer sessions was that Fr McGinnity would regularly go on about the countless healings and miracles that were supposed to have taken place in the House of Prayer. Half the stories made Patrick laugh, as until then he had never seen a shred of evidence.

'The water out in the fountain in the front was supposed to have been delivered by the angels in heaven, according to Fr McGinnity. But I now know Tony Fitzpatrick used to fill a canister from a tap at the back of the House and fill it up, and this was the water that was supposed to be curing people,' said Patrick. 'Fr McGinnity was talking about people dipping their hands into the water and getting cured of warts and silly nonsense like this. Their piles were being cured and this kind of rubbish.'

Patrick said the House of Prayer used to make money from this too, as people had to buy special plastic bottles inside the shop with *Our Lady Queen of Peace* written on them. 'According to Fr McGinnity, the water was blessed from heaven, and there were special privileges and gifts granted and healings through the holy water. It was a tap! Tony Fitzpatrick used to fill it up with a watering can every time the crowds were coming. And they would all drink the water and would be dipping their heads in it.'

The family of an American man, 21-year-old Jed Michael, claimed he was cured of a rare blood clotting disorder and speech impediment by Christina Gallagher. When his father was talking to Patrick on the phone, the American told him: 'She must be the greatest saint of all time. We are going to give her $800,000 in thanksgiving.'

Patrick said he rang Gallagher to give her the good news. But if he was expecting to hear gratitude, he was disappointed. 'She very sourly answered me and said "$800,000! They are worth $10 million. They could easily give me a couple of million. After all, I cured him. They own the biggest jewellery business in New York."'

Patrick said that he was so in with Gallagher and McGinnity, that they once came to his home as a reward – and as an incentive for some work they wanted him to do for them. 'We had Mass in this room, and Christina went into a trance,' said Patrick. 'She was kneeling by the couch and threw her hands back and was looking up at the ceiling, and just at the gold curtains there she said Our Lady appeared to her. There were angels apparently flying all over the room.'

Fr McGinnity later read out a message that Gallagher supposedly received from the Virgin Mary just for Patrick. 'Our Lady was holding baby Jesus in her arms and she was smiling down at me at this end of the room,' said Patrick. 'Her face lit up completely in front of me. She told Christina it seems that God the Father had chosen me to give glory to her son Jesus.' Today, of course, Patrick doesn't believe a word of it.

Soon after this house visit, Patrick received a phone call from Fr McGinnity telling him that a meeting with Archbishop Seán Brady – now Cardinal Brady – had been arranged to try to promote Christina in the eyes of the Primate of All Ireland. The priest wanted Patrick to go to help the cause, but Patrick was less than enthusiastic. The meeting was in the middle of the week and he was extremely busy. 'But it's for Our Lady, I have it all set up and the flights are booked,' insisted Fr McGinnity.

Patrick duly flew to Dublin, and was driven to Fr McGinnity's home in Knockbridge by the priest's sister. Fr McGinnity was very excited. 'He said Mass that day, and did not go through any of the histrionics he would normally go through. It was a straight forward Mass. He was in a hurry obviously and he did not go though any jerking.'

They met Archbishop Brady at 3pm that day in 2001. 'I could see he was very close to Fr McGinnity, and it was all "Gerry" and "Seán".' Patrick remembered that Fr McGinnity told the Archbishop a 'pack of lies' that day, exaggerating everything to do with Christina Gallagher. 'I said on the way home, "Father, those were lies you were telling the Archbishop," and he turned to me and said: "We have to bend the truth a little for Christina's sake."'

Gallagher was on the phone continually to Fr McGinnity as they drove back to Co. Louth, desperately wanting to know everything that happened at the meeting. She was not happy when she heard that Archbishop Brady ended the meeting by saying that all decisions on Christina Gallagher's authenticity as a visionary would ultimately have to be made by the head of her own diocese, Archbishop Neary of Tuam. She lost her temper declaring: 'That bastard Neary!'

Patrick was aware that Gallagher had in the past claimed that Neary and all the bishops who criticised her were 'under the influence of Satan'. This was a fact that was told to Cardinal Brady by former followers of the House of Prayer in the secret meeting held in May 2008. But still the Cardinal did nothing to stop his priest, Fr McGinnity, associating with her.

Six months after his and Fr McGinnity's meeting with Archbishop Brady, Patrick attended a meeting with the Papal Nuncio, Giuseppe Lazzarotto. This meeting was set up by former Justice Minister, Seán Doherty, who had become one of Christina Gallagher's followers. Seán Doherty died of a brain haemorrhage, aged 60, in June 2005. 'Every time Seán went to the House of Prayer,

Christina would bring him to the main sitting room and give him the best couch, and would be chatting away. But Seán was afraid of his life at coming forward and proclaiming anything about Christina.'

Patrick visited the Papal Nuncio in Dublin with Seán Doherty, Fr McGinnity and the House of Prayer lawyer, Donal Corrigan. 'McGinnity introduced Corrigan as a leading barrister – when he is only a small-time solicitor. He introduced Seán Doherty as a senior member of the government – when he was only a backbencher at the time. The Papal Nuncio thought he was in the presence of extraordinarily high company.'

Fr McGinnity wanted Christina Gallagher to be proclaimed the greatest mystic in the Church, and for her case to be sent straight to the Vatican, said Patrick. But again the priest was disappointed when the Papal Nuncio said the same thing as Archbishop Brady, that any decision on Gallagher's authenticity would have to go back to Archbishop Neary.

In the meantime, one of Patrick's House of Prayer friends had invited Gallagher and McGinnity to Co. Clare, saying a lot of sick people were keen to meet them. The duo agreed to come to a prayer meeting to be held in the Clare Inn, outside Ennis. Later Tony Fitzpatrick rang to say they would be collecting money at the door. Patrick's friend, who was organising the event, said that would not be appropriate. The prayer meeting had to be cancelled after the organiser was told there was no way Gallagher would travel down if there was no collection box. 'It was as blunt as that,' said Patrick.

When Patrick eventually saw the extension to the House of Prayer, he was overwhelmed. 'I was flabbergasted at the money the extension must have cost. I said if the media sees this, she is finished. No priest could afford that kind of money to stay there.

It was not for the priests at all. I rang McGinnity that night and said: "Father, I have just seen the extension and I have never seen anything so luxurious." He tried to tell me he had never seen it himself, and him up there every Saturday preaching. That was his first excuse.

'I said it was the most luxurious thing I had ever seen and according to [Our Lady's] message it was supposed to be a hermitage for priests. I said, "I thought it would be simple cells, but do you realise there are satellite TVs in there?" It was beyond anything I had seen even in the big hotels. I said: "If the press sees this… I am only ringing you out of concern." He said: "Oh, Christina loves to do everything beautiful for Our Lady."'

The following night Gallagher came on the phone herself and stormed: 'How dare you, you f**ker! How dare you criticise my extension to Fr McGinnity!'

Patrick said it was the first time he had heard her use this type of language, although he had been told she was capable of expletives. He said she tore into him. 'How dare you! It was Our Lord's work and I was criticising Our Lord's work!' She rang back a couple of days later and apologised for losing her cool. 'She was afraid of losing me.'

Her tantrums were not the behaviour normally associated with religious icons. But they were not the only giveaway that Gallagher was not all that she seemed. Patrick, like many other former followers, is convinced Gallagher had plastic surgery in the time he knew her, because of her changing appearance.

Patrick said he had noted marked changes in her face between 1999-2000. She was also sporting a new blonde look. 'She looked years younger. Her face was transformed. I thought… what has she done?'

There were other signs that Patrick should have picked up on. 'Christina would come out and throw her arms around me like a big heap, and I would be suffocated by the smell of perfume. She was also a total hypochondriac when I knew her. She was even going around in a wheelchair for a while.'

Patrick looks back on many of the schemes run by the House of Prayer as nothing but money-making exercises. He heard that the windows appeal raised an astonishing €1.5 million. 'The fundraising was so clever. People thought they were getting their own private window in the House of Prayer, and yet there were only five windows in the chapel. She said Our Lady wanted the decades of the rosary portrayed in the windows. But they were grand windows before.' He said the new ones probably only cost about €60,000, which left an enormous profit.

Similarly, huge amounts of money were made from an appeal to build a chain of sister Houses of Prayer across Ireland, but the promised centres in Ulster, Munster and Leinster never materialised. 'She was travelling around counties collecting money. Then she gave the excuse, after collecting all the money, that she would not get planning permission, and she started this craic about the chain Houses in the US.'

Patrick said he was invited to one such fundraising meeting in Cashel, Co. Tipperary, in 2004. It was attended by Gallagher, Noel Guinan and Tony Fitzpatrick. 'They were looking for donations and they collected $800,000 that night. Cheque books were being pulled out all over place.' Patrick said the man who organised the meeting had a lot of wealthy friends.

Patrick recalls that he was treated 'like dirt' by Josie Butler, because he arrived late, but Christina was 'hugging and kissing' him. 'They made a fortune that night for a House of Prayer that was supposed to be in Cashel.'

Patrick said Christina Gallagher also had another source of income – people leaving her money in their wills. 'Lots of people who are dead gave her piles of money, because they preyed on nursing homes. She used to send her people round nursing homes talking to old people and collecting money.'

Patrick finally stopped going to the House of Prayer, two years before the scandal over Gallagher's wealth broke. When the *Sunday World* exposés began he rang Gallagher and she stormed: 'That bastard McCrory!' She then said: 'I have nothing, nothing.' Gallagher told him not to speak to anyone. She rang back five minutes later and said: 'If anyone contacts you, tell them there is going to be High Court action.'

Patrick later rang John Rooney and got even more expletives: 'Get off my f**king phone! How dare you ring me?'

Today, looking back over his long association with the House of Prayer, Patrick says the thing that perhaps appals him most was the threats Fr McGinnity used to make to those who the priest claimed did not show enough gratitude to Christina Gallagher at being 'cured' at Achill. 'Fr McGinnity used to do this on a regular basis. I remember being disgusted about McGinnity going on about a woman who was cured of cancer because of Christina and never came back to give thanksgiving and God punished her. The cancer came back and she died. He said it in public. I nearly fell off the chair. There was no compassion.'

Patrick believes that many of Gallagher's predictions simply came from information she gleaned from the TV, particularly when it came to natural disasters. He was told that she was 'forever glued' to CNN and other news and documentary channels at night. She would give her 'predictions' to Fr McGinnity and 'he was so stupid he would write it all down.' Patrick said: 'It's hard to know how much he went along with her. I don't think he is a holy man at all. It was all contrived. He got me to tell lies.'

Patrick said he finally pulled away from the House of Prayer after the ridiculous warning about Texas being destroyed. Today he says: 'I will not rest until I see the doors closed on that place after what I experienced there.'

Epilogue

So what now of the future? Christina Gallagher continues to operate her House of Prayer empire, albeit with far fewer devotees than before. It seems that of those who still follow her, nothing will shake their conviction. They believe Gallagher's claims that everything written about her over the past two years was lies and inventions by the media, despite overwhelming evidence to the contrary. Not once has Gallagher publicly discussed her fabulous homes or her luxurious and opulent lifestyle. Instead, she simply gets her devoted followers to deny everything. If she really had nothing to hide she would have come out long ago with some kind of explanation for her astonishing rags to riches story.

But sadly, there are vulnerable, gullible people out there who will believe anything. We were reminded of that again earlier this year, when people were photographed kissing and praying over a tree stump, because someone said it looked like the Virgin Mary. Two thousand people signed a petition to save the tree stump at the Holy Mary Parish Church, Rathkeale, Co. Limerick, in July. The local priest, Fr Willie Russell, went on radio to say, 'It's just a tree... You can't worship a tree!' But his appeal fell on deaf ears.

As for the Church, it seems it won't change its stance in the immediate future. Archbishop Neary has told former followers that he is powerless to do more, because the House of Prayer is a completely private concern. It is known that he has grown increasingly frustrated at Cardinal Brady's failure to act. But the cardinal, for his part, has done little to stop his own priest, Fr McGinnity, from leaving their diocese most Saturdays to travel to Achill. According to one report, the cardinal did ask Fr McGinnity if he banned him from going to the House of Prayer, would he stop? The priest said he would not.

Meanwhile, Gallagher's former followers are growing in number. People like the Morrisseys, the McCrorys, Anthony Tierney, Christine Adler, Esther, Patrick, Neil, George and Jenny, and many others would like to see priests regularly condemning the House of Prayer from their pulpits. They believe this is the only way to stop people travelling to Achill from their parishes.

Betty Morrissey says today that her visit to Cardinal Brady in May 2008 was the biggest 'waste of time ever' because, as far as she is concerned, nothing whatsoever was accomplished. Similarly, her heartfelt letter, written later that year, urging the Cardinal to act, was just as unsuccessful. 'Our Lady and Our Lord, as per Father McGinnity, were presented to us as threatening, wrathful, vengeful money-hungry deities who are out to seek revenge on us and the whole world if we don't obey the messages,' she told the cardinal. Surely he had to act against such heresies, she said.

The battling pensioner told the cardinal how they were encouraged to vote against the Maastricht Treaty and the Lisbon Treaty, as these were 'Satan's attempt to rule the world'. Such interference by a parish priest in the day to day political concerns of a nation should have drawn some kind of reprimand from his superiors. But they didn't. Even when Betty explained how Fr McGinnity discouraged pilgrims, especially visiting Americans, from visiting recognised shrines, like

Knock, Croagh Patrick and Ballintubber Abbey, there was no action taken by the Church.

Betty also drew attention to Fr McGinnity's sense of self-importance and complete lack of humility. She revealed how he told devotees that his epileptic-type seizures during Mass were 'a gift by God usually reserved for the great saints called "darts of love by the Holy Spirit"'. One monk Betty quoted said: 'That man is full of sanctified pride. Does he consider himself a martyr and saint of the Church already, not having even passed to the next world yet?' But did Cardinal Brady act to reign in his out-of-control priest? The answer was a deafening 'no'.

Unfortunately, no other authorities, such as the Revenue Commissioners, have taken action against the House of Prayer, as yet. Of their long drawn out investigation, a spokesman would only say he could not comment on individual cases. The government, in fact, rather than cracking down on such a questionable, money-making organisation, seemed intent on giving it a helping hand. Many people were angered, early in 2009, when Dermot Ahern, the Minister for Justice, announced that he planned to bring in a new law of blasphemous libel. This would be part of the new Defamation Bill, which is due to go into effect in October 2009. The media and supporters of free speech attacked the move, arguing that cults like the Church of Scientology and others would try to use the new law to silence critics.

Mike Garde, who heads an Irish cult monitoring organisation called Dialogue Ireland, and who has battled the House of Prayer for years, said the new bill would threaten the work of anti-cult campaigners. He said: 'They've tried to prosecute us on the incitement to hatred law before, so I have no doubt that they would seek to use this new law on blasphemous libel.'

The House of Prayer has already used a typical Scientologist tactic to try to stop the *Sunday World*, with its complaints to the Press Council about the newspaper's alleged 'incitement to hatred'. The ridiculous charge was thrown out.

At the moment, there is no crime of blasphemy on the statute books, though it is prohibited by the Constitution. Article 40 of the Constitution, guaranteeing freedom of speech, qualifies it by stating: 'The State shall endeavour to ensure that organs of public opinion, such as the radio, the press, the cinema, while preserving their rightful liberty of expression, including criticism of Government policy, shall not be used to undermine public order or morality or the authority of the State. The publication or utterance of blasphemous, seditious, or indecent material is an offence which shall be punishable in accordance with law.'

Minister for Justice Dermot Ahern proposes to insert a new section into the Defamation Bill, stating: 'A person who publishes or utters blasphemous matter shall be guilty of an offence and shall be liable upon conviction on indictment to a fine not exceeding €100,000.'

'Blasphemous matter' is defined as material 'that is grossly abusive or insulting in relation to matters held sacred by any religion, thereby causing outrage among a substantial number of the adherents of that religion; and he or she intends, by the publication of the matter concerned, to cause such outrage.'

When the Justice Minister's move was announced in April 2009, media commentators argued that the proposed law did not define 'religion'. The Secretary of the National Union of Journalists, Seamus Dooley, called it 'a fatwa against freedom of expression.'

So, there seems little to stop Christina Gallagher from going about her daily business of demanding total submission from all those who follow her. Her essential message down through the years has been a very simple one: do whatever she demands through her messages or you will be damned for all eternity. This unquestioning blind support is just what numerous other cult leaders have demanded in the past. People like David Koresh, of the Branch Davidians in Waco, Texas, who died with 74 members of his sect in a massive self-started fire in 1993. Gallagher's message is that unless you do what she says, 'nothing can save the world'. And doing what she says essentially means giving her money to expand her empire. When Gallagher needed money for an extension in 1996, her message was: 'Make haste to bring about the needs of My House... or a greater calamity will befall Ireland.'

After 20 years of constant and blind devotion to Christina Gallagher, it is unlikely that Fr McGinnity will suddenly see the light. As one priest, who also studied at Maynooth, told me: 'Our attitude to Fr McGinnity is that he has gone off the rails. We feel he has flipped. He is a bright man but a deluded one.'

Former followers now rest all their hopes on other past victims coming forward and telling their stories, particularly those who gave large amounts of money but have, so far, remained silent. The gardaí insist they can only investigate if more victims make a formal complaint. Their previous inquiries came to a halt when the House of Prayer quickly paid back those who had already made complaints. According to past members, there are certain former insiders who have so much explosive information on Christina Gallagher that they could close down the House of Prayer, if they would only speak out. Until now they have been too embarrassed or too frightened to step into the spotlight.

Mike McCrory, the man who started the whole ball

rolling, insists it is time for people to stand up and be counted. He says he cannot understand how former House of Prayer followers – devout people with consciences – can remain silent in light of what they now know. And he often quotes the eighteenth century Irish philosopher Edmund Burke, who said (and there are multiple variations): 'All that is necessary for evil to triumph is for good men to do nothing.' In religious terms, he claims it is impossible for Catholics to follow both the established Church and Christina Gallagher.

For those who are less concerned about the intricacies of Catholic theology than they are about the financial abuse of the elderly, they too claim it is time for victims to speak out.

The world awaits.